C-3424 CAREER EXAMINATION SERIES

This is your
PASSBOOK for...

Code Enforcement Officer

Test Preparation Study Guide
Questions & Answers

NATIONAL LEARNING CORPORATION®

COPYRIGHT NOTICE

This book is SOLELY intended for, is sold ONLY to, and its use is RESTRICTED to individual, bona fide applicants or candidates who qualify by virtue of having seriously filed applications for appropriate license, certificate, professional and/or promotional advancement, higher school matriculation, scholarship, or other legitimate requirements of education and/or governmental authorities.

This book is NOT intended for use, class instruction, tutoring, training, duplication, copying, reprinting, excerption, or adaptation, etc., by:

1) Other publishers
2) Proprietors and/or Instructors of "Coaching" and/or Preparatory Courses
3) Personnel and/or Training Divisions of commercial, industrial, and governmental organizations
4) Schools, colleges, or universities and/or their departments and staffs, including teachers and other personnel
5) Testing Agencies or Bureaus
6) Study groups which seek by the purchase of a single volume to copy and/or duplicate and/or adapt this material for use by the group as a whole without having purchased individual volumes for each of the members of the group
7) Et al.

Such persons would be in violation of appropriate Federal and State statutes.

PROVISION OF LICENSING AGREEMENTS – Recognized educational, commercial, industrial, and governmental institutions and organizations, and others legitimately engaged in educational pursuits, including training, testing, and measurement activities, may address request for a licensing agreement to the copyright owners, who will determine whether, and under what conditions, including fees and charges, the materials in this book may be used them. In other words, a licensing facility exists for the legitimate use of the material in this book on other than an individual basis. However, it is asseverated and affirmed here that the material in this book CANNOT be used without the receipt of the express permission of such a licensing agreement from the Publishers. Inquiries re licensing should be addressed to the company, attention rights and permissions department.

All rights reserved, including the right of reproduction in whole or in part, in any form or by any means, electronic or mechanical, including photocopying, recording, or by any information storage and retrieval system, without permission in writing from the Publisher.

Copyright © 2024 by
National Learning Corporation

212 Michael Drive, Syosset, NY 11791
(516) 921-8888 • www.passbooks.com
E-mail: info@passbooks.com

PUBLISHED IN THE UNITED STATES OF AMERICA

PASSBOOK® SERIES

THE *PASSBOOK® SERIES* has been created to prepare applicants and candidates for the ultimate academic battlefield – the examination room.

At some time in our lives, each and every one of us may be required to take an examination – for validation, matriculation, admission, qualification, registration, certification, or licensure.

Based on the assumption that every applicant or candidate has met the basic formal educational standards, has taken the required number of courses, and read the necessary texts, the *PASSBOOK® SERIES* furnishes the one special preparation which may assure passing with confidence, instead of failing with insecurity. Examination questions – together with answers – are furnished as the basic vehicle for study so that the mysteries of the examination and its compounding difficulties may be eliminated or diminished by a sure method.

This book is meant to help you pass your examination provided that you qualify and are serious in your objective.

The entire field is reviewed through the huge store of content information which is succinctly presented through a provocative and challenging approach – the question-and-answer method.

A climate of success is established by furnishing the correct answers at the end of each test.

You soon learn to recognize types of questions, forms of questions, and patterns of questioning. You may even begin to anticipate expected outcomes.

You perceive that many questions are repeated or adapted so that you can gain acute insights, which may enable you to score many sure points.

You learn how to confront new questions, or types of questions, and to attack them confidently and work out the correct answers.

You note objectives and emphases, and recognize pitfalls and dangers, so that you may make positive educational adjustments.

Moreover, you are kept fully informed in relation to new concepts, methods, practices, and directions in the field.

You discover that you are actually taking the examination all the time: you are preparing for the examination by "taking" an examination, not by reading extraneous and/or supererogatory textbooks.

In short, this PASSBOOK®, used directedly, should be an important factor in helping you to pass your test.

CODE ENFORCEMENT OFFICER

DUTIES
Performs field inspections, investigations and building plan examination to ensure strict adherence and enforce full compliance with legal requirements and provisions of local and state building, plumbing, sewer, heating, ventilation, air-conditioning and zoning laws, codes, ordinances, rules and regulations. Under general supervision, the incumbent of this position performs enforcement work related to quality of life issues such as littering, sanitation, noise, dumping, peddling, and similar activities as outlined in local codes, ordinances, and laws. Where violations are noted, action to secure compliance is instituted. Performs related duties as required.

SUBJECT OF EXAMINATION
Written test will cover knowledge, skills, and/or abilities in such areas as:
1. **Inspection procedures and principles** - These questions test for knowledge of the appropriate practices and methods to use when inspecting various types of building facilities and projects, including proper adherence to plans and codes, dealing with residents, owners and contractors, and inspection record keeping.
2. **Building construction and rehabilitation** - These questions test for knowledge of the various methods and materials used when constructing or renovating various types of buildings and their components.
3. **Understanding and interpreting building plans and requirements** - These questions test for the ability to read, analyze and perform computations based on technical drawings and written technical material related to building facilities and projects. All the information needed to answer the questions will be presented in the written material and/or drawings.
4. **Building, housing and zoning laws and codes** - These questions test for knowledge of, and the ability to apply, provisions of the Building and Residential Codes of State (and the portions of other codes applicable to these two codes), and the general concepts of zoning, including related laws and regulations.
5. **Understanding and interpreting written material** - These questions test how well you comprehend written material. You will be provided with brief reading selections and will be asked questions about the selections. All the information required to answer the questions will be presented in the selections; you will not be required to have any special knowledge relating to the subject areas of the selections.

HOW TO TAKE A TEST

I. YOU MUST PASS AN EXAMINATION

A. *WHAT EVERY CANDIDATE SHOULD KNOW*

Examination applicants often ask us for help in preparing for the written test. What can I study in advance? What kinds of questions will be asked? How will the test be given? How will the papers be graded?

As an applicant for a civil service examination, you may be wondering about some of these things. Our purpose here is to suggest effective methods of advance study and to describe civil service examinations.

Your chances for success on this examination can be increased if you know how to prepare. Those "pre-examination jitters" can be reduced if you know what to expect. You can even experience an adventure in good citizenship if you know why civil service exams are given.

B. *WHY ARE CIVIL SERVICE EXAMINATIONS GIVEN?*

Civil service examinations are important to you in two ways. As a citizen, you want public jobs filled by employees who know how to do their work. As a job seeker, you want a fair chance to compete for that job on an equal footing with other candidates. The best-known means of accomplishing this two-fold goal is the competitive examination.

Exams are widely publicized throughout the nation. They may be administered for jobs in federal, state, city, municipal, town or village governments or agencies.

Any citizen may apply, with some limitations, such as the age or residence of applicants. Your experience and education may be reviewed to see whether you meet the requirements for the particular examination. When these requirements exist, they are reasonable and applied consistently to all applicants. Thus, a competitive examination may cause you some uneasiness now, but it is your privilege and safeguard.

C. *HOW ARE CIVIL SERVICE EXAMS DEVELOPED?*

Examinations are carefully written by trained technicians who are specialists in the field known as "psychological measurement," in consultation with recognized authorities in the field of work that the test will cover. These experts recommend the subject matter areas or skills to be tested; only those knowledges or skills important to your success on the job are included. The most reliable books and source materials available are used as references. Together, the experts and technicians judge the difficulty level of the questions.

Test technicians know how to phrase questions so that the problem is clearly stated. Their ethics do not permit "trick" or "catch" questions. Questions may have been tried out on sample groups, or subjected to statistical analysis, to determine their usefulness.

Written tests are often used in combination with performance tests, ratings of training and experience, and oral interviews. All of these measures combine to form the best-known means of finding the right person for the right job.

II. HOW TO PASS THE WRITTEN TEST

A. NATURE OF THE EXAMINATION

To prepare intelligently for civil service examinations, you should know how they differ from school examinations you have taken. In school you were assigned certain definite pages to read or subjects to cover. The examination questions were quite detailed and usually emphasized memory. Civil service exams, on the other hand, try to discover your present ability to perform the duties of a position, plus your potentiality to learn these duties. In other words, a civil service exam attempts to predict how successful you will be. Questions cover such a broad area that they cannot be as minute and detailed as school exam questions.

In the public service similar kinds of work, or positions, are grouped together in one "class." This process is known as *position-classification*. All the positions in a class are paid according to the salary range for that class. One class title covers all of these positions, and they are all tested by the same examination.

B. FOUR BASIC STEPS

1) Study the announcement

How, then, can you know what subjects to study? Our best answer is: "Learn as much as possible about the class of positions for which you've applied." The exam will test the knowledge, skills and abilities needed to do the work.

Your most valuable source of information about the position you want is the official exam announcement. This announcement lists the training and experience qualifications. Check these standards and apply only if you come reasonably close to meeting them.

The brief description of the position in the examination announcement offers some clues to the subjects which will be tested. Think about the job itself. Review the duties in your mind. Can you perform them, or are there some in which you are rusty? Fill in the blank spots in your preparation.

Many jurisdictions preview the written test in the exam announcement by including a section called "Knowledge and Abilities Required," "Scope of the Examination," or some similar heading. Here you will find out specifically what fields will be tested.

2) Review your own background

Once you learn in general what the position is all about, and what you need to know to do the work, ask yourself which subjects you already know fairly well and which need improvement. You may wonder whether to concentrate on improving your strong areas or on building some background in your fields of weakness. When the announcement has specified "some knowledge" or "considerable knowledge," or has used adjectives like "beginning principles of…" or "advanced … methods," you can get a clue as to the number and difficulty of questions to be asked in any given field. More questions, and hence broader coverage, would be included for those subjects which are more important in the work. Now weigh your strengths and weaknesses against the job requirements and prepare accordingly.

3) Determine the level of the position

Another way to tell how intensively you should prepare is to understand the level of the job for which you are applying. Is it the entering level? In other words, is this the position in which beginners in a field of work are hired? Or is it an intermediate or advanced level? Sometimes this is indicated by such words as "Junior" or "Senior" in the class title. Other jurisdictions use Roman numerals to designate the level – Clerk I, Clerk II, for example. The word "Supervisor" sometimes appears in the title. If the level is not indicated by the title, check the description of duties. Will you be working under very close supervision, or will you have responsibility for independent decisions in this work?

4) Choose appropriate study materials

Now that you know the subjects to be examined and the relative amount of each subject to be covered, you can choose suitable study materials. For beginning level jobs, or even advanced ones, if you have a pronounced weakness in some aspect of your training, read a modern, standard textbook in that field. Be sure it is up to date and has general coverage. Such books are normally available at your library, and the librarian will be glad to help you locate one. For entry-level positions, questions of appropriate difficulty are chosen – neither highly advanced questions, nor those too simple. Such questions require careful thought but not advanced training.

If the position for which you are applying is technical or advanced, you will read more advanced, specialized material. If you are already familiar with the basic principles of your field, elementary textbooks would waste your time. Concentrate on advanced textbooks and technical periodicals. Think through the concepts and review difficult problems in your field.

These are all general sources. You can get more ideas on your own initiative, following these leads. For example, training manuals and publications of the government agency which employs workers in your field can be useful, particularly for technical and professional positions. A letter or visit to the government department involved may result in more specific study suggestions, and certainly will provide you with a more definite idea of the exact nature of the position you are seeking.

III. KINDS OF TESTS

Tests are used for purposes other than measuring knowledge and ability to perform specified duties. For some positions, it is equally important to test ability to make adjustments to new situations or to profit from training. In others, basic mental abilities not dependent on information are essential. Questions which test these things may not appear as pertinent to the duties of the position as those which test for knowledge and information. Yet they are often highly important parts of a fair examination. For very general questions, it is almost impossible to help you direct your study efforts. What we can do is to point out some of the more common of these general abilities needed in public service positions and describe some typical questions.

1) General information

Broad, general information has been found useful for predicting job success in some kinds of work. This is tested in a variety of ways, from vocabulary lists to questions about current events. Basic background in some field of work, such as sociology or economics, may be sampled in a group of questions. Often these are principles which have become familiar to most persons through exposure rather than through formal training. It is difficult to advise you how to study for these questions; being alert to the world around you is our best suggestion.

2) Verbal ability

An example of an ability needed in many positions is verbal or language ability. Verbal ability is, in brief, the ability to use and understand words. Vocabulary and grammar tests are typical measures of this ability. Reading comprehension or paragraph interpretation questions are common in many kinds of civil service tests. You are given a paragraph of written material and asked to find its central meaning.

3) Numerical ability

Number skills can be tested by the familiar arithmetic problem, by checking paired lists of numbers to see which are alike and which are different, or by interpreting charts and graphs. In the latter test, a graph may be printed in the test booklet which you are asked to use as the basis for answering questions.

4) Observation

A popular test for law-enforcement positions is the observation test. A picture is shown to you for several minutes, then taken away. Questions about the picture test your ability to observe both details and larger elements.

5) Following directions

In many positions in the public service, the employee must be able to carry out written instructions dependably and accurately. You may be given a chart with several columns, each column listing a variety of information. The questions require you to carry out directions involving the information given in the chart.

6) Skills and aptitudes

Performance tests effectively measure some manual skills and aptitudes. When the skill is one in which you are trained, such as typing or shorthand, you can practice. These tests are often very much like those given in business school or high school courses. For many of the other skills and aptitudes, however, no short-time preparation can be made. Skills and abilities natural to you or that you have developed throughout your lifetime are being tested.

Many of the general questions just described provide all the data needed to answer the questions and ask you to use your reasoning ability to find the answers. Your best preparation for these tests, as well as for tests of facts and ideas, is to be at your physical and mental best. You, no doubt, have your own methods of getting into an exam-taking mood and keeping "in shape." The next section lists some ideas on this subject.

IV. KINDS OF QUESTIONS

Only rarely is the "essay" question, which you answer in narrative form, used in civil service tests. Civil service tests are usually of the short-answer type. Full instructions for answering these questions will be given to you at the examination. But in case this is your first experience with short-answer questions and separate answer sheets, here is what you need to know:

1) Multiple-choice Questions

Most popular of the short-answer questions is the "multiple choice" or "best answer" question. It can be used, for example, to test for factual knowledge, ability to solve problems or judgment in meeting situations found at work.

A multiple-choice question is normally one of three types—
- It can begin with an incomplete statement followed by several possible endings. You are to find the one ending which *best* completes the statement, although some of the others may not be entirely wrong.
- It can also be a complete statement in the form of a question which is answered by choosing one of the statements listed.

- It can be in the form of a problem – again you select the best answer.

Here is an example of a multiple-choice question with a discussion which should give you some clues as to the method for choosing the right answer:

When an employee has a complaint about his assignment, the action which will *best* help him overcome his difficulty is to
- A. discuss his difficulty with his coworkers
- B. take the problem to the head of the organization
- C. take the problem to the person who gave him the assignment
- D. say nothing to anyone about his complaint

In answering this question, you should study each of the choices to find which is best. Consider choice "A" – Certainly an employee may discuss his complaint with fellow employees, but no change or improvement can result, and the complaint remains unresolved. Choice "B" is a poor choice since the head of the organization probably does not know what assignment you have been given, and taking your problem to him is known as "going over the head" of the supervisor. The supervisor, or person who made the assignment, is the person who can clarify it or correct any injustice. Choice "C" is, therefore, correct. To say nothing, as in choice "D," is unwise. Supervisors have and interest in knowing the problems employees are facing, and the employee is seeking a solution to his problem.

2) True/False Questions

The "true/false" or "right/wrong" form of question is sometimes used. Here a complete statement is given. Your job is to decide whether the statement is right or wrong.

SAMPLE: A roaming cell-phone call to a nearby city costs less than a non-roaming call to a distant city.

This statement is wrong, or false, since roaming calls are more expensive.

This is not a complete list of all possible question forms, although most of the others are variations of these common types. You will always get complete directions for answering questions. Be sure you understand *how* to mark your answers – ask questions until you do.

V. RECORDING YOUR ANSWERS

Computer terminals are used more and more today for many different kinds of exams.
For an examination with very few applicants, you may be told to record your answers in the test booklet itself. Separate answer sheets are much more common. If this separate answer sheet is to be scored by machine – and this is often the case – it is highly important that you mark your answers correctly in order to get credit.

An electronic scoring machine is often used in civil service offices because of the speed with which papers can be scored. Machine-scored answer sheets must be marked with a pencil, which will be given to you. This pencil has a high graphite content which responds to the electronic scoring machine. As a matter of fact, stray dots may register as answers, so do not let your pencil rest on the answer sheet while you are pondering the correct answer. Also, if your pencil lead breaks or is otherwise defective, ask for another.

Since the answer sheet will be dropped in a slot in the scoring machine, be careful not to bend the corners or get the paper crumpled.

The answer sheet normally has five vertical columns of numbers, with 30 numbers to a column. These numbers correspond to the question numbers in your test booklet. After each number, going across the page are four or five pairs of dotted lines. These short dotted lines have small letters or numbers above them. The first two pairs may also have a "T" or "F" above the letters. This indicates that the first two pairs only are to be used if the questions are of the true-false type. If the questions are multiple choice, disregard the "T" and "F" and pay attention only to the small letters or numbers.

Answer your questions in the manner of the sample that follows:

32. The largest city in the United States is
    A. Washington, D.C.
    B. New York City
    C. Chicago
    D. Detroit
    E. San Francisco

1) Choose the answer you think is best. (New York City is the largest, so "B" is correct.)
2) Find the row of dotted lines numbered the same as the question you are answering. (Find row number 32)
3) Find the pair of dotted lines corresponding to the answer. (Find the pair of lines under the mark "B.")
4) Make a solid black mark between the dotted lines.

VI. BEFORE THE TEST

Common sense will help you find procedures to follow to get ready for an examination. Too many of us, however, overlook these sensible measures. Indeed, nervousness and fatigue have been found to be the most serious reasons why applicants fail to do their best on civil service tests. Here is a list of reminders:

- Begin your preparation early – Don't wait until the last minute to go scurrying around for books and materials or to find out what the position is all about.
- Prepare continuously – An hour a night for a week is better than an all-night cram session. This has been definitely established. What is more, a night a week for a month will return better dividends than crowding your study into a shorter period of time.
- Locate the place of the exam – You have been sent a notice telling you when and where to report for the examination. If the location is in a different town or otherwise unfamiliar to you, it would be well to inquire the best route and learn something about the building.
- Relax the night before the test – Allow your mind to rest. Do not study at all that night. Plan some mild recreation or diversion; then go to bed early and get a good night's sleep.
- Get up early enough to make a leisurely trip to the place for the test – This way unforeseen events, traffic snarls, unfamiliar buildings, etc. will not upset you.
- Dress comfortably – A written test is not a fashion show. You will be known by number and not by name, so wear something comfortable.

- Leave excess paraphernalia at home – Shopping bags and odd bundles will get in your way. You need bring only the items mentioned in the official notice you received; usually everything you need is provided. Do not bring reference books to the exam. They will only confuse those last minutes and be taken away from you when in the test room.
- Arrive somewhat ahead of time – If because of transportation schedules you must get there very early, bring a newspaper or magazine to take your mind off yourself while waiting.
- Locate the examination room – When you have found the proper room, you will be directed to the seat or part of the room where you will sit. Sometimes you are given a sheet of instructions to read while you are waiting. Do not fill out any forms until you are told to do so; just read them and be prepared.
- Relax and prepare to listen to the instructions
- If you have any physical problem that may keep you from doing your best, be sure to tell the test administrator. If you are sick or in poor health, you really cannot do your best on the exam. You can come back and take the test some other time.

VII. AT THE TEST

The day of the test is here and you have the test booklet in your hand. The temptation to get going is very strong. Caution! There is more to success than knowing the right answers. You must know how to identify your papers and understand variations in the type of short-answer question used in this particular examination. Follow these suggestions for maximum results from your efforts:

1) Cooperate with the monitor

The test administrator has a duty to create a situation in which you can be as much at ease as possible. He will give instructions, tell you when to begin, check to see that you are marking your answer sheet correctly, and so on. He is not there to guard you, although he will see that your competitors do not take unfair advantage. He wants to help you do your best.

2) Listen to all instructions

Don't jump the gun! Wait until you understand all directions. In most civil service tests you get more time than you need to answer the questions. So don't be in a hurry. Read each word of instructions until you clearly understand the meaning. Study the examples, listen to all announcements and follow directions. Ask questions if you do not understand what to do.

3) Identify your papers

Civil service exams are usually identified by number only. You will be assigned a number; you must not put your name on your test papers. Be sure to copy your number correctly. Since more than one exam may be given, copy your exact examination title.

4) Plan your time

Unless you are told that a test is a "speed" or "rate of work" test, speed itself is usually not important. Time enough to answer all the questions will be provided, but this does not mean that you have all day. An overall time limit has been set. Divide the total time (in minutes) by the number of questions to determine the approximate time you have for each question.

5) Do not linger over difficult questions

If you come across a difficult question, mark it with a paper clip (useful to have along) and come back to it when you have been through the booklet. One caution if you do this – be sure to skip a number on your answer sheet as well. Check often to be sure that you have not lost your place and that you are marking in the row numbered the same as the question you are answering.

6) Read the questions

Be sure you know what the question asks! Many capable people are unsuccessful because they failed to *read* the questions correctly.

7) Answer all questions

Unless you have been instructed that a penalty will be deducted for incorrect answers, it is better to guess than to omit a question.

8) Speed tests

It is often better NOT to guess on speed tests. It has been found that on timed tests people are tempted to spend the last few seconds before time is called in marking answers at random – without even reading them – in the hope of picking up a few extra points. To discourage this practice, the instructions may warn you that your score will be "corrected" for guessing. That is, a penalty will be applied. The incorrect answers will be deducted from the correct ones, or some other penalty formula will be used.

9) Review your answers

If you finish before time is called, go back to the questions you guessed or omitted to give them further thought. Review other answers if you have time.

10) Return your test materials

If you are ready to leave before others have finished or time is called, take ALL your materials to the monitor and leave quietly. Never take any test material with you. The monitor can discover whose papers are not complete, and taking a test booklet may be grounds for disqualification.

VIII. EXAMINATION TECHNIQUES

1) Read the general instructions carefully. These are usually printed on the first page of the exam booklet. As a rule, these instructions refer to the timing of the examination; the fact that you should not start work until the signal and must stop work at a signal, etc. If there are any *special* instructions, such as a choice of questions to be answered, make sure that you note this instruction carefully.

2) When you are ready to start work on the examination, that is as soon as the signal has been given, read the instructions to each question booklet, underline any key words or phrases, such as *least, best, outline, describe* and the like. In this way you will tend to answer as requested rather than discover on reviewing your paper that you *listed without describing*, that you selected the *worst* choice rather than the *best* choice, etc.

3) If the examination is of the objective or multiple-choice type – that is, each question will also give a series of possible answers: A, B, C or D, and you are called upon to select the best answer and write the letter next to that answer on your answer paper – it is advisable to start answering each question in turn. There may be anywhere from 50 to 100 such questions in the three or four hours allotted and you can see how much time would be taken if you read through all the questions before beginning to answer any. Furthermore, if you come across a question or group of questions which you know would be difficult to answer, it would undoubtedly affect your handling of all the other questions.

4) If the examination is of the essay type and contains but a few questions, it is a moot point as to whether you should read all the questions before starting to answer any one. Of course, if you are given a choice – say five out of seven and the like – then it is essential to read all the questions so you can eliminate the two that are most difficult. If, however, you are asked to answer all the questions, there may be danger in trying to answer the easiest one first because you may find that you will spend too much time on it. The best technique is to answer the first question, then proceed to the second, etc.

5) Time your answers. Before the exam begins, write down the time it started, then add the time allowed for the examination and write down the time it must be completed, then divide the time available somewhat as follows:
   - If 3-1/2 hours are allowed, that would be 210 minutes. If you have 80 objective-type questions, that would be an average of 2-1/2 minutes per question. Allow yourself no more than 2 minutes per question, or a total of 160 minutes, which will permit about 50 minutes to review.
   - If for the time allotment of 210 minutes there are 7 essay questions to answer, that would average about 30 minutes a question. Give yourself only 25 minutes per question so that you have about 35 minutes to review.

6) The most important instruction is to *read each question* and make sure you know what is wanted. The second most important instruction is to *time yourself properly* so that you answer every question. The third most important instruction is to *answer every question*. Guess if you have to but include something for each question. Remember that you will receive no credit for a blank and will probably receive some credit if you write something in answer to an essay question. If you guess a letter – say "B" for a multiple-choice question – you may have guessed right. If you leave a blank as an answer to a multiple-choice question, the examiners may respect your feelings but it will not add a point to your score. Some exams may penalize you for wrong answers, so in such cases *only*, you may not want to guess unless you have some basis for your answer.

7) Suggestions
   a. Objective-type questions
      1. Examine the question booklet for proper sequence of pages and questions
      2. Read all instructions carefully
      3. Skip any question which seems too difficult; return to it after all other questions have been answered
      4. Apportion your time properly; do not spend too much time on any single question or group of questions

5. Note and underline key words – *all, most, fewest, least, best, worst, same, opposite,* etc.
6. Pay particular attention to negatives
7. Note unusual option, e.g., unduly long, short, complex, different or similar in content to the body of the question
8. Observe the use of "hedging" words – *probably, may, most likely,* etc.
9. Make sure that your answer is put next to the same number as the question
10. Do not second-guess unless you have good reason to believe the second answer is definitely more correct
11. Cross out original answer if you decide another answer is more accurate; do not erase until you are ready to hand your paper in
12. Answer all questions; guess unless instructed otherwise
13. Leave time for review

b. Essay questions
1. Read each question carefully
2. Determine exactly what is wanted. Underline key words or phrases.
3. Decide on outline or paragraph answer
4. Include many different points and elements unless asked to develop any one or two points or elements
5. Show impartiality by giving pros and cons unless directed to select one side only
6. Make and write down any assumptions you find necessary to answer the questions
7. Watch your English, grammar, punctuation and choice of words
8. Time your answers; don't crowd material

8) Answering the essay question

Most essay questions can be answered by framing the specific response around several key words or ideas. Here are a few such key words or ideas:

M's: manpower, materials, methods, money, management
P's: purpose, program, policy, plan, procedure, practice, problems, pitfalls, personnel, public relations

a. Six basic steps in handling problems:
1. Preliminary plan and background development
2. Collect information, data and facts
3. Analyze and interpret information, data and facts
4. Analyze and develop solutions as well as make recommendations
5. Prepare report and sell recommendations
6. Install recommendations and follow up effectiveness

b. Pitfalls to avoid
1. *Taking things for granted* – A statement of the situation does not necessarily imply that each of the elements is necessarily true; for example, a complaint may be invalid and biased so that all that can be taken for granted is that a complaint has been registered

2. *Considering only one side of a situation* – Wherever possible, indicate several alternatives and then point out the reasons you selected the best one
3. *Failing to indicate follow up* – Whenever your answer indicates action on your part, make certain that you will take proper follow-up action to see how successful your recommendations, procedures or actions turn out to be
4. *Taking too long in answering any single question* – Remember to time your answers properly

IX. AFTER THE TEST

Scoring procedures differ in detail among civil service jurisdictions although the general principles are the same. Whether the papers are hand-scored or graded by machine we have described, they are nearly always graded by number. That is, the person who marks the paper knows only the number – never the name – of the applicant. Not until all the papers have been graded will they be matched with names. If other tests, such as training and experience or oral interview ratings have been given, scores will be combined. Different parts of the examination usually have different weights. For example, the written test might count 60 percent of the final grade, and a rating of training and experience 40 percent. In many jurisdictions, veterans will have a certain number of points added to their grades.

After the final grade has been determined, the names are placed in grade order and an eligible list is established. There are various methods for resolving ties between those who get the same final grade – probably the most common is to place first the name of the person whose application was received first. Job offers are made from the eligible list in the order the names appear on it. You will be notified of your grade and your rank as soon as all these computations have been made. This will be done as rapidly as possible.

People who are found to meet the requirements in the announcement are called "eligibles." Their names are put on a list of eligible candidates. An eligible's chances of getting a job depend on how high he stands on this list and how fast agencies are filling jobs from the list.

When a job is to be filled from a list of eligibles, the agency asks for the names of people on the list of eligibles for that job. When the civil service commission receives this request, it sends to the agency the names of the three people highest on this list. Or, if the job to be filled has specialized requirements, the office sends the agency the names of the top three persons who meet these requirements from the general list.

The appointing officer makes a choice from among the three people whose names were sent to him. If the selected person accepts the appointment, the names of the others are put back on the list to be considered for future openings.

That is the rule in hiring from all kinds of eligible lists, whether they are for typist, carpenter, chemist, or something else. For every vacancy, the appointing officer has his choice of any one of the top three eligibles on the list. This explains why the person whose name is on top of the list sometimes does not get an appointment when some of the persons lower on the list do. If the appointing officer chooses the second or third eligible, the No. 1 eligible does not get a job at once, but stays on the list until he is appointed or the list is terminated.

X. HOW TO PASS THE INTERVIEW TEST

The examination for which you applied requires an oral interview test. You have already taken the written test and you are now being called for the interview test – the final part of the formal examination.

You may think that it is not possible to prepare for an interview test and that there are no procedures to follow during an interview. Our purpose is to point out some things you can do in advance that will help you and some good rules to follow and pitfalls to avoid while you are being interviewed.

What is an interview supposed to test?

The written examination is designed to test the technical knowledge and competence of the candidate; the oral is designed to evaluate intangible qualities, not readily measured otherwise, and to establish a list showing the relative fitness of each candidate – as measured against his competitors – for the position sought. Scoring is not on the basis of "right" and "wrong," but on a sliding scale of values ranging from "not passable" to "outstanding." As a matter of fact, it is possible to achieve a relatively low score without a single "incorrect" answer because of evident weakness in the qualities being measured.

Occasionally, an examination may consist entirely of an oral test – either an individual or a group oral. In such cases, information is sought concerning the technical knowledges and abilities of the candidate, since there has been no written examination for this purpose. More commonly, however, an oral test is used to supplement a written examination.

Who conducts interviews?

The composition of oral boards varies among different jurisdictions. In nearly all, a representative of the personnel department serves as chairman. One of the members of the board may be a representative of the department in which the candidate would work. In some cases, "outside experts" are used, and, frequently, a businessman or some other representative of the general public is asked to serve. Labor and management or other special groups may be represented. The aim is to secure the services of experts in the appropriate field.

However the board is composed, it is a good idea (and not at all improper or unethical) to ascertain in advance of the interview who the members are and what groups they represent. When you are introduced to them, you will have some idea of their backgrounds and interests, and at least you will not stutter and stammer over their names.

What should be done before the interview?

While knowledge about the board members is useful and takes some of the surprise element out of the interview, there is other preparation which is more substantive. It *is* possible to prepare for an oral interview – in several ways:

1) Keep a copy of your application and review it carefully before the interview

This may be the only document before the oral board, and the starting point of the interview. Know what education and experience you have listed there, and the sequence and dates of all of it. Sometimes the board will ask you to review the highlights of your experience for them; you should not have to hem and haw doing it.

2) Study the class specification and the examination announcement

Usually, the oral board has one or both of these to guide them. The qualities, characteristics or knowledges required by the position sought are stated in these documents. They offer valuable clues as to the nature of the oral interview. For example, if the job involves supervisory responsibilities, the announcement will usually indicate that knowledge of modern supervisory methods and the qualifications of the candidate as a supervisor will be tested. If so, you can expect such questions, frequently in the form of a hypothetical situation which you are expected to solve. NEVER go into an oral without knowledge of the duties and responsibilities of the job you seek.

3) Think through each qualification required

Try to visualize the kind of questions you would ask if you were a board member. How well could you answer them? Try especially to appraise your own knowledge and background in each area, *measured against the job sought*, and identify any areas in which you are weak. Be critical and realistic – do not flatter yourself.

4) Do some general reading in areas in which you feel you may be weak

For example, if the job involves supervision and your past experience has NOT, some general reading in supervisory methods and practices, particularly in the field of human relations, might be useful. Do NOT study agency procedures or detailed manuals. The oral board will be testing your understanding and capacity, not your memory.

5) Get a good night's sleep and watch your general health and mental attitude

You will want a clear head at the interview. Take care of a cold or any other minor ailment, and of course, no hangovers.

What should be done on the day of the interview?

Now comes the day of the interview itself. Give yourself plenty of time to get there. Plan to arrive somewhat ahead of the scheduled time, particularly if your appointment is in the fore part of the day. If a previous candidate fails to appear, the board might be ready for you a bit early. By early afternoon an oral board is almost invariably behind schedule if there are many candidates, and you may have to wait. Take along a book or magazine to read, or your application to review, but leave any extraneous material in the waiting room when you go in for your interview. In any event, relax and compose yourself.

The matter of dress is important. The board is forming impressions about you – from your experience, your manners, your attitude, and your appearance. Give your personal appearance careful attention. Dress your best, but not your flashiest. Choose conservative, appropriate clothing, and be sure it is immaculate. This is a business interview, and your appearance should indicate that you regard it as such. Besides, being well groomed and properly dressed will help boost your confidence.

Sooner or later, someone will call your name and escort you into the interview room. *This is it.* From here on you are on your own. It is too late for any more preparation. But remember, you asked for this opportunity to prove your fitness, and you are here because your request was granted.

What happens when you go in?

The usual sequence of events will be as follows: The clerk (who is often the board stenographer) will introduce you to the chairman of the oral board, who will introduce you to the other members of the board. Acknowledge the introductions before you sit down. Do not be surprised if you find a microphone facing you or a stenotypist sitting by. Oral interviews are usually recorded in the event of an appeal or other review.

Usually the chairman of the board will open the interview by reviewing the highlights of your education and work experience from your application – primarily for the benefit of the other members of the board, as well as to get the material into the record. Do not interrupt or comment unless there is an error or significant misinterpretation; if that is the case, do not hesitate. But do not quibble about insignificant matters. Also, he will usually ask you some question about your education, experience or your present job – partly to get you to start talking and to establish the interviewing "rapport." He may start the actual questioning, or turn it over to one of the other members. Frequently, each member undertakes the questioning on a particular area, one in which he is perhaps most competent, so you can expect each member to participate in the examination. Because time is limited, you may also expect some rather abrupt switches in the direction the questioning takes, so do not be upset by it. Normally, a board member will not pursue a single line of questioning unless he discovers a particular strength or weakness.

After each member has participated, the chairman will usually ask whether any member has any further questions, then will ask you if you have anything you wish to add. Unless you are expecting this question, it may floor you. Worse, it may start you off on an extended, extemporaneous speech. The board is not usually seeking more information. The question is principally to offer you a last opportunity to present further qualifications or to indicate that you have nothing to add. So, if you feel that a significant qualification or characteristic has been overlooked, it is proper to point it out in a sentence or so. Do not compliment the board on the thoroughness of their examination – they have been sketchy, and you know it. If you wish, merely say, "No thank you, I have nothing further to add." This is a point where you can "talk yourself out" of a good impression or fail to present an important bit of information. Remember, *you close the interview yourself.*

The chairman will then say, "That is all, Mr. _____, thank you." Do not be startled; the interview is over, and quicker than you think. Thank him, gather your belongings and take your leave. Save your sigh of relief for the other side of the door.

How to put your best foot forward

Throughout this entire process, you may feel that the board individually and collectively is trying to pierce your defenses, seek out your hidden weaknesses and embarrass and confuse you. Actually, this is not true. They are obliged to make an appraisal of your qualifications for the job you are seeking, and they want to see you in your best light. Remember, they must interview all candidates and a non-cooperative candidate may become a failure in spite of their best efforts to bring out his qualifications. Here are 15 suggestions that will help you:

1) Be natural – Keep your attitude confident, not cocky

If you are not confident that you can do the job, do not expect the board to be. Do not apologize for your weaknesses, try to bring out your strong points. The board is interested in a positive, not negative, presentation. Cockiness will antagonize any board member and make him wonder if you are covering up a weakness by a false show of strength.

2) Get comfortable, but don't lounge or sprawl

Sit erectly but not stiffly. A careless posture may lead the board to conclude that you are careless in other things, or at least that you are not impressed by the importance of the occasion. Either conclusion is natural, even if incorrect. Do not fuss with your clothing, a pencil or an ashtray. Your hands may occasionally be useful to emphasize a point; do not let them become a point of distraction.

3) Do not wisecrack or make small talk

This is a serious situation, and your attitude should show that you consider it as such. Further, the time of the board is limited – they do not want to waste it, and neither should you.

4) Do not exaggerate your experience or abilities

In the first place, from information in the application or other interviews and sources, the board may know more about you than you think. Secondly, you probably will not get away with it. An experienced board is rather adept at spotting such a situation, so do not take the chance.

5) If you know a board member, do not make a point of it, yet do not hide it

Certainly you are not fooling him, and probably not the other members of the board. Do not try to take advantage of your acquaintanceship – it will probably do you little good.

6) Do not dominate the interview

Let the board do that. They will give you the clues – do not assume that you have to do all the talking. Realize that the board has a number of questions to ask you, and do not try to take up all the interview time by showing off your extensive knowledge of the answer to the first one.

7) Be attentive

You only have 20 minutes or so, and you should keep your attention at its sharpest throughout. When a member is addressing a problem or question to you, give him your undivided attention. Address your reply principally to him, but do not exclude the other board members.

8) Do not interrupt

A board member may be stating a problem for you to analyze. He will ask you a question when the time comes. Let him state the problem, and wait for the question.

9) Make sure you understand the question

Do not try to answer until you are sure what the question is. If it is not clear, restate it in your own words or ask the board member to clarify it for you. However, do not haggle about minor elements.

10) Reply promptly but not hastily

A common entry on oral board rating sheets is "candidate responded readily," or "candidate hesitated in replies." Respond as promptly and quickly as you can, but do not jump to a hasty, ill-considered answer.

11) Do not be peremptory in your answers

A brief answer is proper – but do not fire your answer back. That is a losing game from your point of view. The board member can probably ask questions much faster than you can answer them.

12) Do not try to create the answer you think the board member wants

He is interested in what kind of mind you have and how it works – not in playing games. Furthermore, he can usually spot this practice and will actually grade you down on it.

13) Do not switch sides in your reply merely to agree with a board member

Frequently, a member will take a contrary position merely to draw you out and to see if you are willing and able to defend your point of view. Do not start a debate, yet do not surrender a good position. If a position is worth taking, it is worth defending.

14) Do not be afraid to admit an error in judgment if you are shown to be wrong

The board knows that you are forced to reply without any opportunity for careful consideration. Your answer may be demonstrably wrong. If so, admit it and get on with the interview.

15) Do not dwell at length on your present job

The opening question may relate to your present assignment. Answer the question but do not go into an extended discussion. You are being examined for a *new* job, not your present one. As a matter of fact, try to phrase ALL your answers in terms of the job for which you are being examined.

Basis of Rating

Probably you will forget most of these "do's" and "don'ts" when you walk into the oral interview room. Even remembering them all will not ensure you a passing grade. Perhaps you did not have the qualifications in the first place. But remembering them will help you to put your best foot forward, without treading on the toes of the board members.

Rumor and popular opinion to the contrary notwithstanding, an oral board wants you to make the best appearance possible. They know you are under pressure – but they also want to see how you respond to it as a guide to what your reaction would be under the pressures of the job you seek. They will be influenced by the degree of poise you display, the personal traits you show and the manner in which you respond.

ABOUT THIS BOOK

This book contains tests divided into Examination Sections. Go through each test, answering every question in the margin. We have also attached a sample answer sheet at the back of the book that can be removed and used. At the end of each test look at the answer key and check your answers. On the ones you got wrong, look at the right answer choice and learn. Do not fill in the answers first. Do not memorize the questions and answers, but understand the answer and principles involved. On your test, the questions will likely be different from the samples. Questions are changed and new ones added. If you understand these past questions you should have success with any changes that arise. Tests may consist of several types of questions. We have additional books on each subject should more study be advisable or necessary for you. Finally, the more you study, the better prepared you will be. This book is intended to be the last thing you study before you walk into the examination room. Prior study of relevant texts is also recommended. NLC publishes some of these in our Fundamental Series. Knowledge and good sense are important factors in passing your exam. Good luck also helps. So now study this Passbook, absorb the material contained within and take that knowledge into the examination. Then do your best to pass that exam.

EXAMINATION SECTION

EXAMINATION SECTION
TEST 1

DIRECTIONS: Each question or incomplete statement is followed by several suggested answers or completions. Select the one that BEST answers the question or completes the statement. *PRINT THE LETTER OF THE CORRECT ANSWER IN THE SPACE AT THE RIGHT.*

1. Concrete with a slump of 2 inches would *most likely* be used for

    A. floors
    B. thin wall sections
    C. columns
    D. deep beams

    1.____

2. The structure above the roof of a building which encloses a stairway is called a

    A. scuttle
    B. bulkhead
    C. penthouse
    D. shaft

    2.____

3. A #4 reinforcing bar has a diameter, in inches, of *approximately*

    A. 1/4   B. 3/8   C. 1/2   D. 5/8

    3.____

4. A spandrel beam will usually be found

    A. at the wall
    B. around stairs
    C. at the peak of a roof
    D. underneath a column

    4.____

5. Oil is applied to the inside surfaces of concrete forms to

    A. prevent loss of water from the concrete
    B. obtain smoother concrete surfaces
    C. make stripping easier
    D. prevent honeycombing

    5.____

6. A retaining wall is built with a batter.
   Of the following conditions, the one which *most likely* applies to the wall is

    A. it is out of plumb
    B. it is thinner at top than at bottom
    C. neither surface is vertical
    D. both surfaces are vertical

    6.____

7. Two cubic yards of sand and four cubic yards of broken stone are to be used to make 1:2:4 concrete.
   If all the aggregate is used, the number of bags of cement that would be required is

    A. 1   B. 9   C. 18   D. 27

    7.____

8. A rectangular plot is 30 feet wide by 60 feet long. The length of the diagonal, in feet, is *most nearly*

    A. 68   B. 67   C. 66   D. 65

    8.____

9. Wood floor joists are supported on masonry walls which have a clear spacing of 17'0". The number of rows of cross-bridging required is

    A. 4   B. 3   C. 2   D. 1

    9.____

10. When painting wood, the puttying of nail holes and cracks should be done

    A. *after* the priming coat is dry
    B. *before* the priming coat is applied
    C. *while* the priming coat is still wet
    D. *after* the finish coat is applied

11. The material that would normally be used to make a corbel in a brick wall is

    A. brick   B. wood   C. steel   D. concrete

12. Headers and trimmers are used in the construction of

    A. footings   B. walls   C. floors   D. arches

13. In the design of stairs, the designer should consider

    A. maximum height of riser only
    B. minimum width of tread only
    C. product of riser height by tread width only
    D. all of the above

14. A reduction in the required number of columns in a building can be made by using one of the following types of beam. Which one?

    A. floor   B. girder   C. cantilever   D. jack

15. Doors sheathed in metal are known as _____ doors.

    A. kalamein   B. tin-clad   C. bethlehem   D. flemish

16. A coat of plaster which is scratched deliberately would *most likely* be

    A. used in two-coat work only
    B. the first coat placed
    C. the second coat placed
    D. condemned by the inspector

17. A concealed draft opening is

    A. *good* because it improves the appearance of a room
    B. *bad* because it might be accidentally blocked up
    C. *good* because it can be used to regulate the flow of fresh air
    D. *bad* because it is a fire hazard

18. A groove is cut in the underside of a stone sill. This is done to

    A. keep rain water from running down the wall
    B. allow the insertion of dowels
    C. improve the mortar bond
    D. reduce the weight of the sill

19. Of the following, the one which would LEAST likely be used in conjunction with the others is

    A. rafter
    B. collar beam
    C. ridgeboard
    D. tail beam

20. The dimensions of a 2 x 4 when dressed are, *most nearly*,

    A. 2 x 4
    B. 1 1/2 x 3 1/2
    C. 1 5/8 x 3 5/8
    D. 1 3/4 x 3 1/2

21. The story heights of a building could be MOST readily determined from

    A. a plan view
    B. an elevation view
    C. a plot map
    D. all of the above

22. Honeycombing in concrete is *most likely* to occur

    A. if the forms are vibrated
    B. near the top of the forms
    C. if the mix is stiff
    D. if the concrete is well-spaded

23. A weather joint in brick work is one in which the mortar is

    A. flush with the face of the lower brick and slopes inward
    B. flush with the face of the upper brick and slopes inward
    C. recessed a fixed distance behind the face of the brick
    D. flush with the face of upper and lower brick but curves inward between the two bricks

24. A 12 inch brick wall is constructed using stretchers only.
    The PRINCIPAL objection to such a wall is with

    A. appearance
    B. construction difficulties
    C. bond
    D. dimensional problems

25. To prevent sagging joists from damaging a brick wall in the event of a fire, it is BEST to

    A. anchor the joists firmly in the wall
    B. make a bevel cut on the end of the joists
    C. use bridal irons to support the joists
    D. box out the wall for the joists

26. Flashing would *most likely* be found in a

    A. footing   B. floor   C. ceiling   D. parapet

27. Vermiculite is used in plaster to

    A. reduce weight
    B. permit easier cleaning
    C. give architectural effects
    D. reduce the mixing water required

28. The volume in cubic feet of a room 8'6" wide by 10'6" long by 8'8" high is *most nearly*

    A. 770   B. 774   C. 778   D. 782

29. A slab of concrete is 2'0" by 3'0" by 8" thick.
    The weight of the slab is, in pounds, *most nearly*

    A. 450   B. 500   C. 550   D. 600

30. Wainscoting is USUALLY found on

    A. floors   B. walls   C. ceilings   D. roofs

31. A piece of wood covering the plaster below the stool of a window is called a(n)

    A. apron   B. sill   C. coping   D. trimmer

32. English bond is used in

    A. plastering   B. papering   C. roofing   D. bricklaying

33. In plastering, coves would *most likely* be found where

    A. wall meets ceiling   B. one wall meets another
    C. wall meets floor   D. wall meets column

34. Fire stopping is usually accomplished by

    A. installing self-closing doors
    B. bricking up the space between furring at floors
    C. installing wire glass
    D. using fire resistive materials throughout the building

35. A Class 1 (fireproof structure) building has floor sleepers of wood. This is

    A. *not permitted*
    B. *permitted*
    C. *permitted* if the space between sleepers is filled with incombustible material
    D. *permitted* if a wearing surface similar to asphalt tile is applied to the wooden flooring

KEY (CORRECT ANSWERS)

1.	A	16.	B
2.	B	17.	D
3.	C	18.	A
4.	A	19.	D
5.	C	20.	C
6.	B	21.	B
7.	D	22.	C
8.	B	23.	A
9.	C	24.	C
10.	A	25.	B
11.	A	26.	D
12.	C	27.	A
13.	D	28.	B
14.	C	29.	D
15.	A	30.	B

31. A
32. D
33. A
34. B
35. C

TEST 2

DIRECTIONS: Each question or incomplete statement is followed by several suggested answers or completions. Select the one that BEST answers the question or completes the statement. *PRINT THE LETTER OF THE CORRECT ANSWER IN THE SPACE AT THE RIGHT.*

1. Joints on interior surfaces of brick walls are usually flush joints EXCEPT when the walls are to be

    A. painted
    B. plastered
    C. waterproofed
    D. dampproofed

2. The headers in a brick veneer wall serve

    A. both a structural and an architectural purpose
    B. a structural purpose only
    C. an architectural purpose only
    D. NO structural or architectural purpose

3. Of the following, the one which is NOT usually classified as interior wood trim is

    A. apron   B. ribbon   C. jamb   D. base mold

4. Single-strength glass would *most likely* be found in

    A. single light sash
    B. doors in fire walls
    C. doors in fire partitions
    D. multi-light sash

5. The one of the following items that is LEAST related to the others is

    A. newel   B. riser   C. nosing   D. sill

6. In a plastered room, grounds for plaster are LEAST likely to be used

    A. at baseboards
    B. around windows
    C. around doors
    D. at the top of wainscoting

7. Of the following types of walls, the type which is *most likely* an interior wall is _____ wall.

    A. curtain   B. faced   C. panel   D. fire

8. *Boxing* is *most likely* to be performed by a

    A. mason
    B. plasterer
    C. plumber
    D. painter

9. Linseed oil is classified as a

    A. vehicle
    B. thinner
    C. drying oil
    D. pigment

10. Curing of concrete would be MOST critical when the temperature and humidity are, respectively,

    A. 75° and 80%
    B. 80° and 90%
    C. 85° and 10%
    D. 90° and 95%

11. Of the following items, the item which is LEAST related to the others is

    A. putty
    B. sash weight
    C. glazier's points
    D. lights

12. Assume that a wood-frame house has studs of 2 x 4's.
    Placing the studs so that the wider dimension is parallel to the wall is

    A. *good* because it provides a wider nailing surface for sheathing and lathing
    B. *bad* because it reduces the open space available for windows
    C. *good* because it stiffens the frame
    D. *bad* because it reduces the load-carrying capacity of the studs

13. Government anchors are used in one of the following types of construction. Which one?

    A. Wood frame
    B. Steel beams supported on masonry bearing walls
    C. Wooden joists on masonry bearing walls
    D. Steel frame with steel joists

14. When rivet holes in structural steel fail to match up by an eighth of an inch, the BEST thing to do is

    A. ignore the mismatch and force the rivet into the hole
    B. enlarge the holes with a drift pin
    C. ream the holes to a larger diameter
    D. use a smaller sized rivet

15. The BEST way to use two angles to make a lintel is

16. A single channel section would *most likely* be used for a

    A. floor beam
    B. girder
    C. spandrel beam
    D. column

17. An oil-base paint is usually thinned with

    A. linseed oil
    B. turpentine
    C. a drying oil
    D. a resin

18. Red lead is often used as a pigment in metal priming paints PRIMARILY because it

    A. provides good coverage
    B. presents a good appearance
    C. makes painting easier
    D. is a rust inhibitor

19. Knots in wood that is to be painted

   A. require no special treatment
   B. should be painted with the priming paint before the priming paint is applied to the rest of the wood
   C. should be coated with linseed oil before any painting is done
   D. should be coated with shellac before any painting is done

20. A dove-tail anchor would *most likely* be used to bond brick veneer with a _____ wall.

   A. brick   B. concrete   C. wood frame   D. concrete block

21. A rafter is MOST similar in function to a

   A. joist   B. stud   C. sill   D. girder

22. In steel construction, it is usually MOST important to mill the ends of

   A. beams   B. girders   C. columns   D. lintels

23. Furring tile is usually set so that the air spaces in the tile are

   A. continuous in a vertical direction
   B. continuous in a horizontal direction
   C. closed off at the ends of each tile
   D. set at random

24. When plastering a wall surface of glazed tile, it is MOST important that the tile

   A. be wet   B. be dry
   C. be scored   D. joints be raked

25. In a peaked roof, the run of a rafter is

   A. less than the length of the rafter
   B. greater than the length of the rafter
   C. equal to the length of the rafter
   D. dependent upon the slope of the rafter

26. Construction of a dormer window does NOT usually involve

   A. cut rafters   B. rafter headers
   C. trimmer rafters   D. hip rafters

27. In a four-ply slag roof,

   A. there is no overlap of the roofing felt
   B. a uniform coating of pitch or asphalt is placed on top of the top layer of felt
   C. slag is placed between the layers of felt
   D. there is no need to use flashing

28. Copper wire basket strainers would *most likely* be used by a

   A. carpenter   B. plumber   C. painter   D. roofer

29. Splices of columns in steel construction are usually made

    A. at floor level
    B. two feet above floor level
    C. two feet below floor level
    D. midway between floors

30. In plumbing, a lead bend is usually used in the line from a

    A. slop sink   B. shower
    C. water closet   D. kitchen sink

31. The location of leaks in gas piping may be BEST detected by use of a

    A. match   B. heated filament
    C. soapy water solution   D. guinea pig

32. The one of the following items that would be MOST useful in eliminating water hammer from a water system is a

    A. magnesium anode   B. surge tank
    C. clean out   D. quick-closing valve

33. The MAIN purpose of a fixture trap is to

    A. catch small articles that may have accidentally dropped in the fixture
    B. prevent back syphonage
    C. make it easier to repair the fixture
    D. block the passage of foul air

34. In a certain district, the area of a building may be no longer than 55% of the area of the lot on which it stands. On a rectangular lot 75 ft. by 125 ft., the maximum permissible area of building is, in square feet, *most nearly*

    A. 5148   B. 5152   C. 5156   D. 5160

35. The allowable tensile stress in steel is 18,000 pounds per square inch. The maximum permissible tensile load in a 1-inch diameter steel bar is, in pounds, *most nearly*

    A. 13,500   B. 13,800   C. 14,100   D. 14,400

KEY (CORRECT ANSWERS)

1. B
2. C
3. B
4. D
5. D

6. D
7. D
8. D
9. A
10. C

11. B
12. D
13. B
14. C
15. A

16. C
17. B
18. D
19. D
20. B

21. A
22. C
23. B
24. C
25. A

26. D
27. B
28. D
29. B
30. C

31. C
32. B
33. D
34. C
35. C

TEST 3

DIRECTIONS: Each question or incomplete statement is followed by several suggested answers or completions. Select the one that BEST answers the question or completes the statement. *PRINT THE LETTER OF THE CORRECT ANSWER IN THE SPACE AT THE RIGHT.*

1. The ends of a joist in a brick building are cut to a bevel. This is done PRINCIPALLY to prevent damage to

    A. joist   B. floor   C. sill   D. wall

2. Of the following, the wood that is MOST commonly used today for floor joists is

    A. long leaf yellow pine   B. douglas fir
    C. oak   D. birch

3. Quarter sawed lumber is preferred for the best finished flooring PRINCIPALLY because it

    A. has the greatest strength
    B. shrinks the least
    C. is the easiest to nail
    D. is the easiest to handle

4. Of the following, the MAXIMUM height that would be considered acceptable for a stair riser is

    A. 6 1/2"   B. 7 1/2"   C. 8 1/2"   D. 9 1/2"

5. The part of a tree that will produce the DENSEST wood is the _____ wood.

    A. spring   B. summer   C. sap   D. heart

6. Lumber in quantity is ordered by

    A. cubic feet   B. foot board measure
    C. lineal feet   D. weight and length

7. A *chase* in a brick wall is a

    A. pilaster   B. waterstop   C. recess   D. corbel

8. *Parging* refers to

    A. increasing the thickness of a brick wall
    B. plastering the back of face brickwork
    C. bonding face brick to backing blocks
    D. leveling each course of brick

9. In brickwork, muriatic acid is commonly used to

    A. increase the strength of the mortar
    B. etch the brick
    C. waterproof the wall
    D. clean the wall

10. Cement mortar can be made easier to work by the addition of a small quantity of

    A. lime   B. soda   C. litharge   D. plaster

11. Joints in brick walls are tooled

    A. immediately after each brick is laid
    B. after the mortar has had its initial set
    C. after the entire wall is completed
    D. 28 days after the wall has been built

12. If cement mortar has begun to set before it can be used in a wall, the BEST thing to do is to

    A. use the mortar immediately as is
    B. add a small quantity of lime
    C. add some water and mix thoroughly
    D. discard the mortar

13. The BEST flux to use when soldering galvanized iron is

    A. killed acid   B. sal-ammoniac
    C. muriatic acid   D. resin

14. The type of solder that would be used in *hard soldering* is _____ solder.

    A. bismuth   B. wiping   C. 50-50   D. silver

15. Roll roofing material is usually felt which has been impregnated with

    A. cement   B. mastic   C. tar   D. latex

16. The purpose of flashing on roofs is to

    A. secure roofing materials to the roof
    B. make it easier to lay the roofing
    C. prevent leaks through the roof
    D. insulate the roof from excessive heat

17. The type of chain used with sash weights is _____ link.

    A. flat   B. round
    C. figure-eight   D. basketweave

18. The material that would be used to seal around a window frame is

    A. oakum   B. litharge   C. grout   D. calking

19. The function of a window sill is *most nearly* the same as that of a

    A. jamb   B. coping   C. lintel   D. buck

20. Lightweight plaster would be made with

    A. sand   B. cinders   C. potash   D. vermiculite

21. The FIRST coat of plaster to be applied on a three-coat plaster job is the _____ coat.

    A. brown   B. scratch   C. white   D. keene

22. The FIRST coat of plaster over rock lath should be a _____ plaster. 22._____

   A. gypsum B. lime
   C. Portland cement D. pozzolan cement

23. The PRINCIPAL reason for covering a concrete sidewalk with straw or paper after the concrete has been poured is to 23._____

   A. prevent people from walking on the concrete while it is still wet
   B. impart a rough, non-slip surface to the concrete
   C. prevent excessive evaporation of water in the concrete
   D. shorten the length of time it would take for the concrete to harden

24. Concrete is *rubbed* with a(n) 24._____

   A. emery wheel B. carborundum brick
   C. sandstone D. alundum stick

25. To prevent concrete from sticking to forms, the forms should be painted with 25._____

   A. oil B. kerosene C. water D. lime

26. One method of measuring the consistency of a concrete mix is by means of a _____ test. 26._____

   A. penetration B. flow
   C. slump D. weight

27. A chemical that is sometimes used to prevent the freezing of concrete in cold weather is 27._____

   A. alum B. glycerine
   C. calcium chloride D. sodium nitrate

28. The one of the following that is LEAST commonly used for columns is 28._____

   A. wide flange beams B. angles
   C. concrete-filled pipe D. "I" beams

29. Fire protection of steel floor beams is MOST frequently accomplished by the use of 29._____

   A. gypsum block B. brick
   C. rock wool fill D. vermiculite gypsum plaster

30. A *Pittsburgh lock* is a(n) 30._____

   A. emergency door lock B. sheet metal joint
   C. elevator safety D. boiler valve

31. Of the following items, the one which is NOT used in making fastenings to masonry or plaster walls is a(n) 31._____

   A. lead shield B. expansion bolt
   C. rawl plug D. steel bushing

32. The term *bell and spigot* USUALLY refers to 32._____

   A. refrigerator motors B. cast iron pipes
   C. steam radiator outlets D. electrical receptacles

33. In plumbing work, a valve which allows water to flow in one direction only is commonly known as a _____ valve.

   A. check   B. globe   C. gate   D. stop

34. A pipe coupling is BEST used to connect two pieces of pipe of

   A. the same diameter in a straight line
   B. the same diameter at right angles to each other
   C. different diameters at a 45° angle
   D. different diameters in a 1/8th bend

35. One method of testing fuses is to connect a pair of test lamps in the circuit in such a manner that the test lamp will light up if the fuse is good and will remain dark if the fuse is bad. In the illustration, 1 and 2 are fuses. In order to test if fuse 1 is bad, test lamps should be connected between

   A. A and B   B. B and D   C. A and D   D. C and B

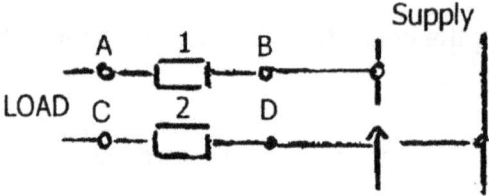

36. Operating an incandescent electric light bulb at less than its rated voltage will result in

   A. shorter life and brighter light
   B. longer life and dimmer light
   C. brighter light and longer life
   D. dimmer light and shorter life

37. In order to control a lamp from two different positions, it is necessary to use

   A. two single pole switches
   B. one single pole switch and one four-way switch
   C. two three-way switches
   D. one single pole switch and one four-way switch

38. The PRINCIPAL reason for the grounding of electrical equipment and circuits is to

   A. prevent short circuits   B. insure safety from shock
   C. save power   D. increase voltage

39. The ordinary single-pole flush wall type switch must be connected

   A. across the line
   B. in the "hot" conductor
   C. in the grounded conductor
   D. in the white conductor

40. A strike plate is MOST closely associated with a

   A. lock   B. sash   C. butt   D. tie rod

41. A room is 7'6" wide by 9'0" long, with a ceiling height of 8'0". One gallon of flat paint will cover approximately 400 square feet of wall.
The number of gallons of this paint required to paint the walls of this room, making no deductions for windows or doors, is *most nearly* _____ gallon.

   A. 1/4   B. 1/3   C. 3/4   D. 1

42. The cost of a certain job is broken down as follows:
    Materials $375
    Rental of equipment 120
    Labor   315
   The percentage of the total cost of the job that can be charged to materials is *most nearly*

   A. 40%   B. 42%   C. 44%   D. 46%

43. By trial, it is found that by using two cubic feet of sand, a 5 cubic foot batch of concrete is produced. Using the same proportions, the amount of sand required to produce 2 cubic yards of concrete is *most nearly* _____ cubic feet.

   A. 20   B. 22   C. 24   D. 26

44. It takes four men six days to do a certain job. Working at the same speed, the number of days it will take three men to do this job is

   A. 7   B. 8   C. 9   D. 10

45. The cost of rawl plugs is $2.75 per gross. The cost of 2,448 rawl plugs is

   A. $46.75   B. $47.25   C. $47.75   D. $48.25

KEY (CORRECT ANSWERS)

1. D	11. B	21. B	31. D	41. C
2. B	12. D	22. A	32. B	42. D
3. B	13. C	23. C	33. A	43. B
4. B	14. D	24. B	34. A	44. B
5. D	15. C	25. A	35. C	45. A
6. B	16. C	26. C	36. B	
7. C	17. A	27. C	37. C	
8. B	18. D	28. B	38. B	
9. D	19. B	29. D	39. B	
10. A	20. D	30. B	40. A	

EXAMINATION SECTION
TEST 1

DIRECTIONS: Each question or incomplete statement is followed by several suggested answers or completions. Select the one that BEST answers the question or completes the statement. *PRINT THE LETTER OF THE CORRECT ANSWER IN THE SPACE AT THE RIGHT.*

1. Assume that a two story building measures 21'6" x 53'7". It is in a district that calls for an open space ratio of .80. The required open space on this lot must be *most nearly* square feet.

    A. 922 B. 1152 C. 1843 D. 2880

    1.____

2. Assume that the elevation at the back of a lot is 127.36 ft. and the elevation at the front of the same lot is 125.49 ft.
    The difference in elevation between front and back of the lot is *most nearly*

    A. 1'10 1/8" B. 1'10 1/4" C. 1'10 3/8" D. 1'10 1/2"

    2.____

3. The sketch below represents the lowest story of a new building. In order for this story to be considered a basement, the elevation of the first floor must be AT LEAST

    A. 131.09 B. 131.14 C. 131.19 D. 131.24

    3.____

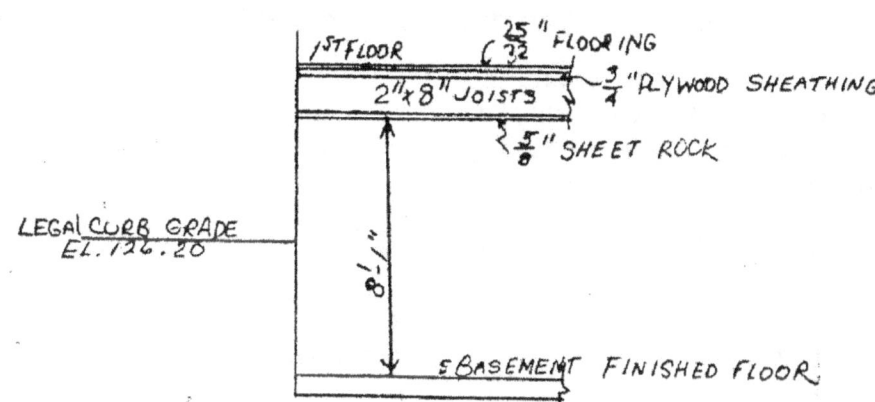

4. The MOST important requirement of a good report is that it should be

    A. properly addressed B. clear and concise
    C. verbose D. spelled correctly

    4.____

5. Of the following, in determining whether a violation should be referred for court action, the MOST important item that should be considered is

    A. the amount of available time you have to process the case
    B. the availability of the inspector
    C. whether or not the owner has indicated a desire to cooperate with the department
    D. whether or not the case is important enough to warrant court action

    5.____

6. In the Zoning Resolution, the size of required side yards would be found in the chapters on

   A. Use Groups
   B. Bulk Regulations
   C. Area Districts
   D. District Boundaries

7. According to the Zoning Resolution, the one of the following that is NOT considered part of the floor area of a building is a(n)

   A. basement
   B. stairwell at floor level
   C. penthouse
   D. attached garage on 1st floor

8. The one of the following that is permitted by the Zoning Resolution as a home occupation is

   A. veterinary medicine
   B. real estate broker
   C. teaching of music
   D. public relations agency

9. For the purpose of determining the number of rooms in a dwelling unit, the Zoning Resolution adds an arbitrary number to the number of *living rooms*.
   Where there are six or less living rooms, this arbitrary number is

   A. 1/2   B. 1   C. 1 1/2   D. 2

10. Assuming the following signs are all 10 square feet in area, the one that is NOT subject to the provisions of the Zoning Resolution is one indicating

    A. a freight entrance to a building
    B. a fund drive for a civic organization
    C. vacancies in an apartment building
    D. a parking area at the rear of a structure

11. On a plan, the symbol ~~~~ represents

    A. earth
    B. wood
    C. metal lath
    D. marble

12. On a plan, the symbol represents

    A. cinder
    B. brick
    C. plywood
    D. rock lath and plaster

13. On a plan, the symbol represents

    A. glass
    B. asphalt shingles
    C. concrete
    D. porcelain enamel

14. A corbel is a form of

    A. cricket
    B. crown molding
    C. cantilever
    D. curtain wall

15. In balloon type framing, the second floor joists rest on a

    A. sole plate
    B. ribband
    C. header
    D. sill

16. Condensation of moisture in inadequately ventilated attics or roof spaces is usually GREATEST in

    A. summer   B. autumn   C. winter   D. spring

17. Of the following combinations of tread and riser, the one that would be acceptable for required stairs in either a new office building or a multiple dwelling is

    A. 9 1/4", 7 1/2"
    B. 9 1/2", 7 1/4"
    C. 9 1/2", 7 3/4"
    D. 10", 8"

18. A meeting rail is a common part of a

    A. door frame
    B. window sash
    C. stairwell
    D. bulkhead

19. If doors in an old building do not close, it is MOST probably an indication that the

    A. frames have shrunk
    B. building has settled
    C. hinges were not set properly
    D. wood used for the doors are of inferior grade

20. Cracks in concrete are not necessarily caused by settlement of a structure. Sometimes they are caused by

    A. shrinkage
    B. curing
    C. hydration
    D. over-troweling

KEY (CORRECT ANSWERS)

1. C
2. D
3. A
4. B
5. C

6. B
7. D
8. C
9. C
10. B

11. A
12. B
13. A
14. C
15. B

16. C
17. C
18. B
19. B
20. A

TEST 2

DIRECTIONS: Each question or incomplete statement is followed by several suggested answers or completions. Select the one that BEST answers the question or completes the statement. *PRINT THE LETTER OF THE CORRECT ANSWER IN THE SPACE AT THE RIGHT.*

1. Required exit doors from a room must open in the direction of egress when the room is occupied by more than _____ persons. 1._____

    A. 15 B. 25 C. 35 D. 50

2. A window in a masonry wall on a lot line 2._____

    A. is not permitted
    B. must have a fire resistive rating of 3/4 hour
    C. must have a fire resistive rating of 1 hour
    D. must have a fire resistive rating of 1 1/2 hours

3. Air entrained concrete is required in all cases for 3._____

    A. garage floors   B. footings
    C. grade beams   D. columns

4. A parapet wall or railing would be required on new non-residential structures where the height of the structure is greater than (give lowest height specified by law) _____ feet. 4._____

    A. 15 B. 19 C. 22 D. 25

5. Of the following statements, the one that is CORRECT is that wood joists may 5._____

    A. not be supported on a fire wall
    B. be supported on a fire wall only if fireproofed wall is used
    C. be supported on a fire wall only if they are separated from each other by at least 4 inches of solid masonry
    D. be supported on a fire wall only if they are separated from each other by at least 12 inches of solid masonry

6. A foundation wall below grade may be of hollow block only if the building 6._____

    A. is a residence
    B. is no more than one story high
    C. is of frame construction
    D. has no cellar or basement

7. The Building Code specifies that lintels are required to be fire-proofed when the opening is more than _____ feet. 7._____

    A. 3 B. 4 C. 5 D. 6

8. In a 12-inch brick wall, the MAXIMUM permitted depth of a chase is 8._____

    A. none B. 4" C. 6" D. 8"

9. Wood joists should clear flues and chimneys by at least 9._____

    A. 1" B. 2" C. 3" D. 4"

10. Fire retarding or enclosure in shafts of all vent ducts are required when they

    A. go through more than one floor
    B. are used for intake as well as exhaust
    C. are more than 144 square inches in area
    D. are in rooms subdivided with wood partitions

11. Assume a builder is unable to complete the pour for a continuous concrete floor slab. The slab is supported by beams and girders.
    The construction joint should be made at a point

    A. over a beam
    B. one quarter of the span length from the beam
    C. one third of the span length from the beam
    D. midway between beams

12. Under required stairs in a Class 3 building,

    A. it is unlawful to locate a closet
    B. a closet is permitted provided that the stringers are fire retarded
    C. a closet is permitted provided that the closet is completely lined with incombustible material
    D. a closet is permitted provided that fireproof wood is used to frame out the closet

13. In New York City, the exit provisions of the State Labor Law apply

    A. only to factories
    B. to factories and warehouses
    C. to factories, warehouses, and restaurants
    D. to all types of uses

14. A Class 3 building, two stories high, may have required stairs enclosed with stud partitions fire retarded with gypsum boards unless the building is used for a

    A. factory   B. storage warehouse
    C. bowling alley   D. department store

15. The one of the following rooms in a *place of assembly* that is required to be sprinklered is a

    A. performer's dressing room
    B. kitchen
    C. service pantry
    D. waiting room

16. Of the following, the FIRST operation in the demolition of a building is the

    A. shoring of the adjoining buildings
    B. erection of railings around stairwells
    C. removal of windows
    D. venting of the roof

17. As used in the Building Code, *consistency* of concrete refers to

    A. composition   B. water-cement ratio
    C. relative plasticity   D. proportion of aggregates

18. One condition that is required for a building to be considered a *Special Occupancy Structure* is that the building is used for

    A. a theater
    B. a church
    C. a restaurant
    D. motor vehicle repairs

19. A wire glass vision panel on a door opening into a fire tower is

    A. not permitted
    B. permitted if the panel has a fire rating of 3/4 hour
    C. permitted if the panel has a fire rating of 3/4 hour and is less than 100 square inches in area
    D. permitted if the panel has a fire rating of 3/4 hour, is less than 100 square inches in area, and is glazed with two thicknesses of wire glass with an air space between

20. One of the requirements that must be met before untreated wood can be used as a subdividing partition in a Class 1 building is that the partition

    A. be no more than 8 feet high
    B. enclose an area less than 200 square feet in size
    C. enclose office space only
    D. be made of a single thickness of wood

KEY (CORRECT ANSWERS)

1.	D	11.	D
2.	B	12.	C
3.	A	13.	A
4.	C	14.	C
5.	C	15.	A
6.	D	16.	C
7.	B	17.	C
8.	B	18.	A
9.	D	19.	A
10.	A	20.	D

TEST 3

DIRECTIONS: Each question or incomplete statement is followed by several suggested answers or completions. Select the one that BEST answers the question or completes the statement. *PRINT THE LETTER OF THE CORRECT ANSWER IN THE SPACE AT THE RIGHT.*

1. There are two criteria required for determining whether a multiple dwelling shall be classified as a *converted dwelling*.
   The FIRST is the number of families originally occupying the dwelling, and the second is the

   A. conjunctive uses
   B. date of erection of the building
   C. classification, whether Class A or B
   D. number of families now occupying the dwelling

2. According to the Multiple Dwelling Law, a *dinette* is NOT considered a living room if its area is _____ sq. ft. or less.

   A. 50   B. 55   C. 59   D. 64

3. Where a building faces only one street, the curb level used for measuring the height of the building is the

   A. lowest curb level in front of the building
   B. highest curb level in front of the building
   C. level of the curb at the center of the front of the building
   D. average of the levels of the lowest and highest curb level in front of the building

4. According to the Multiple Dwelling Code, one of the living rooms in each apartment of a newly created multiple dwelling shall have a MINIMUM floor area of _____ square feet.

   A. 59   B. 110   C. 150   D. 175

5. It is proposed to alter an old law tenement so as to increase the number of apartments. Of the following, the one that MOST completely gives the requirements to be met before the alteration can be approved is: Each new apartment must be provided a

   A. water closet
   B. water closet and a wash basin
   C. water closet, a wash basin, and a bath or shower
   D. water closet, a wash basin, a bath or shower, and centrally supplied heat

6. Gas fueled space heaters may be permitted in lieu of centrally supplied heat.
   One of the following conditions required before the use of space heaters can be permitted is that

   A. each apartment has no more than two living rooms
   B. the building is a Class A multiple dwelling
   C. all apartments are used for single room occupancy
   D. D, the gas line supplying the heater be connected directly to the main so that the tenant cannot control the flow of gas

7. An incinerator is required in all multiple

   A. dwellings
   B. dwellings four or more stories in height
   C. dwellings four or more stories in height and occupied by more than twelve families
   D. dwellings four or more stories in height occupied by more than twelve families and erected after October 1, 1951

8. Tests of required sprinkler systems in a single room occupancy building must be made

   A. monthly   B. quarterly
   C. semi-annually   D. annually

9. An additional apartment may be created on the first floor of a Class A frame converted dwelling provided that no more than two families will occupy this floor and

   A. the entrance hall is sprinklered
   B. the building is brick veneered
   C. there is no basement occupancy
   D. all stairs are enclosed in one hour fire partitions

10. The MAIN feature differentiating a *five tower* from a *fire stair* is the

    A. fire rating of the enclosure walls
    B. use to which the fire tower is put
    C. method of entering the fire tower from the building
    D. height of the fire tower

11. A new elevator shaft is to be built into a non-fireproof multiple dwelling. Of the following materials, the one that has the lowest fire resistance that would be acceptable for the enclosure walls of this shaft is

    A. 3" solid gypsum block
    B. 2" x 4" studs with 5/8" fire code 60 each side
    C. steel studs, wire mesh and 3/4" P.C. plaster
    D. 4" hollow concrete blocks, plastered both sides

12. Of the following statements, the one that is MOST complete and accurate is that a frame extension 70 sq. ft. in area added to a frame multiple dwelling is

    A. not permitted
    B. permitted only if the walls of the extension are brick filled
    C. permitted only if the walls of the extension are brick filled and the extension is to be used solely for bathrooms
    D. permitted only if the walls of the extension are brick filled, the extension is to be used solely for bathrooms and the walls are at least 3 ft. from the side lot lines

13. Assume it is proposed to extend a business use in a non-fireproof multiple dwelling by erecting an extension at the rear of the building.
    The roof the extension is required to be fireproof

    A. in all cases
    B. when the business use requires a combustible occupancy permit
    C. when there are fire escapes above the extension
    D. if the business use is a factory

14. In a Class A dwelling, two water closets may

    A. be placed in one compartment only in old law tenements
    B. be placed in one compartment in either old law or new law tenements
    C. be placed in one compartment in all types of apartment houses
    D. not be placed in one compartment

15. According to the Multiple Dwelling Law, a janitor is NOT required when the maximum number of families occupying the dwelling is

    A. 6   B. 9   C. 12   D. 15

16. The first floor above the lowest cellar in a non-fireproof multiple dwelling does NOT have to be fireproof if

    A. the cellar is used only for incombustible storage
    B. there are two means of egress from the cellar
    C. the building is no more than three stories in height
    D. the dwelling is occupied by no more than nine families

17. In a converted multiple dwelling, ventilation of a room on the top story may be obtained by

    A. a skylight
    B. a duct with a wind blown hood
    C. a duct with an electrically operated fan
    D. by a window only and no other method is acceptable

18. It is proposed to build a closet under the stairs leading to the second floor in a non-fireproof new law tenement. This is

    A. not permitted
    B. permitted only if the entire closet is built of non-combustible materials
    C. permitted only if the closet is used for non-combustible storage
    D. permitted if the closet is built of fire-retarded partitions and the soffit of the stairs is also fire-retarded

19. For multiple dwellings erected after April 18, 1929, a ladder from a fire escape to a roof is NOT required when

    A. the building is three stories or less in height
    B. the roof is built of incombustible material
    C. the fire escape is on the front of the building
    D. there is no safe access from the roof to another building

20. It is proposed to convert a Class B multiple dwelling used for summer resort occupancy to year-round Class B use. This conversion is

    A. illegal
    B. legal provided the exits comply with the requirements for Class B use
    C. legal provided the exits and toilet facilities comply with the requirements for Class B use
    D. legal provided the exits, toilet facilities, and ventilation requirements comply with the requirements for Class B use

KEY (CORRECT ANSWERS)

1. B
2. B
3. C
4. C
5. D

6. B
7. D
8. D
9. B
10. C

11. A
12. A
13. C
14. A
15. C

16. C
17. A
18. A
19. C
20. A

EXAMINATION SECTION
TEST 1

DIRECTIONS: Each question or incomplete statement is followed by several suggested answers or completions. Select the one that BEST answers the question or completes the statement. *PRINT THE LETTER OF THE CORRECT ANSWER IN THE SPACE AT THE RIGHT.*

1. The basis of differentiating between a *Class A* and a *Class B* multiple dwelling is

    A. the date when the building was erected
    B. the size of the building
    C. whether residents are permanent or transient
    D. the number of families living in the building

    1.____

2. The basis of differentiating between a *cellar* and a *basement* is

    A. whether or not there are windows
    B. the relationship of its height to curb level
    C. the ventilation available
    D. the number of exists provided

    2.____

3. The MINIMUM horizontal dimension permitted for a living room in an apartment house erected after 1929 is

    A. 8'0"   B. 8'6"   C. 9'0"   D. 9'6"

    3.____

4. It is proposed to build a garage for two cars for use by the tenants in a three-family dwelling. The garage will be on the same lot as the dwelling.
Of the following, the statement that MOST completely gives the type or types of construction that would be permitted for the garage is _____ with concrete roof.

    A. frame or block walls with flat wood roof or block walls with wood peak roof, or block walls
    B. block walls with flat wood roof or block walls with wood peak roof or block walls
    C. block walls with wood peak roof or block walls
    D. block walls

    4.____

5. A restaurant is permitted in a hotel of non-fireproof construction providing that

    A. there are automatic sprinkler heads in the kitchen
    B. there are two means of egress from the kitchen
    C. the kitchen has windows opening to a required yard
    D. the walls of the kitchen have one hour fire rating

    5.____

6. The one of the following that is considered a *living room* is a

    A. bathroom   B. foyer
    C. public room   D. kitchen

    6.____

7. In certain types of occupancies, gas-fueled space heaters may be used instead of a central heating system. One of the requirements that MUST be met in order that space heaters be permitted in an apartment is that the

    7.____

29

A. building be of fireproof construction
B. apartment must consist of two or more living rooms
C. building is not a tenement
D. apartment has two means of egress

8. Where a parapet wall is required, the MINIMUM height permitted is

   A. 3'0"   B. 3'6"   C. 4'0"   D. 4'6"

9. Ceilings over boilers in converted dwellings MUST be fire-retarded with

   A. two layers of 3/8" sheet rock
   B. wire lath and 3/4" cement mortar
   C. 3/8" rock lath and 1/2" gypsum mortar
   D. 3/8" sheet rock with #26 U.S. gage stamped metal

10. A fire alarm signal is required in all multiple dwellings which have the following type of occupancy:

    A. tenement   B. hotel
    C. converted dwelling   D. single room

11. The multiple dwelling law requires that every living room be ventilated by windows having an area of at least 10% of the floor surface of the room. Assume that a certain living room is 10'6" long by 9'6" wide.
    Of the following, the MINIMUM window size that would be acceptable is

    A. 3'2" x 3'6"   B. 3'4" x 3'6"
    C. 3'4" x 3'8"   D. 3'6" x 3'8"

12. The multiple dwelling law specifies the minimum area and height of living rooms. The PRINCIPAL reason for this is to

    A. insure adequate light and air
    B. make inspections easier
    C. reduce possibility of serious fires
    D. control the number of occupants

13. The one of the following that is considered a multiple dwelling when located in a building separate from other buildings is a

    A. jail   B. monastery
    C. nurses' residence D. asylum

14. When any part of a building is to be fire-retarded, that part of the building MUST be protected by materials having a fire rating of at least _____ hour(s).

    A. 1   B. 2   C. 3   D. 4

15. A *fire damper* is necessary to

    A. adjust the draft in a chimney
    B. wet down combustible material in case of fire
    C. prevent the passage of heat and smoke through an air duct
    D. control the flame in an incinerator

Questions 16-18.

DIRECTIONS: Questions 16 through 18 must be answered in accordance with the following paragraph.

When constructed within a multiple dwelling, such storage space shall be equipped with a sprinkler system and also with a system of mechanical ventilation in no way connected with any other ventilating system. Such storage space shall have no opening into any other part of the dwelling except through a fireproof vestibule. Any such vestibule shall have a minimum superficial floor area of fifty square feet and its maximum area shall not exceed seventy-five square feet. It shall be enclosed with incombustible partitions having a fire-resistive rating of three hours. The floor and ceiling of such vestibule shall also be of incombustible material having a fire-resistive rating of at least three hours. There shall be two doors to provide access from the dwelling to the car storage space. Each such door shall have a fire-resistive rating of one and one-half hours and shall be provided with a device to prevent the opening of one door until the other door is entirely closed.

16. According to the above paragraph, the one of the following that is REQUIRED in order for cars to be permitted to be stored in a multiple dwelling is a(n)

    A. fireproof vestibule
    B. elevator from the garage
    C. approved heating system
    D. sprinkler system

17. According to the above paragraph, the one of the following materials that would NOT be acceptable for the walls of a vestibule connecting a garage to the dwelling portion of a building is

    A. 3" solid gypsum blocks
    B. 4" brick
    C. 4" hollow gypsum blocks, plastered both sides
    D. 6" solid cinder concrete blocks

18. According to the above paragraph, the one of the following that would be ACCEPTABLE for the width and length of a vestibule connecting a garage that is within a multiple dwelling to the dwelling portion of the building is

    A. 3'8" x 13'0"   B. 4'6" x 18'6"
    C. 4'9" x 14'6"   D. 4'3" x 19'3"

Questions 19-20.

DIRECTIONS: Questions 19 and 20 must be answered in accordance with the following paragraph.

It shall be unlawful to place, use, or to maintain in a condition intended, arranged or designed for use, any gas-fired cooking appliance, laundry stove, heating stove, range or water heater or combination of such appliances in any room or space used for living or sleeping in any new or existing multiple dwelling unless such room or space has a window opening to the outer air or such gas appliance is vented to the outer air. All automatically operated gas appliances shall be equipped with a device which shall shut off automatically the gas supply to the main burners when the pilot light in such appliance is extinguished. A gas range or the cooking portion of a gas appliance incorporating a room heater shall not be deemed an automatically operated gas appliance. However, burners in gas ovens and broilers which can be turned on and off or ignited by non-manual means shall be equipped with a device which shall shut off automatically the gas supply to those burners when the operation of such non-manual means fails.

19. According to the above paragraph, an automatic shut-off device is NOT required on a gas

    A. hot water heater
    B. laundry drier
    C. space heater
    D. range

20. According to the above paragraph, a gas-fired water heater is permitted

    A. only in kitchens
    B. only in bathrooms
    C. only in living rooms
    D. in any type of room

21. A tenant tells an inspector that the spring on the entrance door to his apartment is broken and the door remains open.
    Of the following, the BEST action for the inspector to take, after verifying the facts, is to

    A. tell the tenant to get the janitor to fix it
    B. tell the janitor to get it fixed
    C. tell the landlord to hire someone to fix it
    D. report it as a violation and tell the janitor to get it fixed

22. An owner of a two-family house tells you, an inspector, that he wants to convert his house to a three-family dwelling. He asks you for your advice as to the requirements that must be met for this change.
    You should

    A. inspect the building so that you can give him all the necessary information
    B. refer him to your supervisor for fuller advice
    C. tell him to consult a competent architect
    D. tell him you can't give him the information unless he gives you the plans of the building to check

23. An inspector receiving a complaint from a tenant should consider it as

    A. most likely the result of a quarrel with the landlord
    B. usually an exaggerated statement of the facts
    C. a matter which should be investigated
    D. something to be checked after all other work has been completed

24. In a dispute about a matter covered by the multiple dwelling law, an inspector should carefully AVOID

    A. taking the attitude that the landlord is always wrong
    B. sounding out both the landlord and the tenant when both sides disagree
    C. investigating the basis of the disagreement
    D. getting involved in the matter until both the landlord and the tenant agree on the facts

25. If an inspector does not clearly understand one of the provisions of the multiple dwelling law, he should

    A. interpret it as best he can
    B. get his superior to explain it to him
    C. avoid having to enforce this provision
    D. consider this provision unimportant

26. If a tenant continues to ask an inspector a great many questions, the inspector should

    A. tell the tenant not to ask so many questions because the inspector has too many other things to do
    B. pretend he does not hear the tenant unless the tenant persists
    C. tell the tenant that all questions should be referred to the main office
    D. answer the questions as briefly as he can without creating the impression he is trying to *brush off* the tenant

27. If an inspector is dissatisfied with his assignment, he should

    A. demand that he be re-assigned to another task
    B. slow down his work so that his superior knows he is dissatisfied
    C. continue doing his work as well as he can but request a reassignment at the earliest opportunity
    D. make sure his fellow inspectors know his feelings

28. The MAIN reason why an inspector should know the value of his work is that

    A. he will have more of an incentive to do a better job
    B. he can better explain his job to the public
    C. it will be easier for him to get a promotion
    D. he will be able to ignore minor inspections

29. A landlord has made an unjustified complaint about an inspector to the inspector's superiors.
    In future contacts with this landlord, the inspector should be

    A. cool and distant to avoid more trouble
    B. smiling and friendly to ease matters
    C. courteous and fair in enforcing the law
    D. strict so that the landlord knows he must comply with his orders

30. Assume that an inspector believes that one of the provisions of the multiple dwelling law is unfair.
    The inspector should

    A. refuse to enforce this provision because it is unfair
    B. enforce this provision because it does not matter whether the law is fair or not
    C. refuse to enforce this provision because it is impossible to make the public comply with this provision
    D. enforce the provision because it is the law

31. In wood frame construction, mortise and tenon joints may be illegal. The basis for determining whether or not such a joint is legal is

    A. type of wood
    B. size of members
    C. load carried by the members
    D. age of wood

32. Of the following terms, the one LEAST related to the others is

    A. scuttle   B. buttress   C. bulkhead   D. parapet

33. Of the following terms, the one LEAST related to the others is

    A. egress   B. fire tower
    C. fire wall   D. fire escape

34. A deformed bar would MOST likely be used in

    A. masonry work
    B. steel construction
    C. wood construction
    D. reinforced concrete construction

35. A party wall is a(n)

    A. wall serving two structures
    B. interior wall
    C. retaining wall
    D. wall without openings

36. Of the following types of walls, the one LEAST related to the others is

    A. faced   B. spandrel   C. apron   D. panel

37. A bar bending table would MOST likely be used in the following type of construction:

    A. steel   B. reinforced concrete
    C. wood   D. masonry

38. Of the following terms, the one which is LEAST related to the others is

    A. down-spout   B. ground seat
    C. gutter   D. leader

39. Of the following terms, the one which is LEAST related to the others is

    A. ball-peen   B. doublecut flat
    C. file card   D. rat tail

40. Of the following, the one which is LEAST related to the others is

    A. chase   B. footing   C. pier   D. pile

Questions 41-45.

DIRECTIONS: Questions 41 through 45 are to be answered in accordance with the floor plan of one floor of a converted dwelling shown on the last page of this test.

41. The depth of the linen closet, indicated by the letter S, is

    A. 1'4" B. 1'5" C. 1'6" D. 1'7"

42. The door that should have a fire rating is indicated by the letter

    A. G B. H C. J D. K

43. The walls of the building are of

    A. frame construction B. solid brick
    C. brick and block D. solid block

44. Of the following types of steel sections, the one that MOST closely resembles, in appearance, the steel beams used to support the floor joists is

    A. ⊔ B. ST C. L D. WF

45. The grade of lumber indicated for joists FORMERLY was called #

    A. 1 common B. 1 select C. 2 common D. 2 select

8 (#1)

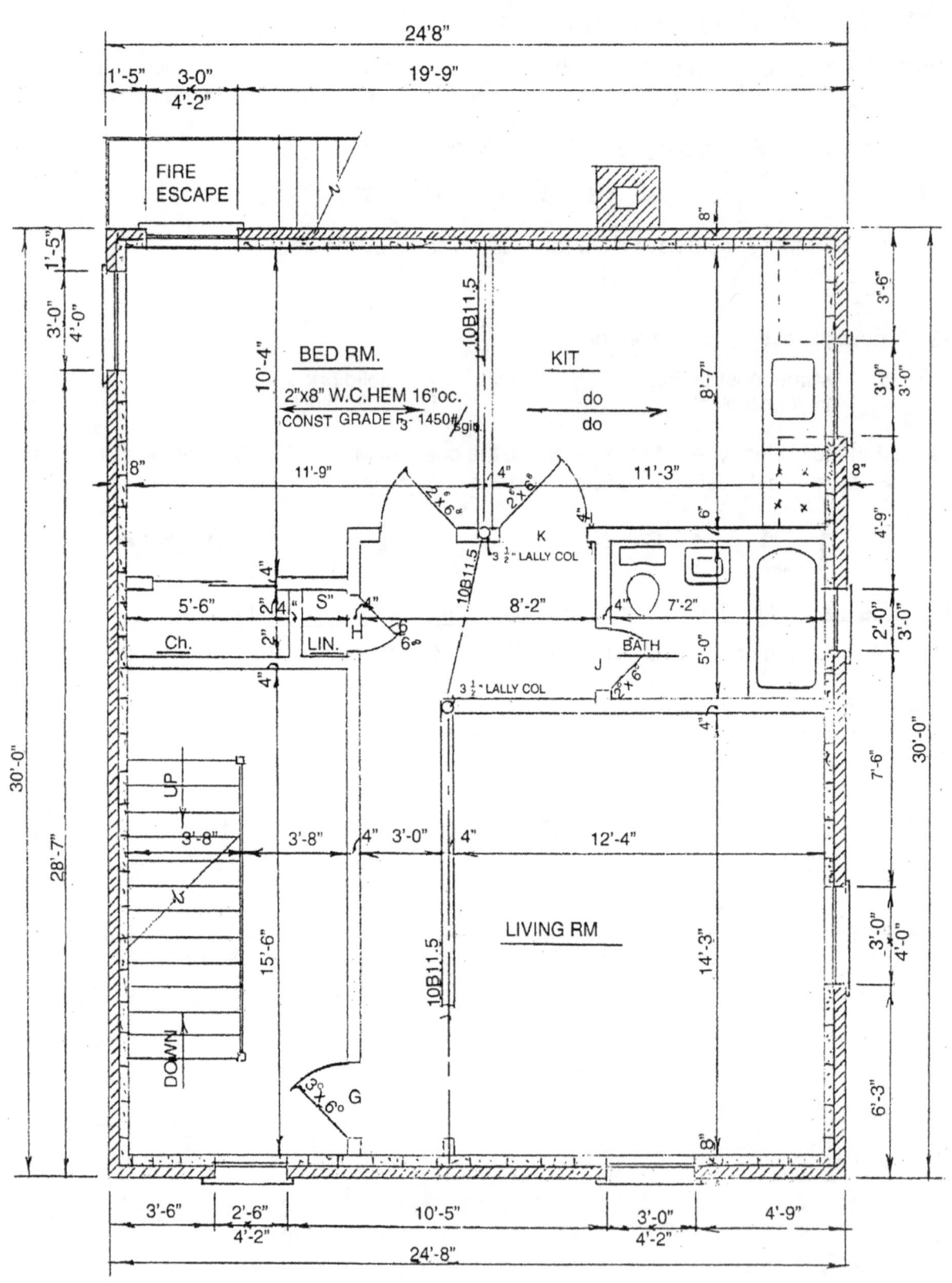

FLOOR PLAN

KEY (CORRECT ANSWERS)

1. C	11. A	21. D	31. B	41. C
2. B	12. A	22. C	32. B	42. A
3. A	13. C	23. C	33. C	43. C
4. D	14. A	24. A	34. D	44. D
5. A	15. C	25. B	35. A	45. A
6. D	16. D	26. D	36. A	
7. B	17. B	27. C	37. B	
8. B	18. C	28. A	38. B	
9. B	19. D	29. C	39. A	
10. D	20. D	30. D	40. A	

EXAMINATION SECTION
TEST 1

DIRECTIONS: Each question or incomplete statement is followed by several suggested answers or completions. Select the one that BEST answers the question or completes the statement. *PRINT THE LETTER OF THE CORRECT ANSWER IN THE SPACE AT THE RIGHT.*

1. A kitchenette is defined as a cooking space having a floor area of LESS than _____ square feet.

    A. 57 B. 58 C. 59 D. 60

2. The one of the following that is classed as a converted dwelling is a(n)

    A. apartment house erected prior to 1929, now used as a hotel
    B. lodging house erected prior to 1913, now used as a multiple dwelling
    C. one-family house erected prior to 1929, now used as a multiple dwelling
    D. rooming house erected prior to 1913, now used as a hotel

3. A *fire-retarded* partition must have a fire-resistive rating of AT LEAST _____ hour(s).

    A. 1 B. 2 C. 3 D. 4

4. The multiple dwelling law states that the total window area of a room must be at least one-tenth of the floor surface area of the room.
   The one of the following types of rooms that is exempted from this provision is a

    A. bedroom   B. kitchen
    C. recreation room   D. bathroom

5. In a non-fireproof multiple dwelling, the HIGHEST story in which a factory may be operated is the

    A. 1st B. 2nd C. 3rd D. 4th

6. In a multiple dwelling under construction, the MINIMUM required width of an entrance hall, from the entrance to the first stair, is

    A. 3'4" B. 3'8" C. 4'0" D. 4'4"

7. Access to a required fire escape, used as a legal second means of egress from an apartment, may be from a

    A. public hall B. kitchen
    C. bathroom   D. closet

8. The basis for differentiating between a *tenement* and any other *Class A multiple dwelling* is

    A. the year in which it was built
    B. the number of families now residing therein
    C. whether residents are permanent or transient
    D. classification of construction

9. In a 6-story multiple dwelling under construction, wood floor joists would NOT be used for

   A. apartments
   B. recreation rooms
   C. toilets
   D. public halls

10. If plans were to be filed now for a change of occupancy, the type of occupancy for which a fire escape is NOT acceptable as a second means of egress is

    A. club house
    B. single room
    C. tenement
    D. garden type maisonette

11. The multiple dwelling law requires self-closing doors between apartments and halls in all Class A multiple dwellings.
    The PRINCIPAL reason for this is to

    A. insure privacy of the tenants
    B. protect other tenants from excessive noise
    C. reduce heat loss
    D. prevent the spread of fire

12. The multiple dwelling law prohibits the erection of a building the height of which is in excess of one and one-half times the width of the widest street on which it faces.
    The MAIN reason for this prohibition is to

    A. insure that tenants will not have to travel too far to the street in case of fire
    B. provide adequate light and air
    C. prevent excessive loadings on the footings
    D. provide adequate water pressure on the top floor

13. The multiple dwelling law requires that the walls of all interior courts shall be built with a light-colored brick. The PRINCIPAL reason for this is that

    A. light-colored brick is easier to clean
    B. more light will be reflected into the apartments
    C. light-colored brick is usually stronger
    D. rain will not penetrate light-colored brick readily

14. The multiple dwelling law requires that every fire escape constructed of material subject to rusting shall be painted with two or more coats of paint of contrasting colors.
    The reason that each coat is required to be of a different color is that

    A. the different pigments in the two coats will better protect the steel from rust
    B. when two colors are used, the sun will not bleach the top color as rapidly as when only one color is used
    C. the contrasting colors make inspection easier
    D. a better bond is obtained between paint of different color

15. The multiple dwelling law requires that every fire escape at the top story of a building shall be provided with a stairway or ladder to the roof, except where the roof is a peak roof with a pitch in excess of twenty degrees. The reason that access to the roof from the fire escape is NOT required where the pitch of the roof is in excess of twenty degrees is that

    A. it would be difficult to walk on a roof with such a slope
    B. a steep roof would tend to catch fire quicker, so people should not be on the roof

C. sparks from a fire would tend to roll down the roof toward any person climbing up the ladder
D. it is almost impossible to anchor a ladder to a steep roof

16. The multiple dwelling law states that for stairs, each tread shall be not less than nine and one-half inches wide; each riser shall not exceed seven and three-quarters inches in height; and the product of the number of inches in the width of the tread and the number of inches in the height of the riser shall be at least seventy and at most seventy-five. The one of the following sets of dimensions that is acceptable for the stairs of a multiple dwelling is tread _____, riser _____. 16.____

    A. 9 3/4"; 7 1/8"   B. 9 1/4"; 8"
    C. 10 1/4"; 7 1/8"   D. 10 1/2"; 7 1/2"

17. The multiple dwelling law prohibits construction of a frame multiple dwelling. The PRINCIPAL reason for this is that 17.____

    A. frame buildings are more susceptible to vermin infection
    B. the heavier loads occurring in multiple dwellings can not be supported in frame buildings
    C. frame buildings, used as multiple dwellings, tend to become slums
    D. fire in a frame building is more dangerous than in other types of buildings

18. The multiple dwelling law states that no radio or other wires shall be attached to any vent line extending above the roof. The PRINCIPAL reason for this prohibition is that 18.____

    A. vent lines are relatively weak structures
    B. wires increase the danger of electric shock due to lightning
    C. low wires are a safety hazard
    D. ventilation will be blocked

19. In a non-fireproof building, the multiple dwelling law requires that certain partitions shall be fire-stopped. This means that 19.____

    A. fireproof doors must be used
    B. the partitions must be constructed of incombustible material
    C. the covering of the studs must be of incombustible material
    D. the spaces between the top of a partition and the ceiling and floors above must be filled with incombustible material

20. The building code states that the floor of a multiple dwelling shall be designed for a live load of 40 pounds per square foot. *Live load* means weight of 20.____

    A. floor joists, beams, and girders
    B. tenants only
    C. tenants and their furniture
    D. floor joists, beams, girders, tenants, and furniture

21. An anonymous complaint is made to the Department of Buildings. This complaint should be

    A. ignored because it is not signed
    B. investigated because it may be valid
    C. filed to see if further complaints of a like nature are made
    D. ignored because only troublemakers make anonymous complaints

22. In order to make certain emergency repairs to an occupied multiple dwelling, a fire escape must be removed. The owner asks you, an inspector, for permission to do this. You should

    A. grant the request, since the only way to make the repair is to remove the fire escape
    B. tell the owner to find another method of making the repair since a fire escape may not be removed
    C. refer the owner to your superiors, since you do not have the authority to grant the request
    D. grant the request only if fire extinguishers are provided to prevent danger of fire

23. The cellar ceiling of a converted multiple dwelling is to be fire-retarded by applying two layers of 1/2" plaster boards to the existing ceiling. The owner tells you that the existing lath is too weak to support the weight of the additional plaster boards. You should

    A. insist that the plaster boards shall be applied on the existing ceiling
    B. tell the owner that the plaster boards will not be necessary since their application would be dangerous
    C. permit installation of only one layer of plaster boards in order to reduce the load on the lath
    D. require that the lath be strengthened first and then that the two layers of plaster boards be applied

24. A tenant has made a complaint that water leaking from a pipe in the apartment above has damaged the ceiling of the tenant's apartment. While the premises are being inspected, the tenant mentions other complaints to you. You should

    A. tell the tenant you are there to inspect the original complaint only
    B. listen courteously to the tenant, but discourage further complaints
    C. check each of the complaints to determine their validity
    D. place a violation on the landlord for all the complaints

25. The public halls of a multiple dwelling were painted two months ago. A tenant has filed a complaint stating that the walls are now peeling and are in a dirty, deteriorated condition. When investigating this complaint, you find that it is justified. You should

    A. test the paint to find out why it peeled so rapidly
    B. notify the landlord to repaint the walls properly
    C. tell the tenant that since the walls were painted within three years, nothing further can be done
    D. refer the complaint to the legal department so that court action may be taken

26. A multiple dwelling is being erected with one wall on a lot line. On the adjoining lot is a two-family house. The owner of this house complaints that the new building is cutting off light and ventilation from the two-family house.
You should

    A. tell the small home owner that nothing can be done since the law permits such construction
    B. tell the small home owner that nothing can be done since two-family houses are not within your jurisdiction
    C. stop construction of the multiple dwelling since it is illegal to block ventilation of another house
    D. tell the small home owner to sue the city for the decrease in the value of his property

27. The approved plans for a converted multiple dwelling call for fireproofing the stair enclosure with metal lath and cement plaster. The contractor would like to substitute two layers of 1/2 inch plaster board since this has the same fire-resistive rating as the lath and plaster.
The inspector should

    A. permit this, since the fire ratings are the same
    B. deny this, since the structural strengths may not be the same
    C. permit this only if an amended plan showing the substitution is approved
    D. permit this only if the structural strengths and the fire-resistive ratings are the same

28. During a routine inspection of a multiple dwelling, an inspector discovers that a fire door has been blocked open.
The FIRST action of the inspector should be to

    A. order the owner or his representative to remove the blocking immediately
    B. notify the owner in writing that a violation of the law exists on the premises
    C. warn the tenants that a fire hazard exists
    D. remove the blocking himself

29. When writing a report of an investigation of a tenant's complaint, the item that you should consider LEAST important for inclusion in the report is the

    A. name of tenant   B. apartment number
    C. age of building   D. location of building

30. A tenant asks you about the procedures the Department of Buildings uses in processing a violation complaint.
You should

    A. refer the tenant to your superiors since they are the only ones permitted to give official information
    B. tell the tenant that such information is none of his business
    C. give the tenant the information in as concise a manner as possible
    D. explain completely and in detail all the ramifications of departmental procedure

31. In investigating the adequacy of the exits of a multiple dwelling, the LEAST important item to check is the

    A. location of exits
    B. width of stairs
    C. size of stair platforms
    D. number of treads and risers

32. In a 8-story fireproof multiple dwelling of skeleton steel construction, the one of the following members that would be LEAST likely to have a fire-resistive enclosure is a

    A. beam   B. column   C. joist   D. lintel

33. The one of the following that is LEAST related to the others is

    A. pile   B. footing   C. caisson   D. pilaster

34. A pit at the low point of a cellar floor is known as a(n)

    A. sump
    B. well
    C. accumulator
    D. drain

35. The structure above the roof of a building that encloses a stairway is called a

    A. bulkhead
    B. penthouse
    C. mezzanine
    D. stairwell

36. To prevent flying sparks, incinerator chimneys in multiple dwellings are frequently covered with

    A. cement copings
    B. draft hoods
    C. goosenecks
    D. wire mesh

37. A valve used to prevent boiler explosions due to excessive pressure is a _____ valve.

    A. check   B. gate   C. relief   D. fuller

38. The one of the following that is acceptable according to the building code for a 3-hour fire partition is 6"

    A. solid brick
    B. solid stone concrete blocks
    C. solid cinder concrete blocks
    D. plain concrete

39. A fire tower is a

    A. means of egress from a building
    B. water tank on the roof of a building
    C. piece of Fire Department equipment
    D. draft space through which fire will spread

Questions 40-45.

DIRECTIONS: Questions 40 through 45, inclusive, refer to the sketch of an apartment building shown on the last page. All questions are to be answered on the basis of this sketch.

40. The dimension of the bedroom indicated by the letter Y is

   A. 9'1 5/16"
   B. 9'1 13/16"
   C. 9'2 3/16"
   D. 9'2 11/16"

41. Following is an abstract of the multiple dwelling law:
   1. Every living room (including bedrooms) shall contain at least 80 square feet of floor space.
   2. Every living room shall be at least eight feet in least horizontal dimension except that any number of bedrooms up to one-half the total number in any apartment containing three or more bedrooms may have a least horizontal dimension of seven feet or more.

   In order to increase the width of the hall, it is necessary to decrease the width of the bedroom indicated by the letter Y.
   The one of the following that is the smallest acceptable width of this room is

   A. 7'0"   B. 7'6"   C. 8'0"   D. 8'6"

42. The columns shown are

   A. wood posts
   B. concrete filled pipes
   C. I beams
   D. built up channels

43. The letter indicating the partition that is MOST likely to be a bearing partition is

   A. M
   B. W
   C. X
   D. There are no bearing partitions

44. The exit door

   A. does not swing in the direction of egress
   B. is too large
   C. will block the stairs
   D. is not fireproof

45. The one of the following general notes that is MOST likely to appear in connection with this plan is:

   A. Masonry walls shall be braced horizontally at maximum intervals of twenty times the wall thickness
   B. Buttresses shall be bonded into the wall by masonry in the same manner as employed in the construction of the wall
   C. Masonry walls shall be anchored at maximum intervals of four feet, to each tier of joists bearing on such walls, by metal anchors
   D. Openings in the masonry wall shall be spanned by a lintel or arch of incombustible materia

8 (#1)

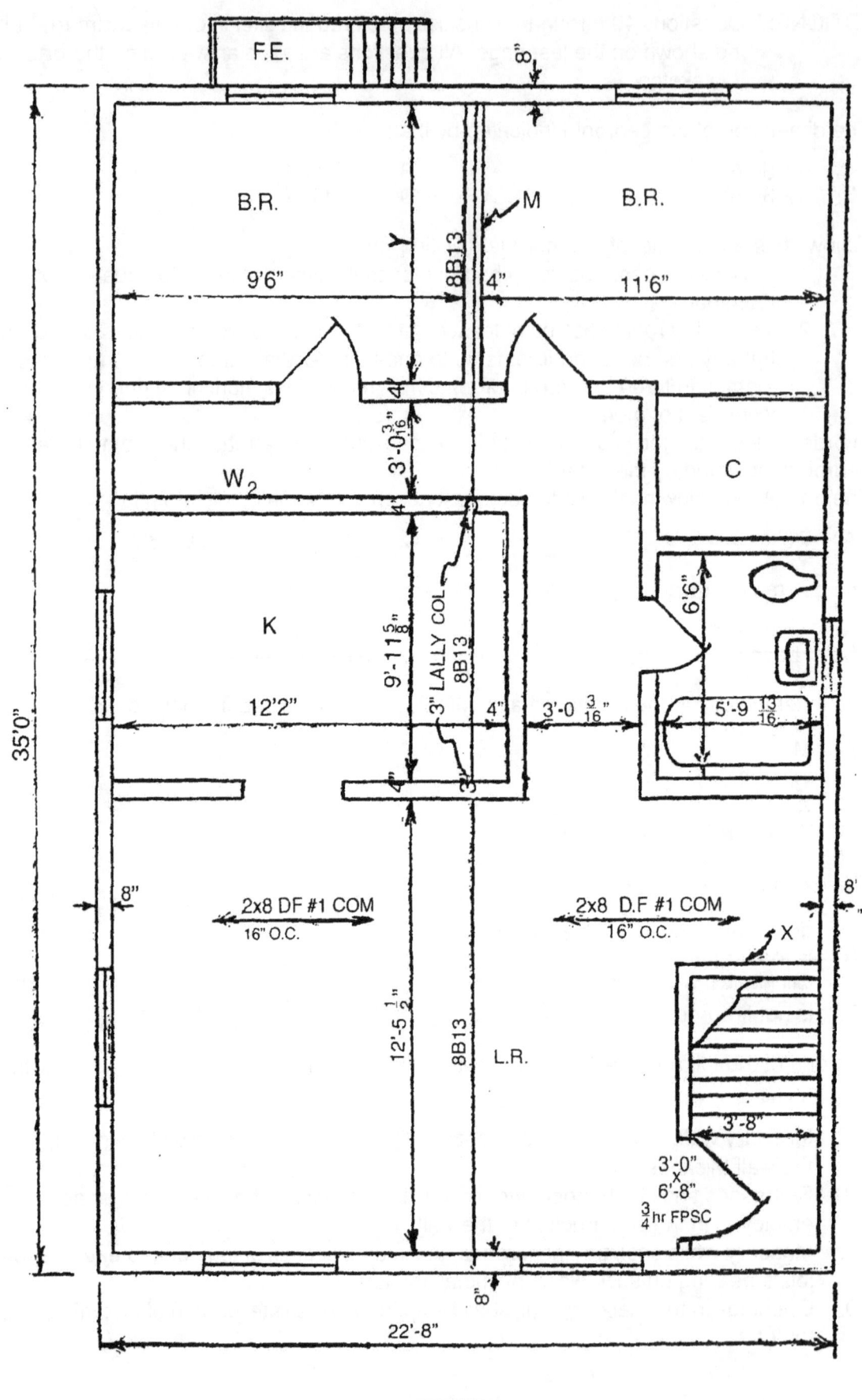

46

KEY (CORRECT ANSWERS)

1. C	11. D	21. B	31. D	41. D
2. C	12. B	22. C	32. D	42. B
3. A	13. B	23. D	33. D	43. D
4. D	14. C	24. C	34. A	44. C
5. B	15. A	25. B	35. A	45. C
6. C	16. C	26. A	36. D	
7. B	17. D	27. C	37. C	
8. A	18. A	28. A	38. C	
9. D	19. D	29. C	39. A	
10. B	20. C	30. C	40. D	

EXAMINATION SECTION
TEST 1

DIRECTIONS: Each question or incomplete statement is followed by several suggested answers or completions. Select the one that BEST answers the question or completes the statement. *PRINT THE LETTER OF THE CORRECT ANSWER IN THE SPACE AT THE RIGHT.*

Questions 1-5.

DIRECTIONS: Questions 1 through 5 are to be answered on the basis of the following statement. Use ONLY the information contained in this statement in answering these questions.

    No multiple dwelling shall be erected to a height in excess of one and one-half times the width of the widest street on which it faces, except that above the level of such height, for each one foot that the front wall of such dwelling sets back from the street line, three feet shall be added to the height limit of such dwelling, but such dwelling shall not exceed in maximum height three feet plus one and three-quarter times the width of the widest street on which it faces.
    Any such dwelling facing a street more than one hundred feet in width shall be subject to the same height limitations as though such dwelling faced a street one hundred feet in width.

1. The MAXIMUM height of a multiple dwelling set back five feet from the street line and facing a 60 foot wide street is _____ feet. 1.____
   A. 60   B. 90   C. 105   D. 165

2. The MAXIMUM height of a multiple dwelling set back six feet from the street line and facing a 120 foot wide street is _____ feet. 2.____
   A. 198   B. 168   C. 120   D. 105

3. The MAXIMUM height of a multiple dwelling is 3.____
   A. 100 ft.   B. 150 ft.   C. 178 ft.   D. unlimited

4. The MAXIMUM height of a multiple dwelling set back 10 feet from the street line and facing a 110 foot wide street is _____ feet. 4.____
   A. 178   B. 180   C. 195   D. 205

5. The MAXIMUM height of a multiple dwelling set back eight feet from the street line and facing a 90 foot wide street is _____ feet. 5.____
   A. 135   B. 147   C. 178   D. 159

Questions 6-10.

DIRECTIONS: Questions 6 through 10 are to be answered on the basis of the following statement. Use ONLY the information contained in this statement in answering these questions.

The number of persons accommodated on any story in a lodging house shall not be greater than the sum of the following components.
   a. 22 persons for each full multiple of 22 inches in the smallest clear width for each means of egress approved by the department, other than fire escapes.
   b. 20 persons for each lawful fire escape accessible from such story.

6. The MAXIMUM number of persons that may be accommodated on a story in a lodging house depends on the

   A. number of lawful fire escapes *only*
   B. number of approved means of egress *only*
   C. smallest clear width in each approved means of egress *only*
   D. number of lawful fire escapes and sum total of smallest clear widths in each approved means of egress

7. The MAXIMUM number of persons that may be accommodated on a story of a lodging house having one lawful fire escape and a sum total of 44 inches in the smallest clear widths of the two approved means of egress is

   A. 20   B. 22   C. 42   D. 64

8. The MAXIMUM number of persons that may be accommodated on a story of a lodging house having two lawful fire escapes and a sum total of 60 inches in the smallest clear width of the approved means of egress is

   A. 64   B. 84   C. 100   D. 106

9. The MAXIMUM number of persons that may be accommodated on a story of a lodging house having one lawful fire escape and a sum total of 33 inches in the smallest clear width of the approved means of egress is

   A. 42   B. 53   C. 64   D. 73

10. The MAXIMUM number of persons that may be accommodated on a story of a lodging house having two lawful fire escapes and two approved means of egress, with 40 inches and 44 inches in the smallest clear widths, respectively, is

    A. 84   B. 104   C. 106   D. 108

11. An employee of the Department of Housing and Buildings may take outside employment in private industry as a(n)

    A. architect
    B. mason
    C. plumber
    D. none of the above

12. The one of the following that is NOT a multiple dwelling is a

    A. college dormitory
    B. dwelling occupied by three families
    C. hospital
    D. lodging house

13. The one of the following that is a Class A multiple dwelling is a

    A. commercial building containing a janitor's apartment
    B. furnished room house

C. hotel
D. tenement

14. A dwelling occupied by one family with five transient roomers is a _____ dwelling.

    A. Class A multiple
    B. Class B multiple
    C. single family private
    D. two-family private

15. The one of the following that is deemed a living room by the multiple dwelling law is a

    A. bathroom
    B. bedroom
    C. dinette, 45 sq. ft. in area
    D. kitchenette, 45 sq. ft. in area

16. The MAXIMUM number of stories to which a new multiple dwelling may be erected without having a passenger elevator is

    A. 4   B. 5   C. 6   D. 7

17. In a new multiple dwelling, which of the following rooms are required to have windows?

    A. Bathroom
    B. Kitchen
    C. Water-closet compartment
    D. All of the above

18. New multiple dwellings three stories or more in height must have hot water supplied during

    A. the hours between 6 A.M. and Midnight *only*
    B. the hours between 8 A.M. and 8 P.M. *only*
    C. the hours between 6 A.M. and Noon and 6 P.M. and Midnight *only*
    D. all hours

19. A winding stair in a new multiple dwelling is

    A. not permitted under any circumstances
    B. permitted under all circumstances
    C. permitted only when the building is more than 6 stories high
    D. permitted only when the building is less than 6 stories high

20. All elevator shaft walls in new multiple dwellings MUST be

    A. at least 4 inches thick
    B. fireproof
    C. hollow
    D. made of gypsum plaster

21. The one of the following statements about new multiple dwellings that is NOT true is:

    A. Boiler rooms in multiple dwellings four stories or more in height must have fireproof doors
    B. Every open roof area must have a guard rail or parapet wall at least 3'6" high
    C. A new multiple dwelling may be placed on the same lot with a frame building
    D. A new multiple dwelling may be used for parking of passenger motor vehicles

22. A tenement within the meaning of the multiple dwelling law is a building erected BEFORE

    A. April 18, 1929 B. April 6, 1948
    C. April 12, 1949 D. March 25, 1952

23. Every entrance hall in a multiple dwelling must be provided with a light of AT LEAST _____ watts.

    A. 5   B. 10   C. 15   D. 40

24. From the entrance to the first stair, every entrance hall in a new multiple dwelling must be, in clear width, AT LEAST

    A. 3'8"   B. 4'   C. 6'   D. 8'

25. A basement in a new multiple dwelling exceeding seven stories in height MUST have AT LEAST one-half of its height _____ curb level and is _____ as a story.

    A. above; counted   B. above; not counted
    C. below; counted   D. below; not counted

26. The lower ends of mitred cross bridging should be nailed to the beams

    A. at the same time that the top ends are nailed
    B. before the rough flooring is placed
    C. after the plastering is complete
    D. after the flooring is placed

27. The maximum distance between lines of bridging should NOT exceed

    A. 10'0"   B. 8'0"   C. 6'6"   D. 4'6"

28. The building code states that it shall be unlawful to corbel walls less than twelve inches thick, except for fire-stopping.
    From this, it may be concluded that

    A. walls 12 inches or more in thickness shall not be corbelled
    B. if a wall is less than 12 inches thick, it is permissible to corbel provided some of the corbelling is used for fire-stopping
    C. fire-stopping shall not be considered to be corbelling
    D. corbelling and fire-stopping are the same

29. The building code states that curtain walls of solid masonry shall be at least eight inches thick for the uppermost thirteen feet and at least twelve inches thick for the next fifty-two feet or fraction thereof below and shall be increased four inches in thickness for each succeeding sixty feet or fraction thereof below.
    This means that the thickness of a solid masonry curtain wall 126 feet high should be AT LEAST

    A. 20 inches throughout its height
    B. 20 inches at the base
    C. 16 inches throughout its height
    D. 16 inches at the base

30. The term *curb cut* refers to

    A. openings in a curb
    B. tire cuts made while parking
    C. surveying marks chiseled in a curb
    D. rental for sidewalk stands

31. A bearing wall is a wall which

    A. carries its own weight *only*
    B. carries load other than its own weight
    C. bears on structural supports at each story
    D. is more than 12 feet high

32. A column is an _____ member.

    A. upright compression   B. inclined compression
    C. upright tension   D. inclined tension

33. A lintel could be broadly classified as a

    A. beam   B. column   C. footing   D. strut

34. A flat slab is MOST commonly used in _____ construction.

    A. sidewalk   B. roadway   C. conduit   D. building

35. Of the following, the member which would MOST likely be supported on a footing is the

    A. beam   B. girder   C. column   D. joist

36. A parapet wall would MOST likely support

    A. a coping   B. roof joists
    C. floor joists   D. partitions

37. Jack arches are used

    A. in ornamental iron work
    B. in fancy stairways
    C. when lintels are omitted
    D. in foundations

38. If green lumber is used for joists, shrinkage will have its MOST serious effect in _____ of joists.

    A. length   B. width   C. depth   D. weight

39. The phrase *concealed draft openings* is MOST likely to be used in connection with

    A. fireplaces   B. flues
    C. fire-stopping D. automatic dampers

40. Of the following terms, the one which is LEAST related to the others is the

    A. jamb   B. strike plate
    C. latch bolt   D. pulley stile

Questions 41-45.

DIRECTIONS: Questions 41 through 45 are to be answered in accordance with the following sketch.

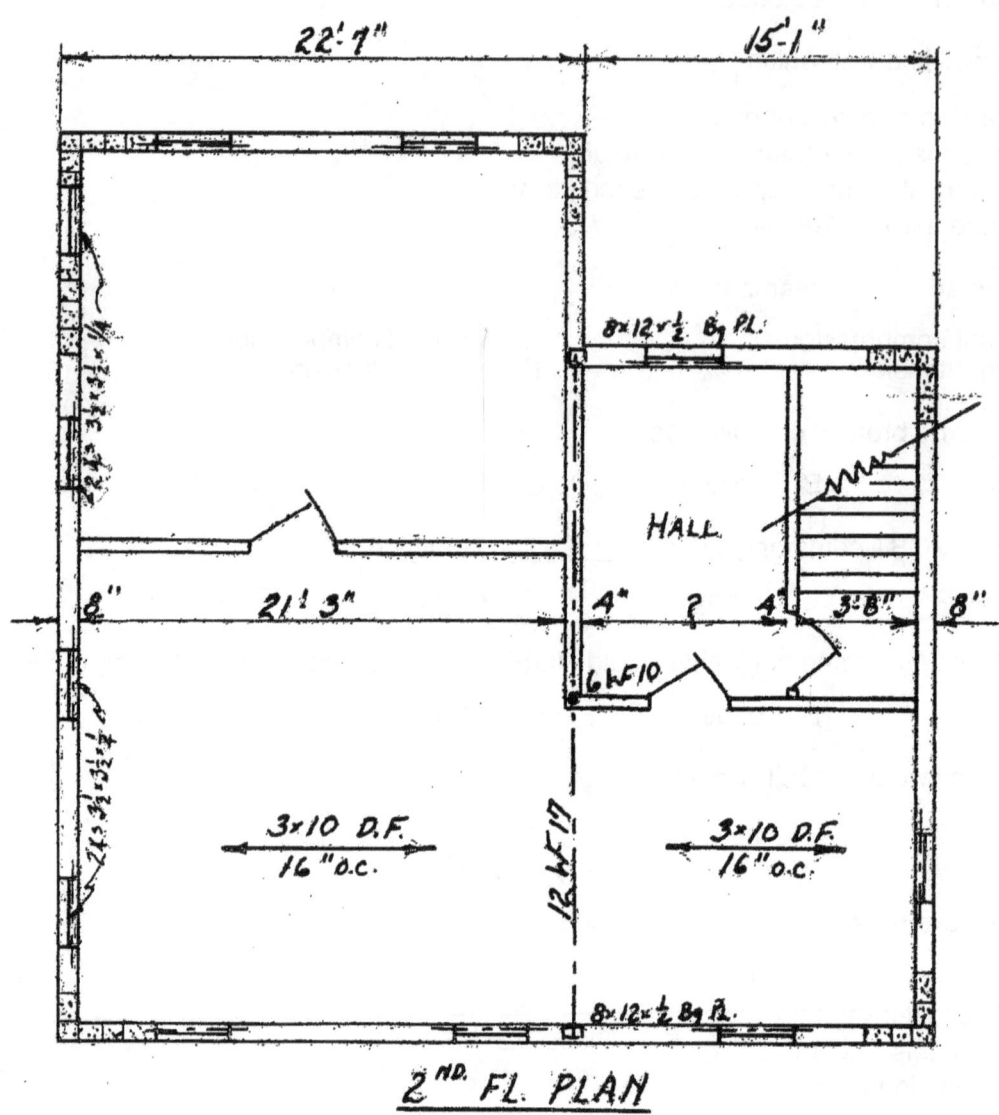

41. The one of the following statements that is CORRECT is: The building

    A. is of fireproof construction
    B. has masonry walls, with wood joists
    C. is of wood frame construction
    D. has timber posts and girders

42. The one of the following statements that is CORRECT is:

    A. The stairway from the ground floor continues through the roof
    B. There are two means of egress from the second floor of this building
    C. The door on the second floor stair landing opens in the direction of egress
    D. The entire stair is shown on this plan

43. The width of the hall is 43.____

    A. 10'3"   B. 10'5"   C. 10'7"   D. 10'9"

44. The lintels shown are 44.____

    A. angles
    B. a channel and an angle
    C. an I-beam
    D. precast concrete

45. The one of the following statements that is CORRECT is: The steel beam is 45.____

    A. supported by columns at the center and at the ends
    B. entirely supported by the walls
    C. supported on columns at the ends only
    D. supported at the center by a column and at the ends by the walls

KEY (CORRECT ANSWERS)

1. C	11. D	21. C	31. B	41. B
2. B	12. C	22. A	32. A	42. C
3. C	13. D	23. C	33. A	43. D
4. A	14. B	24. B	34. D	44. A
5. D	15. B	25. A	35. C	45. D
6. D	16. C	26. D	36. A	
7. D	17. D	27. B	37. C	
8. B	18. A	28. C	38. C	
9. A	19. A	29. B	39. C	
10. C	20. B	30. A	40. D	

EXAMINATION SECTION
TEST 1

DIRECTIONS: Each question or incomplete statement is followed by several suggested answers or completions. Select the one that BEST answers the questions or completes the statement. *PRINT THE LETTER OF THE CORRECT ANSWER IN THE SPACE AT THE RIGHT.*

1. Of the following, the FIRST operation in the demolition of a 4-story building adjacent to the property line is the 1.____

    A. erection of railings around the stairwells
    B. shoring of adjoining buildings
    C. erection of a sidewalk shed
    D. removal of windows

2. Projected sash is defined as a(n) 2.____

    A. double hung window
    B. window that opens inward or outward
    C. architectural projection from a building exterior
    D. storm window

3. Specifications for a reinforced concrete structure call for a roof fill to be placed on the concrete roof slab. Of the following, the PURPOSE of the fill is to 3.____

    A. reduce sound transmission
    B. facilitate drainage
    C. provide a smooth base for insulation
    D. protect the concrete slab

4. The Building Department requires a location survey by a licensed surveyor 4.____

    A. *only* if it is suspected that the building is not in the proper place and may impinge on adjacent property
    B. *only* of the completed foundation
    C. *only* of the completed superstructure
    D. *after* the foundation is completed and a second survey after the building is completed

5. After excavating by a contractor for a footing, the sub-grade soil appears to be below the quality shown on the borings. 5.____
   Of the following types of footings, the one that would be LEAST affected by this condition is a

    A. spread footing B. combined footing
    C. footing on piles D. footing and pier

6. Of the following, the information of GREATEST significance to be recorded for each pile during pile driving is the 6.____

    A. steam pressure and the temperature
    B. condition of the ground at the pile location

C. number of hammer blows at the last inch
D. total number of hammer blows

7. One method of dewatering an excavation for a foundation is by the use of

    A. inverted siphons
    B. well points
    C. line holes
    D. suction heads

8. An excavation for a concrete footing to support a structural steel column was dug 4" too deep.
Of the following, the BEST construction practice would be to

    A. backfill the 4" with stone
    B. backfill the 4" with sand
    C. lower the entire footing 4"
    D. make the footing 4" thicker

9. Spudding, in a pile driving operation, is used PRIMARILY to

    A. remove a broken pile
    B. pass an obstruction
    C. compact the soil in the area
    D. splice piles

10. Where walers and form ties are used in wood formwork for tall vertical concrete walls, the walers are

    A. more closely spaced at the top of the wall than at the bottom
    B. evenly spaced at the top to the bottom of the wall
    C. more closely spaced at the bottom of the wall than at the top
    D. more closely spaced at the middle of the wall than at either the top or the bottom

11. A non-bearing wall unit between columns enclosing a structure is known as a _____ wall.

    A. panel
    B. curtain
    C. apron
    D. spandrel

12. In a multi-story building, standpipes are installed FIRST by the plumber for

    A. water supply
    B. sanitary facilities
    C. fire protection
    D. steam supply

13. It is necessary to burn reinforcing steel while they are in the wood forms in order to change their lengths.
The STANDARD safety precaution to observe during this process is to

    A. fireproof the wood forms
    B. use a low heat flame
    C. have a man stand by with a fire extinguisher
    D. soak a 20-foot radius around the area with water

14. Specifications for a building require that the first floor beams must be in place before backfilling against the foundation walls.
Of the following, the BEST reason for this requirement is that

    A. the utilities up to the first floor level should be in place before backfilling
    B. without the first floor beams in place, the wall may become overstressed
    C. it facilitates the inspection of the first floor construction
    D. it facilitates the inspection of the backfilling operation

14.____

15. The utility line that USUALLY enters the building at the *lowest* elevation is the

    A. electric cable   B. gas lines
    C. water lines   D. plumbing drain

15.____

16. Specifications for a building require that machine excavation for foundation footings be within a foot of final subgrade and the remaining excavation be done by hand. Of the following, the BEST reasons for this requirement is to

    A. prevent cave-ins around the excavation
    B. save the amount of fill needed
    C. prevent disturbing the surrounding excavation
    D. prevent excavation below the subgrade

16.____

17. Of the following outside lines entering a building, the one for which grades must be MOST carefully controlled is the

    A. sewer line   B. water line
    C. gas line   D. electric cable

17.____

18. On a plan, the grades for a building are as follows:
Datum ± 0 (Elev. 24.08')
First floor El + 1' - 0" (Elev. 25.08').
The elevation of a ledge 6'3" below the finished first floor level with respect to datum is

    A. El. - 6.25   B. El. - 5.25
    C. El. + 18.83   D. El. + 17.83

18.____

19. Specifications for a building call for *defective material to be removed from the job site immediately.* The MAIN reason for this is to

    A. prevent accidents
    B. prevent accidental use of the defective material in the construction
    C. insure that the contractor does not make the same mistake again
    D. minimize claims against the department

19.____

20. *Drywall* is installed by

    A. carpenters   B. lathers
    C. plasterers   D. masons

20.____

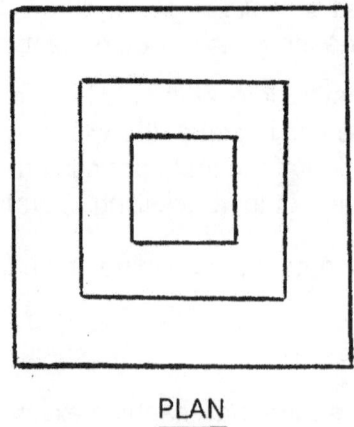

PLAN

21. The Plan of a footing and concrete column is shown above. An elevation of the footing would be shown as: 21.____

A. 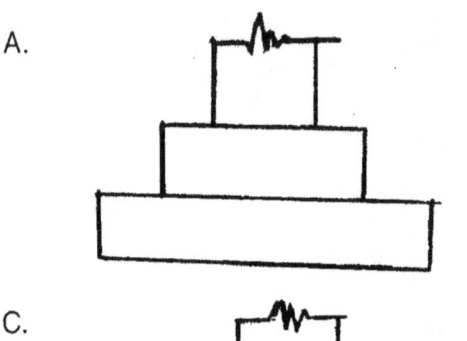 B.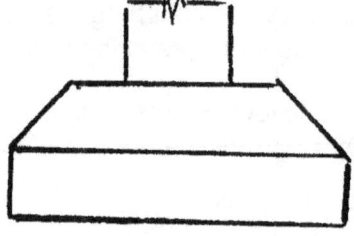

C. 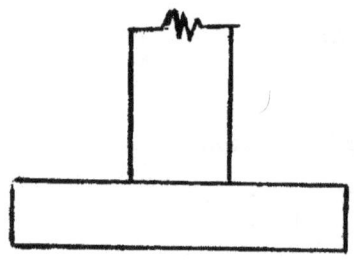 D.

22. Of the following, the BEST sequence to follow in pouring the interior footing, concrete column and basement floor as shown below is pour the footing, 22.____

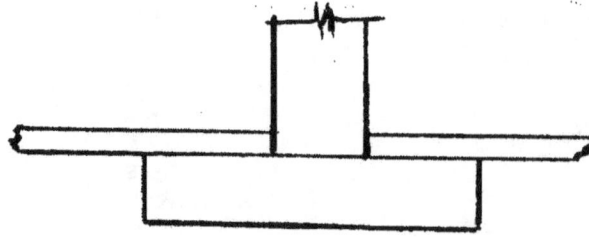

A. and floor in one pour. Pour the column
B. and column in one pour. Pour the floor
C. pour the floor above the footing, pour the column above the floor
D. box out for the floor, pour the column. Pour the floor

23. The PURPOSE of curing concrete is so that the   23.____

    A. forms for the concrete can be stripped quickly
    B. water content will not evaporate too quickly
    C. concrete will harden faster
    D. reinforcing rods will not rust

24. Air-entraining cement may be required so that the resulting concrete will resist   24.____

    A. freezing and thawing   B. hot weather
    C. dampness   D. heavy loads

25. Concrete test cylinders are required to   25.____

    A. provide an indication of the strength of the concrete poured in a specific location
    B. provide a basis of payment
    C. check on the inspector
    D. check the source of material

26. Concrete test cylinders are stored and cured on the job   26.____

    A. so that the contractor can then control the curing
    B. so that the inspector can then control the curing
    C. because the laboratory has no facilities for curing concrete cylinders
    D. because conditions of curing on the job are the same as at the location poured

27. The *water-cement ratio* refers to the quantity of water in a concrete mix as   27.____

    A. cubic feet of water per cubic foot of cement
    B. gallons of water per pound of cement
    C. gallons of water per sack of cement
    D. bags of cement per gallon of water

28. *Slump* of concrete refers to the   28.____

    A. shrinkage of concrete while setting
    B. drop in height relative to a standard testing cone
    C. amount of water introduced into the concrete
    D. cracking or crazing of the surface of concrete

29. Concrete mixes made with lightweight aggregate USUALLY require the addition of an air-entraining agent in order to   29.____

    A. increase the strength of the concrete
    B. reduce the weight of the concrete
    C. obtain the necessary plasticity without added water
    D. save aggregate material

30. Concrete in some instances requires integral waterproofing.   30.____
    This can BEST be achieved by

    A. addition of more cement in the mix
    B. longer vibration
    C. addition of a waterproofing agent to the mix
    D. longer curing period

31. In placing concrete where the vertical drop is greater than 5 feet, the use of an elephant trunk is necessary.
    The BEST reason for using an elephant trunk is to
    A. prevent segregation of the aggregate
    B. prevent waste of material
    C. safeguard health and property
    D. save time and labor

32. According to the Building Code, the maximum size of coarse aggregate for reinforced concrete shall be one-fifth of the narrowest dimension between forms or three-quarters of the clear spacing between reinforcing bars. Of the following, the MAXIMUM sized aggregate permitted for a 12" wall with #6 bars spaced at 3" center to center is
    A. 1 3/4"   B. 1 1/2"   C. 1 1/4"   D. 1"

33. Of the following, the one that is NOT a name for a lightweight aggregate is
    A. Solite   B. Vitralite
    C. Lelite   D. Nitralite

34. High early strength cement is designated as
    A. Type I   B. Type II   C. Type III   D. Type IV

35. The average weight of stone concrete is, MOST NEARLY, _____ lb./cu. ft.
    A. 125   B. 150
    C. 175   D. 200

KEY (CORRECT ANSWERS)

1.	C	16.	D
2.	B	17.	A
3.	B	18.	B
4.	D	19.	B
5.	C	20.	A
6.	C	21.	A
7.	B	22.	D
8.	D	23.	B
9.	B	24.	A
10.	C	25.	A
11.	B	26.	D
12.	C	27.	C
13.	C	28.	B
14.	B	29.	C
15.	D	30.	C

31.	A
32.	B
33.	B
34.	C
35.	B

TEST 2

DIRECTIONS: Each question or incomplete statement is followed by several suggested answers or completions. Select the one that BEST answers the question or completes the statement. *PRINT THE LETTER OF THE CORRECT ANSWER IN THE SPACE AT THE RIGHT.*

1. The Building Code requires that concrete shall be kept in a moist condition, after placing, for at least the FIRST _____ days.

   A. 3   B. 7   C. 14   D. 28

   1.____

2. In concrete work, a dummy joint is SIMILAR in purpose to a(n) _____ joint.

   A. expansion
   B. construction
   C. contraction
   D. shear

   2.____

3. Specifications for concrete usually contain a statement disallowing the *retampering* of concrete. *Retampering* means

   A. adding more water to the drum after ingredients are mixed
   B. vibrating of concrete in the forms
   C. mixing of the remaining concrete after some concrete is taken from the truck
   D. mixing of concrete in the truck after it has partially set and adding water

   3.____

4. Chamfers are placed on a concrete beam PRIMARILY to

   A. save weight
   B. eliminate honeycomb
   C. eliminate sharp corners
   D. save construction costs

   4.____

5. Of the following, the BEST reason for using vibrators in concrete construction is to

   A. increase the workability of the concrete
   B. consolidate the concrete
   C. slow up the setting
   D. speed up the setting

   5.____

6. The concrete test that will BEST determine the consistency of a concrete mix is the

   A. sieve analysis
   B. water-cement ratio test
   C. calorimetric test
   D. slump test

   6.____

7. Specifications for the concrete floor treatment of a building require *dustproofing*. This process consists of

   A. scraping the floor surface to remove loose concrete material that will dust
   B. mopping the floor with a chemical solution that will harden the concrete surface
   C. adding a chemical compound to the concrete mix that will harden the surface of the concrete
   D. grinding the concrete floor with a terrazzo machine that will case harden the surface of the concrete

   7.____

8. In checking the placement of reinforcing steel, it is discovered that reinforcing steel called for on the design drawings is not shown on the reinforcing steel shop drawings. Of the following, the BEST procedure to follow is to

   8.____

A. check the design drawings for the errors
B. check the shop drawings for the errors
C. subtract the missing steel in the field
D. stop all work

9. While a large spread footing of about 50 cubic yards Is being poured, the supply plant breaks down. Concrete is available from another supplier.
The use of the other supplier should

   A. not be approved because the supplier may not be approved
   B. be approved since additional test cylinders can be taken
   C. not be approved since construction joints can be installed where the pour has ended
   D. be approved as the concrete in footings is relatively unimportant

10. Of the following species of lumber, the one MOST likely to be used for concrete formwork is

    A. oak   B. pine   C. maple   D. birch

11. A contractor proposes to install the roofing two days after the concrete roof slab is poured.
This proposal should

    A. *be recommended* as it will speed the construction
    B. *be recommended* as it will cure the concrete better
    C. *not be recommended* as excess water may bulge the roofing
    D. *not be recommended* in cold weather but would be recommended in warm weather

12. For the construction of concrete floors resting on earth, the item that should be MOST carefully checked is that

    A. the earth is dry before pouring
    B. the earth is wet before pouring
    C. all backfill is properly compacted
    D. all backfill is porous soil

13. Cracks in concrete are not necessarily caused by settlement of a structure. Sometimes they are caused by

    A. shrinkage   B. plastic flow
    C. hydration   D. curing

14. Specifications for a building state that reinforcing bars must lap 40 diameters in the concrete.
The length of lap for a number 6 bar should be, MOST NEARLY, _____ inches.

    A. 12   B. 20   C. 30   D. 40

15. Cement stored on the job site that has become caked and lumpy may

    A. be used only for foundations
    B. be used only for slabs on ground
    C. be used anywhere if the lumps are broken up
    D. not be used

16. Of the following statements relating to the plies in plywood, the one that is CORRECT is:

    A. The primary difference between exterior and interior plywood is the quality of the exterior plies.
    B. Exterior plywood has more plies than interior plywood.
    C. Exterior plywood has no surface defects on the outer plies while interior plywood permits surface defects on the outer plies.
    D. Plywood has an odd number of plies.

17. Of the following, the one that is NOT a principal classification of lumber according to the American Lumber Standards is

    A. building
    B. structural
    C. yard
    D. shop

18. Of the following types of lumber, the one that is classified as a hardwood is

    A. cedar
    B. fir
    C. pine
    D. maple

19. When building the formwork for a 12" doubly reinforced concrete wall, the USUAL order of conctruction is to place the

    A. formwork for both faces of the wall; then place the steel
    B. formwork for one face of the wall, place all reinforcing steel, then place the form-work for the other face of the wall
    C. reinforcing steel, then place the formwork for both faces of the wall
    D. formwork for one face of the wall, place the reinforcing steel for one face, place the form-work for the other face of the wall, then place the reinforcing steel for the second face

20. To obtain information concerning the product of a particular major manufacturer of flooring, the BEST of the following sources of information is the

    A. Architectural Standards
    B. ASTM
    C. Sweet's Catalogue
    D. Flooring Institute

21. Of the following, loose lintels would MOST likely be found in the specifications under the item entitled

    A. Ornamental Iron
    B. Miscellaneous Iron
    C. Structural Steel
    D. Hollow Metal Work

22. Galvanized metal lath is metal lath coated with

    A. tin
    B. copper
    C. zinc
    D. nickel

23. In the welding symbol the 2 represents the
    A. spacing between welds in inches
    B. length of the weld in inches
    C. number of sides to be welded
    D. thickness of the throat of the weld in inches

24. The specification for a building states that rib lath should be 3.4 pounds. 24.____
This MEANS 3.4 pounds per

    A. square foot
    B. linear foot of a 3 foot roll
    C. square yard
    D. 10 square feet

25. Terrazzo floors are laid with brass dividing strips PRIMARILY for the purpose of 25.____

    A. preventing slipping
    B. appearance
    C. preventing irregular cracking
    D. easy screeding

26. The PURPOSE of a chase is to 26.____

    A. support stair stringers
    B. accomodate pipes in a wall
    C. accomodate flashing in a parapet
    D. provide venting

27. In masonry work, a bull nose brick would be located at 27.____

    A. an inside corner   B. an outside corner
    C. the key of an arch   D. the roof of a boiler setting

28. The addition of lime to cement mortar improves the workability of mortar and 28.____

    A. increases the strength
    B. decreases the shrinkage
    C. decreases the weight
    D. increases the watertightness

29. Brickwork must be cleaned after completion of setting by 29.____

    A. scrubbing with soap solution and water
    B. wire brushing
    C. washing with muriatic solution
    D. sand blasting

30. In a multi-story building, weep holes in cavity wall brick construction are USUALLY 30.____
placed in the brickwork

    A. above all masonry openings
    B. at foundation level only
    C. at the parapet only
    D. at every floor

31. A brick wall which consists of all stretcher courses is said to be built with a _____ Bond. 31.____

    A. Flemish   B. Running
    C. English   D. Common

32. The whitish deposit frequently seen on brick walls can USUALLY be avoided by

   A. using brick that contains more soluable salts
   B. keeping the water-mortar ratio high
   C. adding muriatic acid to the mortar
   D. constructing properly filled weathertight joints

33. Specifications for a building require brick to be wet before using.
    Of the following, the BEST reason for this requirement is that wetting

   A. makes it easier to place brick
   B. cleans the brick
   C. prevents absorption of moisture from the mortar
   D. shows up flaws in the brick that would otherwise be hidden

34. In checking the ingredients that are to go into the concrete for a footing that is being poured, you notice that there is 5% too much cement.
    Of the following, the BEST action to take in this situation is to

   A. do nothing
   B. condemn the footing
   C. increase the amount of sand in the mix
   D. order core borings taken of the finished footing

35. The soil conditions for a new building are MOST frequently checked by

   A. augering
   B. soundings
   C. rodding
   D. borings

KEY (CORRECT ANSWERS)

1.	B	16.	D
2.	C	17.	A
3.	D	18.	D
4.	C	19.	B
5.	B	20.	C
6.	D	21.	B
7.	B	22.	C
8.	B	23.	B
9.	B	24.	C
10.	B	25.	C
11.	C	26.	B
12.	C	27.	B
13.	A	28.	B
14.	C	29.	C
15.	D	30.	D

31. B
32. D
33. C
34. A
35. D

EXAMINATION SECTION
TEST 1

DIRECTIONS: Each question or incomplete statement is followed by several suggested answers or completions. Select the one that BEST answers the question or completes the statement. *PRINT THE LETTER OF THE CORRECT ANSWER IN THE SPACE AT THE RIGHT.*

1. Of the following reasons for inspection of construction, the one that applies MOST to inspectors in the department is to

    A. coordinate work of the different crafts
    B. avoid extra construction costs
    C. insure adherence to standards of materials and craftsmanship
    D. speed completion of the work

    1.____

2. Of the following statements, the one that is CORRECT is that it is

    A. not important for an inspector to maintain good, personal relations with contractors because contractors might attempt to take advantage of the inspector
    B. important for an inspector to maintain good personal relations with contractors because it will then be easier to obtain cooperation from them
    C. not important for an inspector to maintain good personal relations with contractors because contractors must comply with the Code in any case
    D. important for an inspector to maintain good personal relations with contractors because the inspector can then eliminate much of the required inspections

    2.____

3. Contractors will many times insist on discussing problems only with the senior construction inspector rather than the district inspector.
    This practice is

    A. *good,* because the contractor will get the correct answer immediately
    B. *poor,* because it tends to undermine the responsibility of the district inspector
    C. *good,* because this gives the senior construction inspector an opportunity to train the men under him
    D. *poor,* because the senior construction inspector cannot be familiar with all the conditions in his area.

    3.____

4. It has been said that the perfect job has never been built. Where litigation with respect to a job arises, the BEST indications that the inspector has made proper inspections are the

    A. statements made by the builder
    B. inspector's district assignments
    C. number of violations filed in a district
    D. inspector's written reports

    4.____

5. Defective material should be removed from the job site immediately.
    The MAIN reason for this is to

    A. prevent accidents due to poor *housekeeping*
    B. prevent *accidental* use of the defective material in the construction

    5.____

C. protect the department from any claim against the department
D. insure that the builder does not make the same mistake again

6. A senior inspector should always explain to newly appointed inspectors the importance of the work to be done by them. The MAIN reason for this is that

   A. the inspectors know what has to be done
   B. if this is not done, inspectors will skip unimportant inspections
   C. an inspector who understands the value of proper inspections will most likely do a better job
   D. inspectors will then not have an excuse for making improper inspections

7. Assume that you find that the inspections and reports made by a newly appointed inspector are consistently below a reasonable standard.
   You should FIRST

   A. ask that the inspector be reassigned to a task he can perform properly
   B. request that the inspector be brought up on charges
   C. prepare a formal memorandum stating the facts so that your superiors will be aware of the situation
   D. try to determine and correct the cause for the sub-standard performance

8. In introducing new policies to inspectors under them, senior inspectors should

   A. describe the new policy in detail to each man individually so that the senior is sure the man knows it
   B. describe the new policy to the men and explain the necessity of the new policy
   C. tell the men your honest opinion of the policy, but also tell them it is the department's orders and must be followed
   D. give the men the new policy in writing so that there can be no excuse that they misunderstood you

9. Cooperation from inspectors working under you can BEST be secured by

   A. siding with the inspectors whenever they have a complaint
   B. being a stern disciplinarian and not letting the inspectors get away with anything
   C. emphasizing to the inspectors that if they want anything done for them, they must come to you
   D. being willing to listen to the inspectors, and helping them where possible

10. It is considered good practice for a supervisor to encourage his subordinates to discuss and participate in the solution of problems.
    The MAIN reason for this is that

    A. the subordinate generally knows more about the individual problem than the supervisor
    B. then two people can share the responsibility instead of only one
    C. this will Increase the job satisfaction of the men and improve morale
    D. it will reduce the work load of the supervisor so that he can spend more time on more important matters

11. Of the following, the one MOST important quality required of a good supervisor is

    A. ambition   B. leadership   C. friendliness   D. popularity

12. When an inspector submits a poorly written report, the senior inspector should

    A. discuss the report with the inspector as soon as possible after it has been submitted
    B. call a meeting of all inspectors to explain how reports should be written
    C. wait a few days to see if other reports turned in by the inspector are written the same way
    D. rewrite the report properly himself

13. A senior inspector who is very lenient with his men will find A senior inspector who is very lenient with his men will find that

    A. the men will cooperate more readily with him
    B. there will be a higher quality of performance from the men
    C. the men will have less respect for the senior inspector
    D. the men will get along better among themselves

14. It is often said that a supervisor can delegate authority, but never responsibility. This means MOST NEARLY that

    A. a supervisor must do his own work if he expects it to be done properly
    B. a supervisor can assign some one else to do his work, but in the last analysis, the supervisor himself must take the blame for any actions followed
    C. authority and responsibility are two separate things that cannot be borne by the same person
    D. it is better for a supervisor never to delegate his authority

15. Of the following, the MOST important characteristic of a good senior inspector is

    A. the ability to make friends with the men under him
    B. fairness in dealing with the men under him
    C. willingness to be on the men's side in their complaints against the Department
    D. willingness to overlook mistakes made by the men under him

16. The BEST relationship between the senior inspector and his inspectors exist when

    A. they stick together against adverse criticism made by the department heads
    B. the senior inspector respects the inspectors' rights
    C. the senior inspector will *cover* for the inspectors' faults
    D. the senior inspector avoids enforcing the rules he knows the men do not like

17. With regard to public relations, the MOST important item should be emphasized in an employee training program is that

    A. each inspector is a public relations agent
    B. an inspector should give the public all the information it asks for
    C. it is better to make mistakes and give erroneous information then to tell the public that you do not know the correct answer to their problem
    D. public relations is so specialized a field that only persons specially trained in it should consider it

18. Senior inspectors should regularly visit the districts covered by the inspectors under them in order to

    A. make sure their inspectors know that they are being watched
    B. give people an opportunity to speak directly to the *person in charge*
    C. observe the work of their inspectors to see that they meet proper standards
    D. get the public acquainted with them

19. The one of the following statements that is CORRECT is:

    A. When a stupid question is asked of you by the public, it should be disregarded.
    B. If you insist on formality between you and the public, the public will not be able to ask stupid questions that cannot be answered.
    C. The public should be treated courteously, regardless of how stupid their questions may be.
    D. You should explain to the public how stupid their questions are.

20. Assume that during field inspections, senior inspectors are constantly being asked questions about their job.
    In this respect, the inspector should remember that

    A. entering into conversation with people not connected with the job will leave the impression that city employees do little work
    B. efficiency can best be demonstrated by appearing to be too busy to answer questions
    C. supervisors should take every opportunity to tell the public how busy they really are
    D. the attitudes of the public are often formed by their personal contact's with city employees

21. The condition MOST likely to improve the morale of the inspectional force is

    A. liberal time allowances
    B. recognition of each individual's own efforts by the department
    C. overlooking of minor infractions of rules
    D. allowing the men to do the job in whatever manner they feel proper

22. As a senior inspector, you find that, in error you have reprimanded one of your inspectors.
    You should

    A. ignore the error, but be more careful in the future
    B. make up for it in the future by ignoring his next mistake
    C. find something else wrong
    D. apologize to the man for your mistake

23. As a senior inspector, assume that you have to settle a complaint made by a property owner against one of your inspectors. The PROPER thing to do would be to

    A. back up your inspector, telling the owner he is wrong
    B. tell the owner you will protect him against unjustified violations
    C. listen to both inspector and owner to get at the truth
    D. tell the owner you will check into the matter at your earliest convenience

24. Assume a suggestion is made by one of your inspectors for improving inspectional procedures.
Of the following, the BEST course to follow is to

   A. tell the inspector that the present method used has always been followed and is therefore the best way
   B. check the inspector's suggestion, and if it is good pass it on to the chief inspector
   C. have the man write a report to the superintendent with regard to the suggestion
   D. hold a meeting with the other inspectors to see whether they like the suggestion

25. With respect to anonymous complaints, it is

   A. *good practice* to investigate them since they may be valid
   B. *poor practice* to investigate them since anyone who is not honest enough to sign his name is probably just a trouble maker
   C. *good practice* to investigate them to keep your inspectors *on their toes*
   D. *poor practice* to investigate them since this gives your inspectors the feeling they are being spied upon

26. Members of the public frequently ask about departmental procedures.
Of the following, it is BEST to

   A. advise the public to put the question in writing so that he can get a proper formal reply
   B. refuse to answer, because this is a confidential matter
   C. explain the procedure as briefly as possible
   D. attempt to avoid the issue by discussing other matters

27. In making an inspection on an alteration job, you should

   A. avoid conversation with the foreman on the job
   B. try to get the foreman to talk as much as possible so that he will tell you all the things that are wrong with the job
   C. give the appearance of listening to the foreman but actually ignoring most of what he says
   D. listen to what the foreman has to say, but discourage undue conversation

28. Of the following, the one that would LEAST likely occur as a result of planning of your work is

   A. anticipation of problems before they occur
   B. necessity of frequently putting in overtime to solve problems
   C. better job coordination
   D. ability to meet deadlines for reports

29. In evaluating the quality of an inspector, a senior inspector should be LEAST interested in

   A. whether the man is adaptable to different situations
   B. the man's dependability
   C. how the man gets along with his co-workers and the public
   D. the number of reports the man turns in

30. In instituting disciplinary action against an inspector, the senior inspector should avoid   30.____
   A. taking extenuating circumstances into account
   B. explaining the serious consequences of the infraction
   C. being firm and positive
   D. delay once a decision is reached

KEY (CORRECT ANSWERS)

1.	C	16.	B
2.	B	17.	A
3.	B	18.	C
4.	D	19.	C
5.	B	20.	D
6.	C	21.	B
7.	D	22.	D
8.	B	23.	C
9.	D	24.	B
10.	C	25.	A
11.	B	26.	C
12.	A	27.	D
13.	C	28.	B
14.	B	29.	D
15.	B	30.	D

EXAMINATION SECTION
TEST 1

DIRECTIONS: Each question or incomplete statement is followed by several suggested answers or completions. Select the one that BEST answers the question or completes the statement. *PRINT THE LETTER OF THE CORRECT ANSWER IN THE SPACE AT THE RIGHT.*

1. It is the policy of the department to hold each inspector responsible for formal work assignments given to him.
   Of the following, the BEST reason for this is that it
   A. enables division personnel to keep track of the work schedule
   B. encourages inspectors to be careful with written documents
   C. increases the speed with which inspections are carried out
   D. provides a double check on the time sheet records of inspectors

   1.____

2. Assume that you are faced with delays caused by absences of team members due to illness.
   Of the following, the BEST means of handling this problem is to
   A. have your team members keep an accurate record of their absences so that you will be able to identify anyone who is becoming accident-prone
   B. insist on prompt notification at all times when someone on your tea is absent because of illness
   C. require that your team members submit a memorandum informing you of the days on which they will be absent
   D. take over all tasks assigned to your team members when they are absent

   2.____

3. Assume that one of the men on your team tells you that he has a problem and would like to discuss it with you privately. During the course of this meeting, it becomes apparent that the man's difficulty stems from conflicts he is having with his wife.
   Of the following, the BEST course of action that you, his supervisor, should take in this situation is to
   A. advise the employee to meet with your superior, who might be able to give him more objective advice
   B. gather enough facts to advise the man about definite solutions for his problem
   C. help the man analyze what the problem is but leave the decision to him
   D. tell the man that you can talk to him only about problems that are job-related

   3.____

4. Sometimes it may be advantageous for a senior inspector to let the inspectors under his supervision participate in the development of decisions that must be made about the team's activities.
   The one of the following that is LEAST likely to result when team members participate in supervisory decisions is that the inspectors may

   4.____

A. be able to show leadership
B. have a chance to feel creative
C. require closer supervision
D. take more responsibility for minor problems

5. Of the following, the CHIEF reason that the senior inspector should take disciplinary measures as soon as possible after a subordinate inspector's violation of department rules is that
   A. delay will make the senior inspector seem lax
   B. the inspector is more likely to accept the discipline a justified
   C. the supervisor may forget about the offense
   D. there is less likelihood that other inspectors will find out about the offense

6. Assume that you have been directed to institute a new procedure for writing reports about violations encountered during the inspections conducted by the team of which you are in charge. You have heard, through the grapevine, that several of the experienced inspectors on the team have objections to this new procedure.
   Of the following, the BEST course of action for you to take FIRST in this situation is to
   A. issue a written order to put the new procedure into effect
   B. meet with all the inspectors on your team to discuss the procedure
   C. modify the procedure to make it acceptable to all of your inspectors
   D. postpone institution of the new procedure

7. Assume that the head of your unit expects to be out for a week because of illness. You are to act as head of the unit for that time.
   In determining what to do about those inspection duties that you were originally scheduled to perform and which should not be postponed, it would be MOST advisable to
   A. assign them to the inspector who needs training in this area
   B. assign them to the inspector with the most seniority
   C. attempt to do as many of them as possible yourself
   D. divide them among all inspectors who have the time and ability

8. The one of the following situations that is LEAST likely to result from poor planning and organization of an inspection unit's work is that
   A. inspectors will be uncertain about their responsibilities
   B. job performance will be poor
   C. the work will be completed at a steady monotonous pace
   D. there will be a high turnover rate in the unit's staff

9. Of the following, the BEST course of action to take in order to avoid charges of favoritism when making job assignments is to
   A. delegate the authority to make assignments to a well-liked experienced inspector
   B. keep records which may demonstrate proper distribution and rotation of assignments

C. select the oldest inspectors for the most desirable assignments
D. tell the men that, if they have any gripes about their assignments, they should see the supervising inspector

10. Of the following, the MOST important reason for a senior inspector to receive communications from the supervising inspector before they are transmitted to the inspectors is that he can
    A. avoid discussing communications with his subordinates
    B. exercises close supervision over every detail of the inspectors' assignments
    C. limit the amount of information received by his subordinates
    D. maintains his position in the chain of command

11. If an organization has rules that are clear but excessively detailed and rigid, the one of the following which is MOST likely to occur is that
    A. employees will tend to ignore the rules
    B. records of performance will be more difficult to maintain
    C. supervisors will have more difficulty in applying the rules to individual situations
    D. use of individual judgment and discretion will be decreased

12. An effective senior inspector strives to build up the feeling that he and his men are on the same team. The imposition of discipline may serious endanger the relationship built up between him and his men.
    The one of the following steps that the senior inspector may take to insure that the imposition of discipline will NOT cause any deterioration of his relationship with his subordinates is to
    A. avoid disciplinary action, except for very serious offenses
    B. delegate simple disciplinary problems to a competent, experienced inspector
    C. discipline his men in groups so that they will feel as if they were part of a team
    D. impose discipline in as impersonal way as possible

13. Suppose that one of the inspectors under the supervision of a senior inspector is repeatedly late for work. Despite the inspector's habitual lateness, he manages to complete his work assignments on schedule.
    Of the following, the MOST advisable action for the senior inspector to take in this situation is to
    A. ask one of the other inspectors to speak to him about his attendance
    B. ignore the inspector's habitual lateness as long as he does his work properly
    C. reprimand the inspector privately and follow through to see whether his attendance improves
    D. tell him in the presence of the other inspectors that he must improve his attendance record

14. Assume that you are informed by your superior that all reports prepared by your team should be checked by you when possible before their submission to a supervising inspector.
Of the following, the BEST course of action to take if you are too busy to look at all these reports and they have to be sent out right away is to
   A. delegate the responsibility for checking the reports to someone you have carefully instructed in the need for neat and accurate reports
   B. request additional staff from another unit to help you review these reports
   C. send the reports out without checking them and attach an explanatory note, telling your superior that you have not had time to look at them
   D. tell our men to review one another's reports and initial them

15. Assume that a senior inspector notices that another senior inspector divides his team's workload in what seems to him to be an inefficient manner. He decides to report this to the supervising inspector.
Of the following, an accurate evaluation of the action taken by the senior inspector in this situation is that it is GENERALLY
   A. *good* practice, mainly because the supervising inspector is the only person authorized to make this senior inspector divide the work according to standard procedure
   B. *good* practice, mainly because the senior inspector needs close supervision to adequately carry out his responsibilities
   C. *poor* practice, mainly because the senior inspector should have consulted other senior inspectors about this situation
   D. *poor* practice, mainly because the senior inspector should understand that other senior inspectors may manage their operations differently

16. Assume that you have heard a rumor that department rules are about to be changed in a manner which will make certain types of inspections more complicated.
Of the following, the BEST action for you to take in this situation is to
   A. ask the members of your staff, individually, if they have heard such a rumor
   B. call a meeting of your staff to tell them such a change is rumored
   C. make plans to change your unit's procedures to adapt to the new methods
   D. await official confirmation or denial of the rumor

17. Assume that one of the inspectors under your supervision has been doing an excellent job but no longer seems to have any interest in the work. He complains to you that he finds the work boring.
Of the following, the MOST advisable action for you to take FIRST is to
   A. ask some of his fellow inspectors to discuss the matter with him
   B. attempt to vary his assignments and give him more complex assignments
   C. remind him that his evaluation by superiors may depend in part on the interest he shows in his work
   D. suggest that the inspector be transferred to another division

5 (#1)

18. The BEST way for you to prepare the inspectors in your unit to handle special assignments speedily and make decisions in an emergency is to
    A. follow each employee's work very carefully so you know where he is least efficient
    B. give them the freedom to make decisions in their everyday work
    C. refuse to accept work that is turned in late
    D. set deadlines ahead of the time when regularly assigned work is actually due so they will learn to work efficiently

18.____

19. Suppose you are supervising several inspectors. One of the inspectors has recently transferred to your unit. You discover that although he generally prepares his reports in a fairly correct way, he does not follow the prescribed procedure that you have taught the other inspectors.
    In this situation, the one of the following that it would be BEST for you to do is to
    A. allow him to use his own procedure if it is accurate and efficient
    B. refer him to your supervisor
    C. discuss the matter with all the inspectors and let them decide which procedure they wish to follow
    D. tell him to follow the procedure used by the other inspectors

19.____

20. Assume that you have one of your most competent inspectors working on a new type of project. As you are reviewing his work, you notice he has made some errors.
    You should
    A. correct the errors yourself, otherwise the inspector will get discouraged
    B. ignore the errors; they are probably not important, especially when the inspector is first learning the job
    C. tell the inspector about the errors; he will probably learn from them
    D. tell the inspector about the errors; then he will be aware that he is careless

20.____

21. Assume that your unit has been given a special assignment to make an original study. You plan to give this assignment to two of your most competent inspectors.
    The BEST way to start them on this work is to
    A. ask the two inspectors how they think the work can be done in a most effective way
    B. do some of the work with the inspectors to make sure they do not make any mistakes
    C. tell the inspectors they will be held directly responsible for the success of the study
    D. write up detailed instructions and give them to the inspectors who will do the work

21.____

6 (#1)

22. Of the following steps in setting up an employee training program, the one which should PRECEDE the others is to 22.____
    A. assemble all the materials needed in the training program
    B. decide what training methods would be most effective
    C. determine what facilities are available for training purposes
    D. outline the areas that would be covered in the training program

23. Assume that you find it necessary to retrain an older, experienced inspector because you are giving this inspector a different kind of assignment. 23.____
    Of the following, the problem that is MOST likely to arise when retraining such a staff member is that the
    A. instructor will have disciplinary problems with this employee
    B. instructor will know less than this staff member
    C. employee at this status often lacks motivation to be retrained
    D. younger men will be unable to keep up with the performance of this employee

24. Assume that an inspector has recently been transferred from another unit and is now on your team. 24.____
    Of the following, the BEST method for you to use to determine whether this man needs any additional instruction or training is to
    A. ask him whether he is having difficulty with the work you assign to him
    B. ask the man's former supervisor whether he was a competent inspector
    C. review the way he handles the various tasks that you assign to him
    D. send this man into the field with one of your inspectors and have him evaluate the newly assigned inspector

25. Instituting a program of on-the-job training may sometimes present problems for the supervisor because, when first initiated, such training 25.____
    A. does not take place under actual working conditions
    B. is less instructive than formal training sessions
    C. may result in a decrease in the authority of the supervisor
    D. may slow down the unit's work

26. Suppose that you are approached by a newly appointed inspector who asks you to make an inspection visit with him because he is unsure of the procedure. 26.____
    The one of the following that you should do FIRST is to
    A. agree to make the visit with him
    B. refer him to the supervisor for help
    C. report him to the supervisor for incorrect behavior
    D. tell him to do the best he can and offer to help him write up the report

27. Suppose that you are writing up your inspection reports in your office on a particular day. A fellow inspector, who has left his identification at home, asks if he may use your identification card and badge in order to perform his scheduled inspections. 27.____

Of the following, you should
- A. allow him to use your identification since he is an inspector
- B. offer to perform the inspections for him if he will write the reports
- C. refuse his request and suggest he explain the situation to the supervisor
- D. tell him you need your identification for yourself

28. Assume that you are assigned to handle telephone complaints. After you have attempted to handle a complaint from a belligerent caller, the caller asks your name, saying that he is going to report you to your superior for being insolent to him.
It would be BEST for you to
- A. give the caller a false name so he will stop bothering you
- B. give the caller your name and explain the circumstances to your superior afterwards
- C. refuse to give the caller your name
- D. tell the caller that you have not been insolent to him

28.____

29. As a senior inspector, you are permitted to hold an outside job as long as it is NOT
- A. dangerous
- B. in conflict with the performance of your inspection duties
- C. mentally or physically taxing
- D. paid at a rate higher than your inspector job

29.____

30. Of the following, the MOST important reason that graphs and charts are used in reports to present material that can be treated statistically is that such material
- A. is easier to understand when it is presented in graph or chart form
- B. looks more impressive when it is presented in graph or chart form
- C. requires less time to prepare when it is presented in a graph or chart form instead of written out
- D. take up less space in graph or chart form than when it is written out

30.____

KEY (CORRECT ANSWERS)

1.	A	11.	D	21.	A
2.	B	12.	D	22.	D
3.	C	13.	C	23.	C
4.	C	14.	A	24.	C
5.	B	15.	D	25.	D
6.	B	16.	D	26.	B
7.	D	17.	B	27.	C
8.	C	18.	B	28.	B
9.	B	19.	D	29.	B
10.	D	20.	C	30.	A

TEST 2

DIRECTIONS: Each question or incomplete statement is followed by several suggested answers or completions. Select the one that BEST answers the question or completes the statement. *PRINT THE LETTER OF THE CORRECT ANSWER IN THE SPACE AT THE RIGHT.*

1. If an inspector finds a discrepancy between the plans and specifications, he should
    A. always follow the plans
    B. ask for an interpretation
    C. always follow the specifications
    D. follow the plans if the difference is in dimensions

    1.____

2. In performing field inspectional work, an inspector is the contact man between the public and the agency, and it is his job to secure compliance through the maximum utilization of persuasion and education and the minimum application of coercion.
According to this statement, an inspector performing inspectional duties should
    A. seek to obtain voluntary compliance and use coercion only as a last resort
    B. be conciliatory on all issues of non-compliance and not take an attitude of firmness and authority
    C. maintain a strictly impersonal attitude in the exercise of his duties at all times
    D. use the threat of legal action to secure conformance with specified requirements

    2.____

3. The BEST way for a supervising inspector to determine whether a new inspector is learning his work properly is to
    A. ask the other men how this man is making out
    B. question him directly on details of the work
    C. assume that if he asks no questions, he knows the work
    D. inspect and follow up on the work which is assigned to him

    3.____

4. In assigning his men to various jobs, the BEST principle for a supervising inspector to follow is to
    A. study the men's abilities and assign them accordingly
    B. rotate a man from job to job until you find one which he can do well
    C. assign each of them to a job and let them adjust to it in their own way
    D. assume that men appointed to the position can do all parts of the work equally well

    4.____

5. Good inspection methods require that the inspector
    A. be observant and check all details
    B. constantly check with the engineer who designed the job
    C. apply specifications according to his interpretations
    D. permit slight job variation to establish good public relations

    5.____

6. An inspector inspecting a large job under construction inspected plumbing at 9 A.M., heating at 10 A.M., and ventilation at 11 A.M., and did his officework in the afternoon. He followed the same pattern daily for months.
This procedure is
   A. *bad*, because not enough time is devoted to plumbing
   B. *bad*, because the tradesmen know when the inspections will occur
   C. *good*, because it is methodical and he does not miss any of the trades
   D. *good*, because it gives equal amount of time to the important trades

6.____

7. The BEST way to evaluate the overall state of completion of a construction project is to check the progress estimate against the
   A. inspection worksheet
   B. construction schedule
   C. inspector's checklist
   D. equipment maintenance schedule

7.____

8. When a contractor fails to adhere to an approved progress schedule, he should
   A. revise the schedule without delay
   B. ask for an extension of time on account of delays
   C. adopt such additional means and methods of construction as will make up for time lost
   D. take no immediate action with the hope that sufficient time will be available later on that will assure the completion in accordance with the schedule

8.____

9. The usual contract for agency work includes a section entitled instructions to bidders, which states that the
   A. contractor agrees that he has made his own examination and will make no claim for damages on account of errors or omissions
   B. contractor shall not make claims for damages of any discrepancy, error or omission in any plans
   C. estimates of quantities and calculations are guaranteed by the agency to be correct and are deemed to be a representation of the conditions affecting the work
   D. plans, measurement, dimensions, and conditions under which the work is to be performed are guaranteed by the agency

9.____

10. A lump sum type of contract may require the contractor to submit a schedule of unit price.
The BEST reason for this is that it
   A. prevents the lump sum from being too high
   B. simplifies the selection of the lowest bidder
   C. enables the estimators to check the total cost
   D. provides a means of making equitable partial payments

10.____

11. A contractor on a large construction project USUALLY receives partial payments based on
    A. estimates of completed work
    B. actual cost of materials delivered and work completed
    C. estimates of material delivered and not paid for by the contractor
    D. the breakdown estimate submitted after the contract was signed and prorated over the estimated duration of the contract

11.____

12. In order to avoid disputes over payments for extra work in a contract for construction, the BEST procedure to follow would be to
    A. have contractor submit work progress reports daily
    B. insert a special clause in the contract specifications
    C. have a representative on the job at all times to verify conditions
    D. allocate a certain percentage of the cost of the job to cover such expenses

12.____

13. A fixed amount of money is generally withheld from the contractor for a definite period after the completion of construction.
    The BEST reason for this is
    A. that the money will be available for taxes due
    B. to penalize the contractor for poor work
    C. that it is a security for the repair of any defective work
    D. that the money will be available for modifications in the design of the structure

13.____

14. Prior to the installation of equipment called for in the specifications, the contractor is USUALLY required to submit for approval
    A. sets of shop drawings
    B. a set of revised specifications
    C. a detailed description of the methods of work to be used
    D. a complete list of skilled and unskilled tradesmen he proposes to use

14.____

15. During the actual construction work, the CHIEF value of a construction schedule is to
    A. insure that the work will be done on time
    B. reveal whether production is falling behind
    C. show how much equipment and material is required for the project
    D. furnish data as to the methods and techniques of construction operations

15.____

16. Of the following items, the one which should NOT be included in a proposed work schedule is
    A. a schedule of hourly wage rates and supplementary benefits
    B. an estimated time required for delivery of materials and equipment
    C. the anticipated commencement and completion of the various operations
    D. the sequence and inter-relationship of various operations with those of related contracts

16.____

17. The frequency with which job reports are submitted should depend MAINLY on   17.____
    A. how comprehensive the report has to be
    B. the amount of information in the report
    C. the availability of an experienced man to write the report
    D. the importance of changes in the information included in the report

18. The CHIEF purpose in preparing an outline for a report is usually to insure   18.____
    that
    A. the report will be grammatically correct
    B. every point will be given equal emphasis
    C. principal and secondary points will be properly integrated
    D. the language of the report will be of the same level and include the same
       technical terms

19. The MAIN reason for requiring written job reports is to   19.____
    A. avoid the necessity of oral orders
    B. develop better methods of doing the work
    C. provide a permanent record of what was done
    D. increase the amount of work that can be done

20. Assume you are recommending in a report to your superior that a radical   20.____
    change in a standard maintenance procedure should be adopted.
    Of the following, the MOST important information to be included in this report is
    A. a list of the reasons for making this change
    B. the names of others who favor the change
    C. a complete description of the present procedure
    D. amount of training time needed for the new procedure

KEY (CORRECT ANSWERS)

1.	B		11.	A
2.	A		12.	C
3.	B		13.	C
4.	A		14.	A
5.	A		15.	B
6.	B		16.	A
7.	B		17.	D
8.	C		18.	C
9.	A		19.	C
10.	D		20.	A

READING COMPREHENSION
UNDERSTANDING AND INTERPRETING WRITTEN MATERIAL
EXAMINATION SECTION
TEST 1

DIRECTIONS: Each question or incomplete statement is followed by several suggested answers or completions. Select the one that BEST answers the question or completes the statement. *PRINT THE LETTER OF THE CORRECT ANSWER IN THE SPACE AT THE RIGHT.*

Questions 1-3.

DIRECTIONS: Questions 1 through 3 are to be answered SOLELY on the basis of the following paragraph.

The aging housing inventory presents a broad spectrum of conditions, from good upkeep to unbelievable deterioration. Buildings, even relatively good buildings, are likely to have numerous minor violations rather than the gross and evident sanitary violations of an earlier age. Except for the serious violations in a relatively small number of slum buildings, the task is to deal with masses of minor violations that, though insignificant in themselves, amount in the aggregate to major deprivations of health and comfort to tenants. Caused by wear and tear, by the abrasions of time, and aggravated by neglect, these conditions do not readily yield to the dramatic *vacate and restore* measures of earlier times. Moreover, the lines between *good* and *bad* housing have become blurred in many parts of our cities; we find a range of *shades of gray* blending into each other. Different kinds of code enforcement efforts may be required to deal with different degrees of deterioration.

1. The above passage suggests that code enforcement efforts may have to be
   A. developed to cope with varying levels of housing dilapidation
   B. aimed primarily at the serious violations in slum buildings
   C. modeled on the *vacate and restore* measures of earlier times
   D. modified to reduce unrealistic penalties for petty violations

2. According to the above passage, during former times some buildings had sanitary violations which were
   A. irreparable and minor
   B. blurred and gray
   C. flagrant and obvious
   D. insignificant and numerous

3. According to the above passage, the aging housing stock presents a
   A. great number of rent-controlled buildings
   B. serious problem of tenant-caused deterioration
   C. significant increase in buildings without intentional violations
   D. wide range of physical conditions

Questions 4-5.

DIRECTIONS: Questions 4 and 5 are to be answered SOLELY on the basis of the following passage.

In general, housing code provisions relating to the safe and sanitary maintenance of dwelling units prescribe the maintenance required for foundations, walls, ceilings, floors, windows, doors, stairways, and also the facilities and equipment required in other sections. The more recent codes have, in addition, extensive provisions designed to ensure that the unit be maintained in a rat-free and rat-proof condition. Also, as an example of new approaches in code provisions, one proposed Federal model housing code prohibits the landlord from terminating vital services and utilities except during temporary emergencies or when actual repairs or maintenance are in process. This provision may be used to prevent a landlord from turning off utility services as a technique of self-help eviction or as a weapon against rent strikes.

4. According to the above passage, the more recent housing codes have extensive provisions designed to

   A. maintain a reasonably fire-proof living unit
   B. prohibit tenants from participating in rent strikes
   C. maintain the unit free from rats
   D. prohibit tenants from using lead-based paints

5. According to the above passage, one housing code would permit landlords to terminate vital services during

   A. a rent strike
   B. an actual eviction
   C. a temporary emergency
   D. the planning of repairs and maintenance

Questions 6-8.

DIRECTIONS: Questions 6 through 8 are to be answered SOLELY on the basis of the following passage.

City governments have long had building codes which set minimum standards for building and for human occupancy. The code (or series of codes) makes provisions for standards of lighting and ventilation, sanitation, fire prevention, and protection. As a result of demands from manufacturers, builders, real estate people, tenement owners, and building-trades unions, these codes often have established minimum standards well below those that the contemporary society would accept as a rock-bottom minimum. Codes often become outdated so that meager standards in one era become seriously inadequate a few decades later as society"s concept of a minimum standard of living changes. Out-of-date codes, when still in use, have sometimes prevented the introduction of new devices and modern building techniques. Thus, it is extremely important that building codes keep pace with changes in the accepted concept of a minimum standard of living.

6. According to the above passage, all of the following considerations in building planning would probably be covered in a building code EXCEPT

   A. closet space as a percentage of total floor area
   B. size and number of windows required for rooms of differing sizes
   C. placement of fire escapes in each line of apartments
   D. type of garbage disposal units to be installed

7. According to the above passage, if an ideal building code were to be created, how would the established minimum standards in it compare to the ones that are presently set by city governments?
   They would

   A. be lower than they are at present
   B. be higher than they are at present
   C. be comparable to the present minimum standards
   D. vary according to the economic group that sets them

8. On the basis of the above passage, what is the reason for difficulties in introducing new building techniques?

   A. Builders prefer techniques which represent the rock-bottom minimum desired by society.
   B. Certain manufacturers have obtained patents on various building methods to the exclusion of new techniques.
   C. The government does not want to invest money in techniques that will soon be outdated.
   D. New techniques are not provided for in building codes which are not up-to-date.

Questions 9-11.

DIRECTIONS: Questions 9 through 11 are to be answered SOLELY on the basis of the following paragraph.

When constructed within a multiple dwelling, such storage space shall be equipped with a sprinkler system and also with a system of mechanical ventilation in no way connected with any other ventilating system. Such storage space shall have no opening into any other part of the dwelling except through a fireproof vestibule. Any such vestibule shall have a minimum superficial floor area of fifty square feet, and its maximum area shall not exceed seventy-five square feet. It shall be enclosed with incombustible partitions having a fire-resistive rating of three hours. The floor and ceiling of such vestibule shall also be of incombustible material having a fire-resistive rating of at least three hours. There shall be two doors to provide access from the dwelling, to the car storage space. Each such door shall have a fire-resistive rating of one and one-half hours and shall be provided with a device to prevent the opening of one door until the other door is entirely closed.

9. According to the above paragraph, the one of the following that is REQUIRED in order for cars to be permitted to be stored in a multiple dwelling is a(n)

   A. fireproof vestibule   B. elevator from the garage
   C. approved heating system   D. sprinkler system

10. According to the above paragraph, the one of the following materials that would NOT be acceptable for the walls of a vestibule connecting a garage to the dwelling portion of a building is

    A. 3" solid gypsum blocks
    B. 4" brick
    C. 4" hollow gypsum blocks, plastered both sides
    D. 6" solid cinder concrete blocks

10.____

11. According to the above paragraph, the one of the following that would be ACCEPTABLE for the width and length of a vestibule connecting a garage that is within a multiple dwelling to the dwelling portion of the building is

    A. 3'8" x 13'0"   B. 4'6" x 18'6"
    C. 4'9" x 14'6"   D. 4'3" x 19'3"

11.____

Questions 12-13.

DIRECTIONS: Questions 12 and 13 are to be answered SOLELY on the basis of the following paragraph.

It shall be unlawful to place, use, or maintain in a condition intended, arranged, or designed for use, any gas-fired cooking appliance, laundry stove, heating stove, range or water heater or combination of such appliances in any room or space used for living or sleeping in any new or existing multiple dwelling unless such room or space has a window opening to the outer air or such gas appliance is vented to the outer air. All automatically operated gas appliances shall be equipped with a device which shall shut off automatically the gas supply to the main burners when the pilot light in such appliance is extinguished. A gas range or the cooking portion of a gas appliance incorporating a room heater shall not be deemed an automatically operated gas appliance. However, burners in gas ovens and broilers which can be turned on and off or ignited by non-manual means shall be equipped with a device which shall shut off automatically the gas supply to those burners when the operation of such non-manual means fails.

12. According to the above paragraph, an automatic shut-off device is NOT required on a gas

    A. hot water heater   B. laundry dryer
    C. space heater   D. range

12.____

13. According to the above paragraph, a gas-fired water heater is permitted

    A. only in kitchens   B. only in bathrooms
    C. only in living rooms   D. in any type of room

13.____

Questions 14-18.

DIRECTIONS: Questions 14 through 18 are to be answered SOLELY on the basis of the information contained in the statement below.

No multiple dwelling shall be erected to a height in excess of one and one-half times the width of the widest street on which it faces, except that above the level of such height, for each one foot that the front wall of such dwelling sets back from the street line, three feet shall be added to the height limit of such dwelling, but such dwelling shall not exceed in maximum height three feet plus one and three-quarter times the width of the widest street on which it faces.

Any such dwelling facing a street more than one hundred feet in width shall be subject to the same height limitations as though such dwelling faced a street one hundred feet in width.

14. The MAXIMUM height of a multiple dwelling set back five feet from the street line and facing a 60 foot wide street is _____ feet.

    A. 60   B. 90   C. 105   D. 165

15. The MAXIMUM height of a multiple dwelling set back six feet from the street line and facing a 120 foot wide street is _____ feet.

    A. 198   B. 168   C. 120   D. 105

16. The MAXIMUM height of a multiple dwelling is

    A. 100 ft.   B. 150 ft.   C. 178 ft.   D. unlimited

17. The MAXIMUM height of a multiple dwelling set back 10 feet from the street line and facing a 110 foot wide street is _____ feet.

    A. 178   B. 180   C. 195   D. 205

18. The MAXIMUM height of a multiple dwelling set back eight feet from the street line and facing a 90 foot wide street is _____ feet.

    A. 135   B. 147   C. 178   D. 159

Questions 19-23.

DIRECTIONS: Questions 19 through 23 are to be answered SOLELY on the basis of the following statement.

The number of persons accommodated on any story in a lodging house shall not be greater than the sum of the following components,

  a. 22 persons for each full multiple of 22 inches in the smallest clear width for each means of egress approved by the department, other than fire escapes
  b. 20 persons for each lawful fire escape accessible from such story.

19. The MAXIMUM number of persons that may be accommodated on a story in a lodging house depends on the

    A. number of lawful fire escapes *only*
    B. number of approved means of egress *only*
    C. smallest clear width in each approved means of egress *only*
    D. number of lawful fire escapes and sum total of smallest clear widths in each approved means of egress

20. The MAXIMUM number of persons that may be accommodated on a story of a lodging house having one lawful fire escape and a sum total of 44 inches in the smallest clear widths of the two approved means of egress is

    A. 20   B. 22   C. 42   D. 64

21. The MAXIMUM number of persons that may be accommodated on a story of a lodging house having two lawful fire escapes and a sum total of 60 inches in the smallest clear width of the approved means of egress is

    A. 64   B. 84   C. 100   D. 106

22. The MAXIMUM number of persons that may be accommodated on a story of a lodging house having one lawful fire escape and a sum total of 33 inches in the smallest clear width of the approved means of egress is

    A. 42   B. 53   C. 64   D. 73

23. The MAXIMUM number of persons that may be accommodated on a story of a lodging house having two lawful fire escapes and two approved means of egress, with 40 inches and 44 inches in the smallest clear widths, respectively, is

    A. 84   B. 104   C. 106   D. 108

Questions 24-25.

DIRECTIONS: Questions 24 and 25 are to be answered SOLELY on the basis of the following paragraph.

Though the recent trend toward apartment construction may appear to be the Region's response to large-lot zoning and centralized industry, it really is not. It is mainly a function of the age of the population. Most of the apartments are occupied by one- and two-person families young people out of school but without a family of their own and older people whose children have grown. Both groups have been increasing in number; and, in this Region, they characteristically live in apartments. It is this increased demand for apartments and the simultaneous decrease in demand for one-family houses that dramatically raised the percentage of building permits issued for multi-family housing units from 36 percent in 1977 to 67 percent in 1981. The fact that three-fourths of the apartments were built in the Core between 1977 and 1981 at the same time as the Core was losing population underscores the failure of the apartment boom to slow the outward spread of the population.

24. According to the above paragraph, one of the reasons for the increase in the number of building permits issued for multi-family construction in the City Metropolitan Region is

    A. that workers in industry want to live close to their jobs
    B. an increase in the number of elderly people living in the Region
    C. the inability of many families to afford the large lots necessary to build private homes
    D. the new zoning ordinance made it easier to build apartments

25. According to the above paragraph, the apartment construction boom

    A. increased the population density in the Core
    B. spurred a population shift to the suburbs
    C. did not halt the outward flow of the population from the Core
    D. was most significant in the outer areas of the Region

KEY (CORRECT ANSWERS)

1. A
2. C
3. D
4. C
5. C

6. A
7. B
8. D
9. D
10. B

11. C
12. D
13. D
14. C
15. B

16. C
17. A
18. D
19. D
20. D

21. B
22. A
23. C
24. B
25. C

———

TEST 2

DIRECTIONS: Each question or incomplete statement is followed by several suggested answers or completions. Select the one that BEST answers the question or completes the statement. *PRINT THE LETTER OF THE CORRECT ANSWER IN THE SPACE AT THE RIGHT.*

Questions 1-4.

DIRECTIONS: Questions 1 through 4 are to be answered SOLELY on the basis of the following paragraph.

Although the suburbs have provided housing and employment for millions of additional families since 1950, many suburban communities have maintained controls over the kinds of families who can live in them. Suburban attitudes have been formed by reaction against a perception of crowded, harassed city life and threatening alien city people. As population, taxable income, and jobs have left the cities for the suburbs, the *urban crisis* of substandard housing, declining levels of education and public services, and decreasing employment opportunities has been created. The crisis, however, is not urban at all, but national, and in part a result of the suburban policy that discourages outward movement by the urban poor.

1. According to the above paragraph, the quality of urban life

    A. is determined by public opinion in the cities
    B. has worsened in recent years
    C. is similar to rural life
    D. can be changed by political means

2. According to the above paragraph, suburban communities have

    A. tried to show that the urban crisis is really a national crisis
    B. avoided taking a position on the urban crisis
    C. been involved in causing the urban crisis
    D. been the innocent victims of the urban crisis

3. According to the above paragraph, the poor have

    A. become increasingly sophisticated in their attempts to move to the suburbs
    B. generally been excluded from the suburbs
    C. lost incentive for betterment of their living conditions
    D. sought improvement of the central cities

4. As used in the above paragraph, the word perception means MOST NEARLY

    A. development   B. impression
    C. opposition   D. uncertainty

Questions 5-8.

DIRECTIONS: Questions 5 through 8 are to be answered SOLELY on the basis of the following paragraph.

The concentration of publicly assisted housing in central cities -- because the suburbs do not want them and effectively bar them -- is usually rationalized by a solicitous regard for keeping intact the city neighborhoods cherished by low-income groups. If one accepted this as valid, the devotion of minorities to blighted city neighborhoods in preference to suburban employment and housing would be an historic first. Certainly no such devotion was visible among the millions who have deserted their city neighborhoods in the last 25 years even if it meant an arduous daily trip from the suburbs to their jobs in the cities.

5. The writer implies that MOST poor people

   A. prefer isolation
   B. fear change
   C. are angry
   D. seek betterment

6. The general tone of the paragraph is BEST characterized as

   A. uncertain   B. skeptical   C. evasive   D. indifferent

7. As used in the above paragraph, the word rationalize means MOST NEARLY

   A. dispute   B. justify   C. deny   D. locate

8. According to the above paragraph, publicly assisted housing is concentrated in the central cities PRIMARILY because

   A. city dwellers are unable to find satisfactory housing
   B. deterioration of older housing has increased in recent years
   C. suburbanites have opposed the movement of the poor to the suburbs
   D. employment opportunities have decreased in the suburbs

Questions 9-11.

DIRECTIONS: Questions 9 through 11 are to be answered SOLELY on the basis of the following paragraph.

In recent years, new and important emphasis has been placed upon the maximum use of conservation and rehabilitation techniques in carrying out programs of urban renewal and revitalization. In urban renewal projects where existing structures are hopelessly deteriorated or land uses are incompatible with the community's overall plans, the entire area may be acquired, cleared, and sold for redevelopment. However, where existing structures are basically sound but have deteriorated to the point where they are a blighting influence on the neighborhood, they may be salvaged through a program of rehabilitation and reconditioning.

9. According to the above paragraph, the one of the following which is MOST likely to cause area-wide razing of the buildings in urban renewal programs is

   A. a program of rehabilitation and reconditioning
   B. concerted insistence by landlords and tenants that certain buildings be bulldozed
   C. an inability of community groups to agree on priorities for staged clearance
   D. land use contrary to the community's general plan

10. According to the above paragraph, rehabilitation of structures may take place if

    A. new conservation and rehabilitation techniques are used
    B. salvaging all the buildings in the entire area is hopeless
    C. the community wishes to preserve historic structures
    D. the existing buildings are structurally sound

11. As used in the above paragraph, the word <u>blighting</u> means MOST NEARLY 11.____

    A. ruining   B. infrequent   C. recurrent   D. traditional

Questions 12-13.

DIRECTIONS: Questions 12 and 13 are to be answered SOLELY on the basis of the following paragraphs.

We must also find better ways to handle the relocation of people uprooted by projects. In the past, many renewal plans have foundered on this problem, and it is still the most difficult part of the community development. Large-scale replacement of low-income residents -- many ineligible for public housing -- has contributed to deterioration of surrounding communities. However, thanks to changes in housing authority procedures, relocation has been accomplished in a far more satisfactory fashion. The step-by-step community development projects we advocate in this plan should bring further improvement.

But additional measures will be necessary. There are going to be more people to be moved; and, with the current shortage of apartments, large ones especially, it is going to be tougher to find places to move them to. The city should have more freedom to buy or lease housing that comes on the market because of normal turnover and make it available to relocatees.

12. According to the above paragraphs, one of the reasons a neighborhood may deteriorate is that 12.____

    A. there is a scarcity of large apartments
    B. step-by-step community development projects have failed
    C. people in the given neighborhood are uprooted from their homes
    D. a nearby renewal project has an inadequate relocation plan

13. From the above paragraphs, one might conclude that the relocation phase of community renewal has been improved. 13.____

    A. by changes in housing authority procedures
    B. by development of step-by-step community development projects
    C. through expanded city powers to buy housing for relocation
    D. by the addition of huge sums of money

Questions 14-15.

DIRECTIONS: Questions 14 and 15 are to be answered SOLELY on the basis of the following paragraphs.

Provision of decent housing for the lower half of the population (by income) was thus taken on as a public responsibility. Public housing was to assist the poorest quarter of urban families while the 221(d)(3) Housing Program would assist the next quarter. But limited funds meant that the supply of subsidized housing could not stretch nearly far enough to help this half of the population. Who were to be left out in the rationing process which was accomplished by the sifting of applicants for housing on the part of public and private authorities?

Discrimination on the grounds of race or color is not allowed under Federal law. In all sections of the country, encouragingly, housing programs are found which follow this law to the letter. Yet, housing programs in some cities still suffer from the residue of racial segregation policies and attitudes that for years were condoned or even encouraged.

Some sifting in the 221(d)(3) Housing Program follows the practice of many public housing authorities, the imposition of requirements with respect to character. This is a delicate matter. To fill a project overwhelmingly with broken families, alcoholics, criminals, delinquents, and other problem tenants would hardly make it a wholesome environment. Yet the total exclusion of such families is hardly an acceptable alternative. To the extent this exclusion is practiced, the very people whose lives are described in order to persuade lawmakers and the public to instigate new programs find the door shut in their faces when such programs come into being. The proper balance is difficult to achieve, but society's neediest families surely should not be totally denied the opportunities for rejuvenation in subsidized housing.

14. From the above paragraphs, it can be assumed that the 221(d)(3) Housing Program

 A. served a population earning more than the median income
 B. served a less affluent population than is served by public housing
 C. excludes all problem families from its projects
 D. is a subsidized housing program

15. According to this text, the provision of housing for the poor

 A. has not been completely accomplished with public monies
 B. is never influenced by segregationist policies
 C. is limited to providing housing for only the neediest families
 D. is primarily the responsibility of the Federal government

16. Five hundred persons attended a public hearing at which a proposed public housing project was being considered. Less than half favored the project while the majority opposed the project.
According to the above statement, it is REASONABLE to conclude that

 A. the proposal stimulated considerable community interest
 B. the public housing project was disapproved by the city because a majority opposed it
 C. those who opposed the project lacked sympathy for needy persons
 D. the supporters of the project were led by militants

17. A vacant lot close to a polluted creek is for sale. Two buyers compete. One owns an adjacent factory which provides 300 high paying unskilled jobs. He needs to expand or move from the city. If he expands, he will provide 300 additional jobs. The other is a community group in a changing residential area close by. They hope to stabilize the neighborhood by bringing in new housing. They would build an apartment building with 100 dwelling units on the lot.
According to the above paragraph, it is REASONABLE to conclude that

 A. jobs are more important than housing
 B. there is conflict between the factory owners and the neighborhood group
 C. the neighborhood group will not succeed in stabilizing the area by constructing new housing
 D. the polluted creek should be cleaned up

18. The housing authority faces every problem of the private developer, and it must also assume responsibilities of which private building is free. The authority must account to the community; it must conform to federal regulations; it must provide durable buildings of good standard at low cost; it must overcome the prejudices against public operations, of contractors, bankers, and prospective tenants. These authorities are being watched by anti-housing enthusiasts for the first error of judgment or the first evidence of high costs, to be torn to bits before a Congressional committee.
On the basis of this statement, it would be MOST correct to state that

   A. private builders do not have the opposition of contractors, bankers, and prospective tenants
   B. Congressional committees impede the progress of public housing by petty investigations
   C. a housing authority must deal with all the difficulties encountered by the private builder
   D. housing authorities are no more immune from errors in judgment than private developers

19. Another factor that has considerably added to the city's housing crisis has been the great influx of low-income workers and their families seeking better employment opportunities during wartime and defense boom periods. The circumstances of these families have forced them to crowd into the worst kind of housing and have produced on a renewed scale the conditions from which slums flourish and grow.
On the basis of this statement, one would be justified in stating that

   A. the influx of low-income workers has aggravated the slum problem
   B. the city has better employment opportunities than other sections of the country
   C. the high wages paid by our defense industries have made many families ineligible for tenancy in public housing projects
   D. the families who settled in the city during wartime and the defense build-up brought with them language and social customs conducive to the growth of slums

20. Much of the city felt the effects of the general postwar increase of vandalism and street crime, and the greatly expanded public housing program was no exception. Projects built in congested slum areas with a high incidence of delinquency and crime were particularly subjected to the depredations of neighborhood gangs. The civil service watchmen who patrolled the projects, unarmed and neither trained nor expected to perform police duties, were unable to cope with the situation.
On the basis of this statement, the MOST accurate of the following statements is:

   A. Neighborhood gangs were particularly responsible for the high incidence of delinquency and crime in congested slum areas having public housing programs
   B. Civil service watchmen who patrolled housing projects failed to carry out their assigned police duties
   C. Housing projects were not spared the effects of the general postwar increase of vandalism and street crime
   D. Delinquency and crime affected housing projects in slum areas to a greater extent than other dwellings in the same area

21. Another peculiar characteristic of real estate is the absence of liquidity. Each parcel is a discrete unit as to size, location, rental, physical condition, and financing arrangements. Each property requires investigation, comparison of rents with other properties, and individualized haggling on price and terms.
On the basis of this statement, the LEAST accurate of the following statements is:

    A. Although the size, location, and rent of parcels vary, comparison with rents of other properties affords an indication of the value of a particular parcel
    B. Bargaining skill is the essential factor in determining the value of a parcel of real estate
    C. Each parcel of real estate has individual peculiarities distinguishing it from any other parcel
    D. Real estate is not easily converted to other types of assets

22. In part, at least, the charges of sameness, monotony, and institutionalism directed at public housing projects result from the degree in which they differ from the city's normal housing pattern. They seem alike because their very difference from the usual makes them stand apart.
In many respects, there is considerably more variety between public housing projects than there is between different streets of apartment houses or tenements throughout the city.
On the basis of this statement, it would be LEAST accurate to state that:

    A. There is considerably more variety between public housing projects than there is between different streets of tenements throughout the city
    B. Public housing projects differ from the city's normal housing pattern to the degree that sameness, monotony, and institutionalism are characteristic of public buildings
    C. Public housing projects seem alike because their deviation from the usual dwellings draws attention to them
    D. The variety in structure between public housing projects and other public buildings is related to the period in which they were built

23. The amount of debt that can be charged against the city for public housing is limited by law. Part of the city's restricted housing means goes for cash subsidies it may be required to contribute to state-aided projects. Under the provisions of the state law, the city must match the state's contributions in subsidies; and while the value of the partial tax exemption granted by the city is counted for this purpose, it is not always sufficient.
On the basis of this statement, it would be MOST accurate to state that:

    A. The amount of money the city may spend for public housing is limited by annual tax revenues
    B. The value of tax exemptions granted by the city to educational, religious, and charitable institutions may be added to its subsidy contributions to public housing projects
    C. The subsidy contributions for state-aided public housing projects are shared equally by the state and the city under the provisions of the state law
    D. The tax revenues of the city, unless supplemented by state aid, are insufficient to finance public housing projects

24. Maintenance costs can be minimized and the useful life of houses can be extended by building with the best and most permanent materials available. The best and most permanent materials in many cases are, however, much more expensive than materials which require more maintenance. The most economical procedure in home building has been to compromise between the capital costs of high quality and enduring materials and the maintenance costs of less desirable materials.
On the basis of this statement, one would be justified in stating that:

    A. Savings in maintenance costs make the use of less durable and less expensive building materials preferable to high quality materials that would prolong the useful life of houses constructed from them
    B. Financial advantage can be secured by the home builder if he judiciously combines costly but enduring building materials with less desirable materials which, however, require more maintenance
    C. A compromise between the capital costs of high quality materials and the maintenance costs of less desirable materials makes it easier for a home builder to estimate construction expenditures
    D. The most economical procedure in home building is to balance the capital costs of the most permanent materials against the costs of less expensive materials that are cheaper to maintain

24.____

25. Personnel selection has been a critical problem for local housing authorities. The pool of qualified workers trained in housing procedures is small, and the colleges and universities have failed to grasp the opportunity for enlarging it. While real estate experience makes a good background for management of a housing project, many real estate men are deplorably lacking in understanding of social and governmental problems. Social workers, on the other hand, are likely to be deficient in business judgment.
On the basis of this statement, it would be MOST accurate to state that:

    A. Colleges and universities have failed to train qualified workers for proficiency in housing procedures
    B. Social workers are deficient in business judgment as related to the management of a housing project
    C. Real estate experience makes a person a good manager of a housing project
    D. Local housing authorities have been critical of present methods of personnel selection

25.____

KEY (CORRECT ANSWERS)

1.	B	11.	A
2.	C	12.	D
3.	B	13.	A
4.	B	14.	D
5.	D	15.	A
6.	B	16.	A
7.	B	17.	B
8.	D	18.	C
9.	D	19.	A
10.	D	20.	C

21. B
22. B
23. C
24. B
25. A

THE HOUSING CODE

CONTENTS

		Page
I.	Definitions	1
II.	Background of Housing Codes in the United States	5
III.	Objectives of a Housing Code	6
IV.	Limitations	6
V.	Content	7
VI.	Administrative Elements of a Housing Code	8
VII.	Substantive Provisions of a Housing Code	12

THE HOUSING CODE

Any housing code, regardless of who promulgates it, is basically an environmental health protection code. The hygiene of housing, correspondingly, is the area of environmental health that deals with man's most intimate living environment – his home and his neighborhood. Into the fabric of housing hygiene is woven a wide variety of health, safety, economic, social, and political factors.

Early housing codes primarily considered protecting only man's physical health; hence, they were enforced only in slum areas. More recently the realization has been made that if urban blight and its associated human suffering are to be controlled; the housing codes must consider both physical and mental health and must be administered uniformly throughout the community.

In preparing or revising the housing code, local officials must maintain a level of standards that will not merely be "minimal." These standards should maintain a living environment that contributes positively to healthful individual and family living. The fact that a small portion of housing fails to meet a desirable standard is hardly a legitimate reason for retrogressive modification or abolition of a standard. A housing code is merely a means to an end. The end is the eventual elimination of all substandard conditions within the home and neighborhood. This end cannot be reached if the community adopts an inadequate housing code. The adoption of a housing ordinance that establishes low standards for existing housing serves only to legalize and perpetuate an unhealthy living environment. Wherever local conditions are such that immediate enforcement of some standards within the code would cause undue hardship upon some individuals, it is better to provide a time interval for compliance than to eliminate an otherwise satisfactory standard.

I. Definitions

The following definitions of terms have been excerpted from "APHA - CDC Recommended Housing Maintenance and Occupancy Ordinance" and will be used throughout this manual.

1. **Accessory Building or Structure** shall mean a detached building or structure in a secondary or subordinate capacity from the main or principal building or structure on the same premises.

2. **Appropriate Authority** shall mean that person within the governmental structure of the corporate unit who is charged with the administration of the appropriate code.

3. **Approved** shall mean approved by the local or state authority have such administrative authority?

4. **Ashes** shall mean the residue from the burning of combustible materials.

5. **Attic** shall mean any story situated wholly or partly within the roof, and so designed, arranged or built as to be used for business, storage, or habitation.

6. **Basement** shall mean the lowest story of a building, below the main floor and wholly or partially lower than the surface of the ground.

7. **Building** shall mean a fixed construction with walls, foundation and roof, such as a house, factory, or garage.

8. **Bulk Container** shall mean any metal garbage, rubbish, or refuse container having a capacity of two (2) cubic yards or greater and which is equipped with fittings for hydraulic or mechanical emptying, unloading or removal.

9. **Cellar** shall mean a room or group of rooms totally below the ground level and usually under a building.

10. **Central Heating System** shall mean a single system supplying heat to one (1) or more dwelling unite(s) or more than one (1) rooming unit.

11. **Chimney** shall mean a vertical masonry shaft of reinforced concrete, or other approved noncombustible, heat-resisting material enclosing one (1) or more flues, for the purpose of removing products of combustion from solid, liquid, or gaseous fuel.

12. **Dilapidated** shall mean no longer adequate for the purpose or use for which it was originally intended.

13. **Dormitory** shall mean a building or a group of rooms in a building used for institutional living and sleeping purposes by four (4) or more persons.

14. **Dwelling** shall mean any enclosed space wholly or partly used or intended to be used for living, sleeping, cooking, and eating; provided that temporary housing as hereinafter defined shall not be classified as a dwelling. Industrialized housing and modular construction which conform to nationally accepted industry standards and used or intended for use for living, sleeping, cooking, and eating purposes shall be classified as dwellings.

15. **Dwelling Unit** shall mean a room or group of rooms located within a dwelling forming a single habitable unit with facilities used or intended to be used by a single family for living, sleeping, cooking, and eating purposes.

16. **Egress** shall mean an arrangement of exit facilities to assure a safe means of exit from buildings.

17. **Extermination** shall mean the control and elimination of insects, rodents, or other pests by eliminating their harborage places; by removing or making inaccessible materials that may serve as their food; by poisoning, spraying, fumigating, trapping, or by any other recognized and legal pest elimination methods approved by the local or state authority having such administrative authority.

18. **Fair Market Value** shall mean a price at which both buyers and sellers are willing to do business.

19. **Family** shall mean one or more individuals living together and sharing common living, sleeping, cooking, and eating facilities (See also Household).

20. **Flush Water Closet** shall mean a toilet bowl which is flushed with water which has been supplied under pressure and equipped with a water sealed trap above the floor level.

21. **Garbage** shall mean the animal and vegetable waste resulting from the handling, preparation, cooking, serving, and nonconsumption of food.

22. **Grade** shall mean the finished ground level adjacent to a required window.

23. **Guest** shall mean an individual who shares a dwelling unit in a non-permanent status for not more than thirty (30) days.

24. **Habitable Room** shall mean a room or enclosed floor space used or intended to be used for living, sleeping, cooking, or eating purposes, excluding bathrooms, water closet compartments, laundries, furnace rooms, pantries, kitchenettes and utility rooms of less than fifty (50) square feet of floor space, foyers, or communicating corridors, stairways, closets, storage spaces and workshops, hobby and recreation areas.

25. **Health Officer** shall mean the legally designated health authority of the (Name of Corporate Unit) or his authorized representative. (If the legally designated health authority has a title other than "Health Officer" the title of this authority should be substituted for "Health Officer" in this section and all other sections of this ordinance.)

26. **Heated Water** shall mean water heated to a temperature of not less than 120°F at the outlet.

27. **Heating Device** shall mean all furnaces, unit heaters, domestic incinerators, cooking and heating stoves and ranges, and other similar devices.

28. **Household** shall mean one or more individuals living together in a single dwelling unit and sharing common living, sleeping, cooking, and eating facilities (See also Family).

29. **Infestation** shall mean the presence within or around a dwelling of any insects; rodents, or other pests.

30. **Kitchen** shall mean any room used for the storage and preparation of foods and containing the following equipment: sink or other device for dishwashing, stove or other device for cooking, refrigerator or other device for cool storage of food, cabinets or shelves for storage of equipment and utensils, and counter or table for food preparation.

31. **Kitchenette** shall mean a small kitchen or an alcove containing cooking facilities.

32. **Lead-based Paint** shall mean any paint containing more lead than the level established by the U.S. Consumer Product Safety Commission as being the "safe" level of lead in residential paint and paint products.

33. **Meaning of Certain Words** Whenever the words "dwelling," "dwelling unit," "rooming units," "premises," and "structure" are used in the ordinance they shall be construed as though they were followed by the words "or any part thereof." Words used in the singular include the plural, and the plural the singular, the masculine gender includes the feminine and the feminine the masculine.

34. **Multiple Dwelling** shall mean any dwelling containing more than two dwelling units.

35. **Occupant** shall mean any individual, over one (1) year of age, living, sleeping, cooking, or eating in or having possession of a dwelling unit or a rooming unit; except that in dwelling units a guest shall not be considered an occupant.

36. **Operator** shall mean any person who has charge, care, control, or management of a building, or part thereof, in which dwelling units or rooming units are let.

37. **Ordinary Summer Conditions** shall mean a temperature 10°F below the highest recorded temperature in the locality for prior ten (10) year period.

38. **Ordinary Winter Conditions** shall mean a temperature 15°F above the lowest recorded temperature in the locality for prior ten (10) year period.

39. **Owner** shall mean any person who alone or jointly or severally with others:
    (a) shall have legal title to any premises, dwelling or dwelling unit, with or without accompanying actual possession thereof, or
    (b) shall have charge, care, or control of any premises, dwelling or dwelling unit, as owner or agent of the owner, or as executor, administrator, trustee or guardian of the estate of the owner.

40. **Permissible Occupancy** shall mean the maximum number of individuals permitted to reside in a dwelling unit, rooming unit, or dormitory.

41. **Person** shall mean and include any individual, firm, corporation, association, partnership, cooperative, or governmental agency.

42. **Plumbing** shall mean and include all of the following supplied facilities and equipment: gas pipes, gas burning equipment, water pipes, garbage disposal units, waste pipes, water closets, sinks, installed dishwashers, lavatories, bathtubs, shower baths, installed clothes washing machines, catch basins, drains, vents, and any other similar supplied fixtures, and the installation thereof, together with all connections to water, sewer, or gas lines.

43. **Premises** shall mean a platted lot or part thereof or unplatted lot or parcel of land or plot of land, either occupied or unoccupied by any dwelling or nondwelling structure, and includes any such building, accessory structure, or other structure thereon.

44. **Privacy** shall mean the existence of conditions which will permit an individual or individuals to carry out an activity commenced without interruption or interference, either by sight or sound by unwanted individuals.

45. **Properly Connected** shall mean connected in accordance with all applicable code and ordinances of this (Name of Corporate Unit) as from time to time enforced; provided, however, that the application of this definition shall not require the alteration or replacement of any connection in good working order and not constituting a hazard to life or health.

46. **Rat Harborage** shall mean any conditions or place where rats can live, nest, or seek shelter.

47. **Ratproofing** shall mean a form of construction which will prevent the ingress or egress of rats to or from a given space or building, or from gaining access to food, water, or harborage. It consists of the closing and keeping closed of every opening in foundations, basements, cellars, exterior and interior walls, ground or first floors, roofs, sidewalk gratings, sidewalk openings, and other places that may be reached and entered by rats by climbing, burrowing or other methods, by the use of materials impervious to rat gnawing and other methods approved by the (Appropriate Authority).

48. **Refuse** shall mean all putrescible and nonputrescible solids (except body wastes) including garbage, rubbish, ashes, and dead animals.

49. **Refuse Container** shall mean a watertight container that is constructed of metal, or other durable material impervious to rodents, that are capable of being serviced without creating

insanitary conditions, or such other containers as have been approved by the (Appropriate Authority). Openings into the container such as covers and doors shall be tight fitting.

50. **Rooming House** shall mean any dwelling other than a hotel or motel or that part of any dwelling, containing one (1) or more rooming units, or one (1) or more dormitory rooms and in which persons either individually or as families are housed with or without meals being provided.

51. **Rooming Unit** shall mean any room or group of rooms forming a single habitable unit used or intended to be used for living and sleeping, but not for cooking purposes.

52. **Rubbish** shall mean nonputrescible solid wastes (excluding ashes) consisting of either:
    (a) combustible wastes such as paper, cardboard, plastic containers, yard clippings, and wood; or
    (b) noncombustible wastes such as cans, glass, and crockery.

53. **Safety** shall mean the condition of being reasonably free from danger and hazards which may cause accidents or disease.

54. **Space Heater** shall mean a self contained heating appliance of either the convection type or the radiant type and intended primarily to heat only a limited space or area such as one room or two adjoining rooms.

55. **Supplied** shall mean paid for, furnished by, provided by, or under the control of the owner, operator, or agent.

56. **Temporary Housing** shall mean any tent, trailer, mobile home or any other structure used for human shelter which is designed to be transportable and which is not attached to the ground, to another structure, or to any utility system on the same premises for more than thirty (30) consecutive days.

57. **Toxic Substance** shall mean any chemical product applied on the surface of or incorporated into any structural or decorative material which constitutes a potential hazard to human health at acute

58. **Variance** shall mean a difference between that which is required or specified and that which is permitted.

II. Background of Housing Codes in the United States

To assist municipalities with the development of legislation necessary to regulate the quality of housing, the Committee on the Hygiene of Housing, American Public Health Association, prepared and in 1952, published a proposed housing ordinance. This provided a prototype on which such legislation might be based and has served as the basis for countless housing codes enacted in the United States since that time. Some municipalities enacted it without change. Others made revision by omitting some portions, modifying others, and some times adding new provisions.

One must keep in mind when considering the adoption of any model code that the code is, as stated, merely a model. The community should read and consider each element within the model code to determine its applicability to that community. As previously stated, however, a housing code is merely a means to an end. The end is the eventual elimination of all substandard conditions within the home and the neighborhood. This end cannot be reached if the community adopts an inadequate housing code.

III. Objectives of a Housing Code

The Housing Act of 1949 gave new impetus to existing local, state, and Federal housing programs directed towards the elimination of poor housing and the production of sound and decent housing. In passing this legislation, Congress defined a new national objective by declaring that the general welfare and security of the nation and the health and living standards of its people ... require a decent home and a suitable living environment for every American family. This mandate generated an awareness that the quality of housing and residential environment has an enormous influence upon the physical and mental health and the social well-being of each individual and, in turn, upon the economic, political, and social conditions in every community. Consequently, public agencies, units of government, professional organizations, and others sought ways to ensure that the quality of housing and the residential environment did not depreciate or deteriorate.

It soon became apparent that a new type of legislation was needed, namely, ordinances that regulate the supplied facilities and the maintenance and occupancy of dwellings and dwelling units, or as they are more commonly called, "housing codes." The objective of a housing code is to establish minimum standards essential to make dwellings safe, sanitary, and fit for human habitation by governing the condition and maintenance, the supplied utilities and facilities, and the occupancy.

IV. Limitations

A housing code is limited in its effectiveness by several factors. First, if the housing code does not contain *standards that adequately protect the health and well-being of the individuals*, it cannot be effective. The best trained soldier, if armed only with a pea shooter, can accomplish little positive action in a battle. Similarly, the best trained housing inspector, if not armed with an adequate housing code, can accomplish little good in the battle against urban blight.

A second factor affecting the quality of the housing administration effort is the *budget of the housing group*. If the housing effort is directed, because of limitations of funds and personnel, to the fire-fighting efforts of complaint answering, then the community can expect to lose the battle against urban blight. It is only through a systematic enforcement effort by an adequately sized staff of properly trained inspectors that the battle can be won.

A third factor that can affect the housing effort is the *attitude of the political bodies within the area*. A properly administered housing program will require the upgrading of substandard housing throughout the community. Frequently, this results in political pressures being exerted to prevent the enforcement of the code in certain areas of the city. If the housing effort is backed properly by all political elements, blight can be controlled and eventually eliminated within the community. If, however, the housing program is not permitted to choke out the spreading influence of substandard conditions, urban blight will spread like a cancer, engulfing greater and greater portions of the city. Similarly, an effort directed only at the most serious blocks in the city will merely upgrade those blocks while the blight spreads elsewhere. If a cancer is to be controlled, it must be cut out in its entirety. If urban blight is to be controlled, it also must be cut out in its entirety.

A fourth element that limits the ability of a housing program is *whether or not the housing program is supported fully by the other departments within the city*. Regardless of which city agency administers the housing program, the other city agencies must support the activities of the housing program. In addition, great effort should be expended to obtain the support and cooperation of the community as a whole towards the housing effort. This can be accomplished through public awareness and public information programs. These two programs should never be undersold. They can provide considerable support or considerable resistance to the efforts of the program.

A fifth limitation to an effective housing program is an *inadequately or improperly trained inspectional staff*. The housing inspector should have considerable training and considerable capabilities if the effort is to accomplish much good. He should have a basic knowledge and general understanding of the principles involved in many related areas. He should have the capability of evaluating whether a serious or a minor problem exists in matters ranging from a structural stability of a building to the health and sanitary aspects relating to the structure. A housing inspector cannot be expected to accomplish his job properly unless he is given sufficient training so as to prepare him to be able to make basic judgments regarding the severity of problems. Since the housing inspector is a generalized inspector, it is not intended that he should become an expert in all areas such as building, electrical, or health inspection. It is merely intended that he should be able to distinguish whether a problem warrants immediate referral to another department or whether it can be handled through routine channels.

A sixth item that frequently restricts the effectiveness of a housing administration effort is *the fact that many housing groups fail to do a complete job of evaluation of the housing problems*. In many cases, the inspectional effort is restricted to merely evaluating what conditions exist with little or no thought given to why these conditions exist. If a housing effort is to be successful, it must consider why the homes deteriorated. Was it because of environmental stresses within the neighborhood that need to be eliminated or was it because of apathy developed on the part of the occupants? In either case, if the causative agent is not removed, then the inspector faces an annual problem of maintaining the quality of that residence. It is only by eliminating the causes of deterioration that the quality of the neighborhood can be maintained. These, then, are a few of the principal limitations that affect the quality of a housing administration effort.

V. Content

What then are the general items that should be included in a housing code? Although all comprehensive housing codes or ordinances contain a number of common elements, the provisions of any two or more communities on the same element or elements will usually vary to some extent. This is true whether the codes be national or state models, those of a northern, eastern, southern, or western municipality, or even of two or more communities within the same state or region. These variations stem from differences in local policies, preferences, and to a lesser extent, needs. They are also influenced by the standards set by the related provisions of the diverse building, electrical, and plumbing codes in use in the municipality.

Within any housing code there are generally five major sections. These sections are:

A **Definitions of terms** used in the code.

B **Administrative provisions** showing who is authorized to administer the code and the basic methods and procedures that must be followed in implementing and enforcing the sections of the code. The administrative sections deal with items such as what are reasonable hours of inspections; when service of violation notices is and is not required; how to notify either the absentee owner when he can or cannot be contacted in person or through a legally responsible agent, or the resident-owner or tenant; how to process and conduct hearings; what rules to follow in processing dwellings alleged to be unfit for human habitation; how to occupy or use dwellings finally declared fit.

C **Substantive provisions** specifying the various types of health, building, electrical, heating, plumbing, maintenance, occupancy, and use conditions that constitute violations of the housing code. These provisions can also be and often are grouped into three main categories, namely, (1) minimum facilities and equipment for dwelling units, (2) adequate maintenance of dwellings and dwelling units as well as their facilities and equipment, and (3) the occupancy conditions of dwellings and dwelling units.

D **Court and penalty sections** outlining the basis for court action and the penalty or penalties to which the alleged violator will be subjected if he is proved guilty of violating one or more provisions of the code.

E **Enabling, conflict, and unconstitutionality clauses** providing for the date a new or amended code will take effect, prevalence of more stringent provision when there is a conflict of two codes, severability of any part of the ordinance that might be found unconstitutional and retention of all other parts in full course and effect. In any city following the format of the "APHA - CDC Recommended Housing Maintenance and Occupancy Ordinance," the Health Officer or other supervisor in charge of housing inspections will also adopt appropriate housing rules and regulations from time to time to clarify or further refine the provisions of the ordinance. This has been done, for example, by the Commissioners of Health in Baltimore, Maryland and Milwaukee, Wisconsin, and by the District of Columbia's Department of Licenses and Inspections. In contrast, some municipalities such as Fort Worth, Texas; St. Louis, Missouri; and Chicago, Illinois, have tended to make their housing codes broader in the first place and subsequently have relied more on amendments to their ordinances rather than on numerous rules and regulations. Either method has its advantages, or so local practice will often help determine which is used.

Where the rules and regulations method is used care should be taken that the department is not overburdened with a number of minor rules and regulations. Similarly, a basic housing ordinance that encompasses all rules and regulations might have difficulty because any amendments to it require action by the political element of the community. Some housing groups, in attempting to obtain amendments to the ordinance, have had the entire ordinance thrown out by the political bodies.

VI. Administrative Elements of a Housing Code

The administrative procedures and powers of the housing inspection agency its supervisors and staff which are outlined in a housing code are similar to its other provisions in that all are based upon the police power of the state to legislate for public health and safety. In addition, the administrative provisions, and to a lesser extent, the court and penalty provisions outline how the police power is to be exercised in administering and enforcing the code.

Generally, the administrative elements deal with the procedures to follow for ensuring that the constitutional doctrines of reasonableness, equal protection under the laws, and due process of law are observed. They must also guard against violation of its prohibitions against unlawful search and seizure, impairment of obligations of contract, and unlawful delegation of authority. These factors encompass items of great importance to housing inspection supervisors such as the inspector's right of entry, reasonable hours of inspection, proper service, and the validity of the provisions of the housing codes they administer. All are described and discussed generally, in light of United States Supreme Court and state Supreme Court tests and decisions, in the publication entitled, "The Constitutionality of Housing Codes." This publication is a clear and excellent source of information about the constitutional administration of housing codes.

A. Determination of Legal Owner of Record

In some communities the importance of ascertaining the legal owner of record is not fully understood by the housing inspection supervisors and inspectors. Consequently, they lose cases in court because they have not taken action against the proper party. This problem often arises in connection with "land contract of sale" properties, where the legal deed never passes to the purchaser until he has paid for the property completely. In these cases, the person who is selling the property is the rightful owner and the action should be taken against him.

The method of obtaining the name and address of the legal owner of a property in violation varies from place to place. Ordinarily a check of the city tax records will suffice unless there is reason to believe these are not up to date on the property in question. In the latter case, a further check of county or parish records will turn up the legal owner if state law requires him to register his deed there. If it does not, the advice of the municipal law department should be sought about the next steps to follow.

B. Due Process Requirements

Every notice, complaint, summons, or other type of legal paper concerning alleged housing code violations in a given dwelling or dwelling unit must be legally served on the proper party. This might be the owner, his agent, or the tenant, as required by the code, in order to be valid and to prevent harassment of innocent parties. It is quite customary to require that the notice(s) to correct existing violations and any subsequent notices or letters to the violator be served by certified or registered mail with return receipt requested. The receipt serves as proof of service if the case has to be taken to court.

Due process requirement also calls for clarity and specificity with respect to the alleged violations, both in the violation notices and the court complaint-summons. For this reason, special care must be taken to be complete and accurate in testing the violations and charges. To illustrate, rather than direct the violator "to repair all windows where needed" he should be told exactly which windows and what repairs are involved. Unless he is so advised, his attorney has a built-in defense against the city's case.

The chief limitation on the due process requirement, with respect to service of notices, lies in cases involving immediate threats to health and safety. In these instances, the inspection agency or its representative may, without notice or hearing, issue an order citing the existence of the emergency and requiring such action to be taken as is deemed necessary to meet the emergency.

C. Hearings and the Condemnation Power

The purpose of a hearing is to give the alleged violator an opportunity to be heard, if he wishes, before further action is taken by the housing inspection agency. These hearings may be very informal, involving meetings between a representative of the agency and the person ordered to take corrective action. They may also be formal hearings at which the agency head presides and the city and the defendant both are entitled to and usually are represented by counsel and expert witnesses. Each type will be discussed below.

1. **Informal Hearings** – A violation notice may raise questions in the mind of the violator or may be served on him at a time when personal hardships or other factors prevent him from meeting the terms of the notice. Therefore, many housing codes afford him an opportunity to have a hearing at which he may discuss his questions or problems and seek additional time or some modification of the order. Administered in a firm but understanding manner, these hearings serve as invaluable aids in relieving needless fears of those involved, in showing how the inspection program is designed to help them, and in winning their voluntary compliance.

2. **Formal Hearings**. – These are quasi-judicial hearings—even though the prevailing court rules of evidence do not control—from which an appeal may be taken to court. All witnesses must therefore be sworn, and a stenographic record of the proceedings must be made.

   The formal hearing is used chiefly as the basis for determining whether a dwelling is or is not fit for human habitation, occupancy, or use. In the event it is proved "unfit," the building is condemned as such and the owner is given a designated amount of time either to rehabilitate it completely or to demolish it. Where local funds are available or the new Federal demolition grant program is in effect, if the owner fails to obey the order within the time specified, the municipality may demolish his building and put a lien against the property to cover demolition costs.

   This type of "condemnation" hearing is a very effective means of stimulating prompt and appropriate corrective action when it is administered fairly and firmly. This is particularly true if the community funds are available for demolition action when the owner proves reluctant or unwilling to obey the order.

   In some places, such as Oakland, California, the housing inspection agency is permitted only to order unfit buildings repaired or vacated until they are repaired. In others, such as Jersey City, New Jersey, the local ordinance also empowers the housing inspection agency to order these buildings demolished by the city if the owners fail to repair or demolish.

D. **Special Features for Coping with Common Problems**

1. **Limitation of Occupancy Notification** – This technique was pioneered by Wilmington, Delaware. It makes it mandatory for property owners in the community to obtain legal notice from the housing inspection agency of the maximum number of persons that may occupy each of their dwelling or rooming units. It also requires these owners to have a residence, place of business, or an agent for their properties within the community. The agent should be empowered to take remedial action on any of the properties found in violation. In addition, if the property is sold, the new owner must obtain a new Limitation of Occupancy Notification. The fee charged is nominal.

2. **Request Inspections** – California and Pennsylvania are among the states that permit their municipalities to offer a request inspection service. In return for a fee, the housing inspector will inspect a property for violations of the housing code before its sale so that the buyer can learn its condition in advance. Some communities require owners to notify prospective purchasers of any outstanding notice of violations they have against their property before the sale. If they fail to do so and their properties are in violation, the code holds them liable to civil action by the purchaser and quasi-criminal action by the inspection agency as housing code violators.

3. **Tickets for Minor Offenses** – Denver, Colorado, have used this method of token fines to prod minor violators and first offenders into correcting without the city resorting to court action. There are mixed views about this technique because it is so akin to formal police action. The inspection agency's primary function is to achieve compliance rather than to punish a criminal for a crime that cannot be "corrected" once the damage has been done. Nevertheless, if the action stimulates compliance and reduces the amount of court action needed to achieve it, the ticket technique will undoubtedly spread.

E. **Other Administrative Aids: Forms and Form Letters**

There is tremendous diversity in these aids, yet many small communities have little information about them. The reason for this is that no one in the nation has developed a "housing inspection library" of standard forms and letters.

Before describing a fairly typical set of forms and form letters, it should be stressed that inspectional forms to be used for legal notices must (a) satisfy legal standards of the code, (b) be meaningful to the owner and sufficiently explicit about the extent and location of particular defects, (c) be adaptable to statistical compilation for the governing body reports, and (d) be written in a manner that will facilitate clerical and other administrative usage.

1. **The Daily Report Form** – This form gives the inspection agency an accurate basis for reporting, evaluating, and, if necessary, improving the productivity and performance of its inspectors.

2. **Complaint Form** – This form helps in obtaining full information from the complainant and thus makes the relative seriousness of the problem clear and reduces the number of crank complaints.

3. **No Entry Notice** – This advises occupant or owner that inspector was there and notifies him he must call and make an appointment or face legal action.

4. **Inspection Report Form** – This is the most important form in the agency. It comes in countless varieties ranging from manual, to key punch, to "automated" and from almost complete write-in to almost complete check-off types. If it is designed properly, it will (a) ensure more productivity and more thoroughness by the inspectors, (b) reduce the time spent in writing reports, (c) locate all violations correctly, and (d) reduce time required for typing violation notices. Forms may vary widely in sophistication from a very simple form to those whose components are identified by number for use in processing the case by automation. Some forms are a combined inspection report and notice form in triplicate so that the first page can be used as the notice of violation, the second as the office record, and the third as the guide for reinspection. A covering form letter notifies the violator of the time allowed to correct the conditions listed in the report-notice.

5. **Violation Notice** – This is the legal notice to the owner or tenant that the specified housing code violations in his property or dwelling unit exist and must be corrected within the indicated amount of time. It may be in the form of a letter that includes the list of alleged violations or has a copy of these attached. It may be a standard notice form, or it may be a combined report-notice. Regardless of the type used, each should make the location and nature of all violations clear and specify the exact section of the code that covers each one. The notice must advise the violator of his right to a hearing. It should also indicate that he has a right to be represented by counsel and that failure to obtain counsel will not be accepted as grounds for postponing a hearing or court case.

6. **Hearing Forms** – These should include a form letter notifying violator of date and time set for his hearing, a standard summary sheet on which the supervisor can record the facts presented at an informal hearing, and a hearing decision letter for notifying all concerned of the hearing results. The latter should include the names of the violator, inspector, law department, and any other city official or agency that may be involved in the case.

7. **Reinspection Form Letters or Notices** – These have the same characteristics as the Violation Notice previously referred to except that they cover the follow-up orders given to the violator who has failed to comply with the original notice within the time specified. Some agencies may use two or three types of these form letters to accommodate different degrees of response by the violator. Whether one or several are used, standardization of these will expedite the processing of cases.

8. **Court Complaint and Summons Forms** – These forms advise the alleged violator of the charges against him and summon him to appear in court at the specified time and place. It is essential that the housing inspection agency work closely with the municipal law department in the preparation of these forms so that each is done in exact accord with the rules of court procedure in the state and community.

9. **Court Action Record Form** – This is not a very prevalent form, but it should be, for it provides an accurate running record of the inspection agency's court actions and their results.

If a housing inspection agency does not include all of these forms and form letters in its basic kit, it should move to introduce the needed additions. Although it will take some time to arrive at the best forms to meet local needs, once they are put into use they will result in marked savings of time.

VII. Substantive Provisions of a Housing Code

A discussion of the substantive provisions of a housing code will be divided into three main categories. Discussions follow on each of these categories

A Minimum Facilities and Equipment for Dwelling Units

What are the minimum facilities and equipment that should be required for a dwelling unit? Keep in mind during this discussion that a dwelling unit must have provisions for preparing at least one regularly cooked meal per day within the unit. Minimum equipment should include a kitchen sink in good working condition and properly connected to the water supply system approved by the appropriate authority. It should provide, at all times, an adequate amount of heated and unheated running water under pressure and should be connected to a sewer system approved by the appropriate authority. Cabinets or shelves, or both, for the storage of eating, drinking, and cooking utensils and food should be provided. These surfaces should be of sound construction and made of material that is easily cleanable and that will not impart a toxic or deleterious effect to the food. In addition, a stove and refrigerator should be provided. Within every dwelling there should be a nonhabitable room that affords privacy and is equipped with a flush water closet in good working condition. Within the vicinity of the flush water closet a lavatory sink should be provided. In no case should a kitchen sink be permitted to substitute as a lavatory sink. In addition, within each dwelling unit there should be provided, within a room that affords privacy, either a bathtub or shower or both, in good working condition. As mentioned in the discussion of the kitchen sink, both the lavatory basin and the bathtub or shower or both should be equipped with an adequate amount of heated and unheated water under pressure. Each should be connected to an approved sewer system. Obviously, within each dwelling unit two or more means of egress should be provided to safe and open space at ground level. Provisions should be incorporated within the housing code to meet the safety requirements of the state and community involved. The housing code should spell out minimum standards for lighting and ventilation within each room in the structure. In addition, minimum thermal standards should be provided. Although most codes merely provide the requirement of a given temperature at a given height above floor level, the community should give consideration to the use of "effective temperatures." The effective temperature is a means of incorporating not only absolute temperature in degrees but also humidity and air movement. This mechanism gives a better indication of the comfort index of the room.

B **Adequate Maintenance of Dwellings and Dwelling Units and of Their Facilities and Equipment**

The code should spell out provisions that no person shall occupy or let for occupancy any dwelling or dwelling units that do not comply with stated requirements. Generally, these requirements specify that the structure be in sound condition and good repair regarding foundation, roof, exterior walls, doors, and window space and window condition; that it be damp-free, watertight and reasonably weathertight; that all structural surfaces be sound and in good repair. These provisions basically state that any necessary repairs should be made before the unit is relet to new occupants.

C **The Occupancy Conditions of Dwellings and Dwelling Units**

Occupancy provisions set maximum density standards within dwelling units. Generally, they require a given quantity of square footage of space for sleeping area. Requirements in this section restrict the number of basic families permitted within anyone dwelling unit. They state, in addition, the minimum ceiling heights, and closet space.

The housing code is the basic tool of the housing inspector. This code spells out what he may and may not do. It sets the requirements he will enforce and provides him with his basis for action. A housing effort can be no better than the code allows.

ZONING ORDINANCES IN RELATION TO THE HOUSING INSPECTION

	Page
I. Background of Zoning	1
II. Definitions	2
III. Zoning Objectives	3
IV. What Zoning Cannot Do	4
V. Content of the Ordinance	4
VI. Bulk and Height requirements	5
VII. Yard Requirements	5
VIII. Off street Parking	6
IX. Nonconforming Uses	6
X. Variances	6
XI. Exceptions	7
XII. Administration	7
XIII. How Zoning Can Benefit the Housing Inspector	7
XIV. Example of Zoning and Housing Relationships	8

ZONING ORDINANCES IN RELATION TO THE HOUSING INSPECTION

Zoning is essentially a means of ensuring that a community's hind uses are compatibly located for the health, safety, and general welfare of the community. Experience has shown that some types of controls are needed in order to provide orderly growth in relation to the community plan for development. Just as a capital improvement program governs public improvements such as streets, parks, and other recreational facilities, schools, and public buildings, so zoning governs the planning program with respect to the use of public and private property.

When a person buys or builds a house or other structure in a municipality that has a zoning ordinance in effect, he is presumed to know and obliged by law to comply with the zoning regulations governing the use of buildings and land in the section of the community in which his property is located. If he either erects a structure or converts a house or building that is within that particular district by the local zoning ordinance into another type of use he still has acquired no property right to continue the forbidden use. An example would be the conversion of a single family residence into multifamily units. Even if the owner has obtained a building permit for this work already completed, the building permit would be voided, because the work was started in violation of the zoning code and because a building permit can be valid' only when issued for a lawful purpose. The building inspector is therefore obliged to refuse issuance of a building permit if the proposed work is in violation of the zoning ordinance.

It is very important that the housing inspector know the general nature of zoning regulations, since properties in violation of both the housing code and the zoning ordinance must be brought into full compliance with the zoning ordinance before the housing code can be enforced. In many cases the housing inspector may be able to eliminate some of the properties in violation of the housing code through enforcement of the zoning ordinance.

I. Background of Zoning

Zoning regulations have been used for several centuries. In the early settlement of our country, gunpowder mills and storehouses were prohibited from being located within the heavily populated portions of town, owing to the frequent fires and explosions. Later, zoning took the form of fire districts, and under implied legislative powers, wooden buildings were prohibited from certain sections of the municipality.

Massachusetts passed one of the first zoning laws in 1692. This law authorized Boston, Salem, Charlestown, and certain other market towns in the province to assign certain locations in each town for the establishment of slaughterhouses and still houses for currying of leather.

Act and Resolves of the Province of Massachusetts Bay 1692-93 C. 23

"Be it ordained and enacted by the Governor, Council and Representatives convened in General Court or Assembly, and by the authority of the same,

Sect. 1 That the selectmen of the towns of Boston, Salem, and Charlestown respectively, or other market towns in the province, with two or more justices of the peace dwelling in the town, or two of the next justices of the country, shall at or before the last day of March, one thousand six hundred ninety-three, assign some certain places of the said towns (where it may be least offensive) for the erecting or setting up of slaughterhouses for the killing of all meat, still houses, and houses for trying of tallow and currying of leather (which houses may be erected of timber, the law referring to building with brick or stone not withstanding) and shall cause an entry to be made in the town book of what places shall be by them so assigned, and make known the same by posting it up in some public places of the town; by which houses and places respectively, and no other, all butchers, slaughter men, distillers, chandlers, and curriers shall exercise and practice their respective trades and mysteries; on pain that any butcher or slaughter man transgressing of this act by killing of meat in any other place, for every conviction thereof before one or more justices of the peace, shall forfeit and pay the sum of twenty shillings (shilling worth about 12-16¢); and any distiller, chandler or currier offending against this act, for every conviction thereof before their majesties justices at the general sessions of the peace for the county, shall forfeit and pay the sum of five pounds (a pound equals 20 shillings and was worth somewhere between $2.40 and $3.20); one-third part of said forfeitures to be the use of the majesties for the support of the government of the province and incident charges thereof, one-third to the poor of the town when such offense shall be committed, and the other third to him or them that shall inform and sue for the same ....

II. Definitions

A. Accessory Structure - A detached building or structure in a secondary or subordinate capacity from the main or principal building or structure on the same premises. Example: garage behind a single-family dwelling.

B. Accessory Use - A use incidental and subordinate to the principal use of a structure. Example: a home-located physician's office.

C. Alteration - A change or rearrangement of the structural parts of a building, or an expansion or enlargement of the building.

D. Building Area - That portion of the lot remaining available for construction after all required open space and yard requirements are met.

E. Dwelling - Any enclosed space that is wholly or partially used or intended to be used for living or sleeping by human occupants provided that temporary housing shall not be regarded as a dwelling. Temporary housing is defined as any tent, trailer, mobile home, or any other shelter designed to be transportable and not attached to the ground, to another structure, or to any utility system on the same premises for more than 30 consecutive days.

F. Dwelling, Two Family - A structure containing two dwelling units and designed for occupancy by no more than two families.

G. Dwelling, Multifamily - A residential structure equipped with more than two dwelling units.

H. Dwelling Unit - Any room or group of rooms located within a dwelling and forming a single habitable unit with facilities that are used or intended to be used by a single family for living, sleeping, cooking, and eating.

I. Exception - Sometimes called "special use." An exception is a land use that can be made compatible with a district upon the imposition by the board of adjustment of special provisions covering its development, even though it would not otherwise be permitted in the district. Example: Fire substation being permitted to locate in a residential area.

J. Family - One or more individuals living together and sharing common living, sleeping, cooking, and eating facilities.

K. Home Occupation - An occupation conducted in a dwelling unit subject to the restrictions of the zoning ordinance. Limitations of interest to housing inspectors are the following: (a) Only the occupant or members of his family residing on the premises shall be engaged in the occupation, (b) the home occupation use shall be subordinate to its use for residential purposes and shall not occupy more than 25 per cent of the floor area of the dwelling unit, (c) the home occupation shall not be conducted in an accessory structure, (d) no offensive noise, glare, vibration, heat, smoke, dust, or odor shall be produced.

L. Lot- Parcel of land considered as a unit devoted to either a particular use or to occupancy by a building and its accessory structures.

M. Lot Depth - The average horizontal distance between the front and rear lot line measured at right angles to the structure.

N. Lot Width - The average horizontal distance between the sides of a lot measured at right angles to the lot depth.

O. Nonconforming Use - (a) Use of a building or use of land that does not conform to the regulations of the district in which located. (b) Nonconforming use also means a building or land use that does not conform to the regulations of the district in which the building or land is but that is nevertheless legal since it existed before enactment of the ordinance.

P. Open Space - Unoccupied space that is open to the sky and on the same lot with the building.

Q. Variance - Easing or lessening of the terms of the zoning ordinance by a public body so that relief for hardships will be provided but with the public interest still protected.

Inspectors should refer to the definitions in the zoning ordinance of their municipality for additions and changes.

III. Zoning Objectives

As stated earlier, the purpose of a zoning ordinance is to ensure that the land uses within the community are regulated not only for the health, safety, and welfare of the community but also in keeping with the comprehensive plan for community development. The objectives contained in the zoning ordinance that help to achieve a development providing for the health, safety, and welfare are the following:

A. Regulate Height, Bulk, and Area of Structure. In order to provide established standards of healthful housing within the community, regulations dealing with building heights, lot coverage, and floor areas must be established. These regulations then ensure that adequate natural lighting, ventilation, privacy, and recreational area for children will be realized. These are all fundamental physiological needs that have been determined to be necessary for a healthful environment.

Safety from fires is enhanced because of building separations needed to meet yard and open-space requirements.

Through prescribing minimum lot area per dwelling unit, population density controls are established.

B. Avoid Undue Levels of Noise, Vibration, Glare, Air Pollution, and Odor. By providing land use category districts, these environmental stresses upon the individual can be reduced. As in the first item, the absence of these stresses has been determined to be a fundamental physiological individual need.

C. Lessen Street Congestion Through Off-Street Parking and Off-Street Loading Requirement.

D. Facilitate Adequate Provisions of Water, Sewerage, Schools, Parks, and Playgrounds.

E. Secure Safety From Flooding.

F. Conserve Property Values. Through careful enforcement of the provisions property values will be stabilized and conserved.

IV. What Zoning Cannot Do

In order to understand more fully the difference between zoning and the other devices such as subdivision regulations, building codes, and housing ordinances, the housing inspector must know the things that cannot be accomplished by a zoning ordinance.

Items that cannot be accomplished in a zoning ordinance include:

A. Correcting Existence of Overcrowding or Substandard Housing. Zoning is not retroactive and cannot correct conditions such as those cited. These are corrected through enforcement of a minimum standards housing code.

B. Materials and Methods of Construction. Materials and methods of construction are enforced through the building codes rather than through zoning.

C. Cost of Construction. Quality of construction and hence construction costs are often regulated through deed restrictions or covenants. Zoning does, however, stabilize property values in an area by prohibiting incompatible development such as the location of a heavy industry in the midst of a well-established subdivision.

D. Subdivision Design and Layout. Design and layout of subdivisions as well as provisions for parks and streets are controlled through subdivision regulations.

V. Content of the Ordinance

Zoning ordinances establish districts of whatever size, shape, and number the municipality deems best for carrying out the purposes of the zoning ordinance. Most cities use three major districts: residential, commercial, and industrial. These three may then be subdivided into many sub districts, depending on local conditions. These districts specify the principal and accessory uses, exceptions, and prohibitions.

In general these permitted land uses are based on intensity of land use, a less intense land use being permitted in a more intense district but not vice versa. For example, a single-family residence is a less intense land use than a multifamily dwelling. A multifamily dwelling would not, however, be permitted in a single-family district.

In recent years, some ordinances are being partially based on performance standards rather than solely on land use intensity. For example, some types of industrial developments may be permitted in a less intense use district provided that the proposed land use creates no noise, glare, smoke, dust, vibration, or other environmental stress exceeding acceptable standards and provided further that adequate off street parking, screening, landscaping, and other similar measures are taken.

VI. Bulk and Height Requirements

To further achieve the earlier stated objectives of the zoning ordinance, other regulations within a particular zoning district are imposed to gain control of population densities and to provide adequate light, air, privacy, and other elements needed for a safe and healthy environment.

Most early zoning ordinances stated that within a particular district the height and bulk of any structure could not exceed certain dimensions and specified that dimensions for front, side, and rear yards must be provided. Today some zoning ordinances use floor area ratios for regulation. Floor area ratio is the relationship between the floor space of the structure and the size of the lot on which it is located. For example, a floor area ratio of 1 would permit either a two-story building covering 50 per cent of the lot, or a one-story building covering 100 per cent of the lot. This is illustrated in Figure 1. Other zoning ordinances specify the maximum amount of the lot that can be covered or else merely require that a certain amount of open space must be provided for each structure and leave the flexibility of the location to the builder. Still other ordinances, rather than specify a particular height for the structure, specify an angle of light obstruction within a particular district that will assure air and light to the surrounding structures. An example of this is shown in Figure 2.

VII. Yard Requirements

Zoning ordinances also contain yard requirements that are divided into front, rear, and side yard requirements. These requirements, in addition to stating the lot dimensions, usually designate the amount of setback

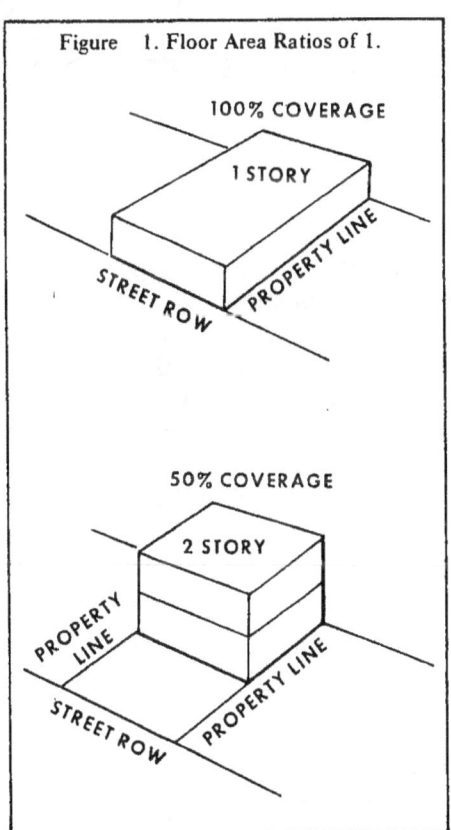

Figure 1. Floor Area Ratios of 1.

required. Most ordinances permit the erection of auxiliary buildings in rear yards provided they are located at stated distances from all lot lines and provided sufficient stated open space is maintained. If the property is a corner lot, additional requirements are set to allow visibility for motorists.

VIII. Off street Parking

Space for off street parking and off street loading is also contained in the ordinance. These requirements are based on standards relating floor space or seating capacity to land use. For example, a furniture store would require fewer off street parking spaces in relation to the floor area than a movie theater would.

IX. Nonconforming Uses

Since zoning is not retroactive, all zoning ordinances must contain a provision for nonconforming uses. If a use has already been established within a particular district before adoption of the ordinance, it must be permitted to continue. Provisions are, however, put into

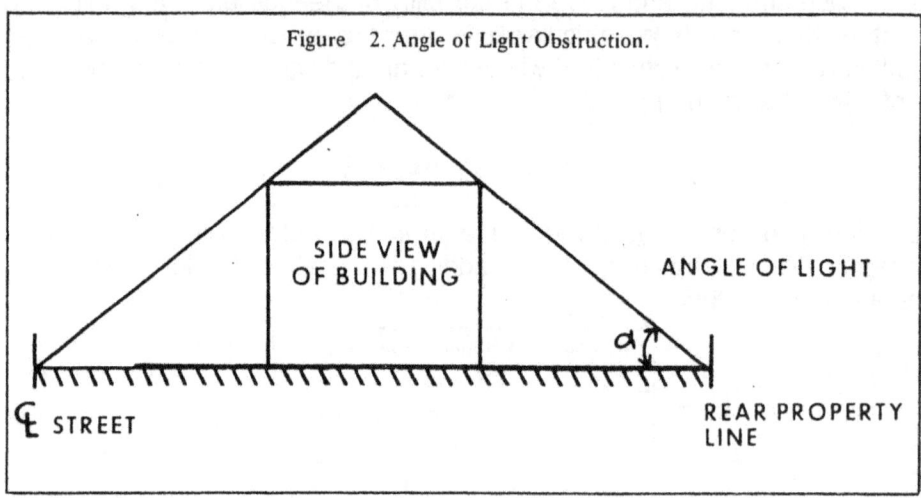

Figure 2. Angle of Light Obstruction.

The ordinance to aid in eliminating nonconforming use. These provisions generally prohibit the following: (1) An enlargement or expansion of the nonconforming uses, (2) reconstruction of the nonconforming use if more than a certain portion is destroyed, (3) resumption of the use after it has been abandoned for a period of specified time, and (4) changing the use to a higher classification or to another nonconforming use. Some zoning ordinances further provide a period of amortization during which the nonconforming land use must be phased out.

X. Variances

Zoning ordinances contain provisions for permitting variances and providing a method of granting these variances subject to certain specified conditions. A variance may be granted when, owing to a particular lot shape, topography, or other lot characteristics, an undue hardship would be imposed on the owner if the exact content of the ordinance is adhered to. For example, assume we have a piece of irregularly shaped property located in a district having the side yard requirements of 20 feet on a side and total lot size requirement of 10,000 square feet. Suppose that our property contains 10,200 feet and thus meets the area requirements; however, let us further assume that, owing to the irregular shape of the property, we can provide side yards of only 15 feet on a side. Since a hardship would be imposed if the exact letter of the law is held to, the zoning board of adjustment could be asked for a variance. Since there is sufficient total open area and since a lessening of the ordinance is not detrimental to the surrounding property, a variance would probably be granted.

Before a variance can be granted, it must be shown that (1) there is a practical hardship, (2) that the variance is needed for the owner to realize a reasonable return on the property, (3) that the original intent of the ordinance will be adhered to, (4) that the character of the neighborhood will not be changed, and (5) that the public's safety and welfare will be preserved.

XI. Exceptions

An exception is often confused with a variance. In every city there are some necessary uses that do not correspond to the permitted land uses within the district. The zoning code recognizes, however, that if proper safeguards were to be provided, these uses would not have a detrimental effect on the district. An example would be a fire substation, which could be permitted in a residential area provided the station house is designed to resemble a residential dwelling and further provided the property is properly landscaped.

XII. Administration

The key man in the zoning process is the zoning inspector, since he must come in contact with each case. In many cases the zoning inspector may also be the building inspector or the housing inspector. Since the building inspector or housing inspector is already in the field making inspections, it is relatively easy for him to check compliance with a zoning ordinance. This compliance can be checked by comparing the actual land use against that allowed for the area and shown on the zoning map.

Each zoning ordinance has a map as a part of the ordinance giving the permitted usage for each block. By taking a copy of this map with him, the inspector can make a preliminary check of the land use in the field. If the use does not conform, the inspector must then check with the Zoning Board to see if the property in question was a "nonconforming use" at the time of passage of the ordinance and if an exception has been granted. In cities where up-to-date records of existing nonconforming uses and exceptions granted are maintained, the inspector can check the use in the field against the records.

When violation is observed and the property owner is duly notified of the violation, he then has the right of hearing before a Zoning Board of Adjustment (sometimes also called the Zoning Board of Appeals). The Board may uphold the zoning enforcement officer or may rule in favor of the property owner. If the action of the zoning enforcement officer is upheld, the property owner may, if he so desires, seek relief through the courts; otherwise the violation will be corrected to conform to the zoning code.

XIII. How Zoning Can Benefit the Housing Inspector

It is of critical importance for the housing inspector, the building inspector, and the zoning inspector to work closely together in cities where these positions and responsibilities are separate. Experience has shown that when illegal conversions or uses of properties occur, these illegally converted properties are often among the most substandard encountered in the city and often contain especially dangerous housing code violations.

In communities where the zoning code is enforced effectively, the resulting zoning compliance in new and existing housing helps advance, as well as sustain, many of the minimum standards of the housing code such as occupancy, ventilation, light, and unimpeded egress. By the same token, building or housing inspectors can often aid the zoning inspector by helping eliminate some nonconforming uses through code enforcement.

XIV. Example of Zoning and Housing Relationships

The following cases will illustrate these relationships:

A Case 1

Two and one-half-story, 13-room house. Originally it had these features:

a Five-room dwelling unit on first floor including a three-piece bathroom.

b Eight-room dwelling unit occupying the second and third floors including one bathroom of three pieces on the second floor. The second and third floors are served by only one staircase.

c Two oil burners, one heating first floor, the other the second and third floors.

It is located in a residential zoning district where two-family housing is the maximum use permitted.

Five years later, while making a regular inspection, the zoning officer found this house in the process of being converted into a three-family use in violation of the zoning ordinance. The owner has already done these things.

a Made second floor into a separate five-room dwelling unit.

b Started converting the three rooms on the third floor into another apartment by:

  1. Installing a three-piece bathroom, 35 square feet in area, against the windowless west wall of the center bedroom, the habitable area being thus reduced to 40 square feet, and setting up the remainder of the area as the living room by providing a coffee table, lamp, and two overstuffed chairs;

  2. Putting in a wall kitchenette consisting of a sink with cold water and a stove, plus a table, lamp, and cupboards in the rear bedroom that is 60 square feet in area;

  3. Equipping the front bedroom that is 90 square feet in size with two beds, chest of drawers, and other bedroom furnishings for two.

He admitted, however, that he had not checked on state tenement house law requirements since he did not realize multiple dwellings of three families or more are covered by this law.

Question: How many violations (either housing or zoning) can you find?

Answer: As a result of these actions by the owner, the house now has one more dwelling unit than is permitted by the zoning ordinance in this residential district and also contains these obvious housing code violations:

(a) Threatened over occupancy of the third-floor dwelling unit (only 190 square feet available, but 250 square feet habitable floor space is the minimum required for two occupants).

(b) Size of the front bedroom inadequate by 30 square feet if it is used by two occupants. The back bedroom lacks the requirements needed for occupancy by one person (70 square feet). If a third person lived in the dwelling unit the minimum required habitable floor area would then become 350 square feet.

(c) The bathroom does not meet the light and ventilation requirements.

(d) The kitchen sink does not have hot water.

(e) No refrigerator is provided.

(f) From the description it sounds as if one might have to go through a sleeping room to reach the bathroom. This would be a violation.

(g) Both the second and third floor units are in violation since they lack two means of egress.

B Case 2

Assume that a three-family dwelling unit is the largest size permitted in the zoning district where the building in question is located. The housing inspector's investigation of the three-story dwelling from cellar to roof showed that it contained:

1. Four dwelling units, two with six rooms each and two with three rooms each.

2. Five families, three in separate dwelling units and the two on the third floor in one unit.

3. A bathroom and a kitchen on the second floor shared by two families.

4. The bathroom and kitchen on the third floor also being shared by two families.

5. Inadequate means of egress from the dwelling unit in the third floor.

Question: If you were the housing inspector, what actions would you take?

Answer: In this situation there are definite housing code violations. The housing inspector also knows there is a zoning violation. Because he knows that the property must meet zoning requirements before complying with the housing code, the inspector would refer this case to the zoning department for action.

The housing inspector should never speak for the zoning department and tell the owner that he is in violation of a zoning ordinance unless he and the zoning inspector are the same individual. The housing inspector should complete his housing inspection and leave. Responsibility for informing the owner of any zoning violation lies with the zoning department.

In this particular case, some housing code violations will be corrected through enforcement of zoning. However, there are still violations of requirements for egress, a third kitchen, and a third bathroom.

After compliance with the zoning ordinance has been obtained, the zoning department should notify the housing inspector so that he can then enforce any housing violations that may still exist.

C Case 3

Mr. Jones, a zoning inspector, gets a report that at 1212 Oak Street the owner, Mr. Smith, is converting his single-family house into two apartments and has already started alterations. Investigations of the zoning map shows that in this district, apartments, up to four, are permitted if 1,500 square feet of open land area is provided for each apartment. Mr. Jones checks and finds that no building permit has been issued. A site investigation reveals that Mr. Smith has only 2,000 square feet of open area available. He then informs Mr. Smith that he is in violation of the zoning ordinance.

Mr. Smith then appeals to the Zoning Board of Adjustment for a variance to allow him to have two apartments even though he does not have the required 3,000 square feet 0 f open area. His appeal is denied by the board since no real hardship exists. As a result, Mr. Smith must rent the property as a single-family dwelling and is unable to recover the money he has already spent in starting alterations.

Discuss:

1. The actions of Mr. Jones.

Answer: Mr. Jones was justified in citing Mr. Smith for a zoning violation since the proposed open area would have been inadequate.

2 The action of the Board of Adjustment.

Answer: The Board of Adjustment was also justified in upholding the zoning regulations. If the board had not acted in this manner, the crowding on this property could well have started deterioration in surrounding properties.

3 The action of Mr. Smith.

Answer: Mr. Smith had no legitimate complaint when the Board ruled against him. If he had first sought to obtain a building permit, as required by law, he would have been told that his proposed alterations would not meet zoning regulations and hence would not have suffered a monetary loss.

D Case 4

Mr. Edwards requests a building permit to change a three-story single-family house into a two-family unit. Since two-family units are permitted in this district and he has sufficient open area, the permit is granted.

Six months later, the housing inspector, while making a systematic code enforcement inspection, finds that the converted house now has an apartment on each of the three floors. The bath on the second floor is shared by families on the second and third floors. This is a violation of the housing code.

Knowing that all the other houses on this street are only one- or two-family units, he also suspects a zoning violation. After returning to the office, he contacts the zoning department and learns that Mr. Edwards is in violation of the zoning ordinance as well as of the housing code.

Question: Which ordinance must be enforced first and why?

Answer: The zoning ordinance must be enforced first, since a zoning ordinance is a "primary" ordinance and determines the land use of a particular property. A housing code ordinance is a "secondary" ordinance and sets standards of residential usage on the property.

E   Case 5

During a routine inspection, the housing inspector finds a house with three families, one of which is living in a cellar apartment.

Question: What actions should he take?

Answer: The inspector should immediately cite the owner for a violation of the ordinance and then follow through to see that the situation is corrected. If the family living in the cellar requires housing assistance as a result of corrective measures taken, the housing inspector should inform them of public agencies available for assistance.

F   Case 6

During a routine inspection of a district zoned for up to three-family use, the housing inspector encounters a house that the owner says contains two dwelling units in addition to his own, and also one rooming unit. The inspector finds a cook stove in the "rooming unit."

Question: What actions should he take?

Answer: Although a rooming unit would be permitted in this district, the addition of a cook stove changes the rooming unit into a dwelling unit.

The inspector should refer this case to the zoning department for immediate action and then follow up for housing violations at a later date.

G   Case 7

The housing inspector is investigating a complaint of alleged housing violations. The owner refuses to admit the inspector inside the building and becomes belligerent.

Question: What should the inspector do next?

Answer: The inspector should remain courteous and not lose his temper. If the inspector is not able to obtain permission to inspect without further arousing the owner, he should leave.

Since recent decisions of the U.S. Supreme Court have dictated the inclusion of requirements to obtain a search warrant in cases where entry to the inspector is denied, the inspector should obtain a warrant. He will then return at a later time with someone to serve the warrant.

H Case 8

During an inspection in July, the housing inspector finds a house that has been converted into two apartments. While checking the basement, he sees that the furnace appears in an unsafe condition. Further checking reveals that there is no provision for heat in the second apartment.

Question: What action should the inspector take since it is July and heat is not now needed. Besides, how does he know that the owner will not install heat before winter?

Answer: The inspector should cite the owner for a violation of the housing code anyway. In his notice of violations, because it is July, he can give the owner sufficient time to comply. He would also send a copy of the letter to the heating inspector for follow up.

I Case 9

During an inspection, the housing inspector is greeted at the door by a 10-year-old boy who is alone. The boy says it is all right to make the inspection.

Question: Should he? Why?

Answer: No. Permission to enter must be obtained from a responsible adult. Suppose that instead of the 10-year-old boy, he had found a 16-year-old girl.

Question: How would these change things? Why?

Answer: It would not change things, since the 16-year-old girl is not considered a responsible adult. For the protection of the inspector, some housing departments would not permit him to enter alone when the house is occupied by only a female, especially one under age.

J Case 10

During his inspections the housing inspector finds a house that has no bathroom but does have an outside pit privy.

Question: What action should be taken?

Answer: The inspector should issue a violation for lack of indoor toilet facilities and follow through the regular steps established. by his housing department. A copy of the violation should also be sent to the health department for any actions that they may wish to take for elimination of the privy.

K Case 11

A number of violations are found in a residence, but the family is occupying the unit under a land purchase contract agreement with the landlord. The owner holds title until enough rent is paid to equal the sale price. The repairs needed are more than the family can afford and are such that the building should be declared unfit for occupancy. The family now has $2,000 worth of equity in the property.

Questions: What actions should the inspector take? Who is responsible for repairs? Who will lose money?

Answer: The inspector would cite the owner of record for a housing violation, since the owner of record is responsible for repairs. If the owner will not bring the building into compliance with the code, the building should be posted as unfit for habitation and the family removed.

The family buying will probably lose in this situation. Before contracting to buy, they should have obtained a certificate of inspection from the housing department showing any violations existing at the time of purchase.

L Case 12

The property at 112 East Street is owned by an out-of-state individual. The housing inspector found the property unfit for habitation and has had the family renting the property removed. The house is now vacant and the out-of-town owners will not make the repairs since the cost of the necessary

repairs would be too great in relation to the value of the property. The property is in an area that will probably be included in a future urban renewal project within the next few years.

Complaints have been made to the housing department by the neighbors that the house has its windows broken out and its doors broken open. Children play inside during the day and have almost set the building on fire several times. Moreover, vagrants occasionally sleep inside at night.

Question: What action would you take if you were the housing inspector?

Answer: After following standard department procedures, the housing inspector should recommend, that the house be demolished and this cost assessed as a lien against the property. If allowed to remain, the house will be a detriment to surrounding properties and also to the neighborhood.

M Case 13

During a routine inspection, you find a house with very poor premises sanitation and evidence of roaches, flies, and rats. The property meets minimum housing standards otherwise.

Question: What action can you take?

Answer: The action depends on local regulations and procedures. In many communities the housing program is organizationally located within the health department. In that case, the housing inspector would probably follow through in requiring elimination of the infestation. If the housing inspection program were located within a department other than the health department, the housing inspector may refer the case to the health department for action.

N Case 14

While making a systematic code inspection, the housing inspector encounters a lady who questions the inspector regarding his findings on the house next door, which she is sure is much worse than hers.

Question: How should the inspector deal with the lady?

Answer: The inspector must be very courteous and tactful in his conversation and inform her that he is not permitted to discuss his survey findings for other properties.

THE BUILDING AND ITS MAKEUP

TABLE OF CONTENTS

	Page
BUILDING CONSTRUCTION	1
Introduction	1
General Construction Principles	1
Types of Building Construction	2
Building Materials and Contents	3
Building Code Requirements	7
Involvement of Ceilings	8
Building Elements	8
Interior Finish	9
MATERIALS	11
Introduction	11
Properties of Materials	11
Classes of Materials	12
UTILITY SYSTEMS	17
Introduction	17
Heating, Ventilation and Air Conditioning	18
Electrical	21

THE BUILDING AND ITS MAKEUP

BUILDING CONSTRUCTION

Introduction

In many cases the design, construction, and use of the building contributes to the initiation and severity of serious building fires. For these reasons, a knowledge of buildings, how they are constructed, and with what kinds of materials, is important to the fire investigator.

A knowledge and use of the correct terminology of building construction also is important in the writing of accurate reports, as well as in courtroom appearances. As an example, the investigator should know and be able to describe the similarities and the differences between spandrels, beams, and girders.

Sometimes in getting at the fire cause, it is necessary to "reconstruct" the arrangement and condition of the room or area of fire involvement to understand the development and spread of the fire. To do this "reconstruct", it is necessary to know what kinds of building materials and construction were likely to have been present prior to the fire damage. (Where there are similar rooms or areas available in the same or similar buildings, such as in hotels or garden apartments, a method to "reconstruct" is to examine undamaged units.)

General Construction Principles

The fire investigator should be familiar with the basic principles of building construction.

The initial concern of fire resistance provisions in building codes is that the building should not collapse as a result of a fire. Secondarily, the structure should limit the fire to an area of acceptable size.

Some elements of the system are more vulnerable to fire than others. When a fire occurs, the building is only as stable as the weakest (to fire) element.

All loads must be transmitted continuously to ground. This is accomplished by a multitude of structural components and connections in the structure. The importance of the connections varies. In some cases, the failure of a connection may have only a local effect. In other cases, the failure may be catastrophic in that a building collapse may occur.

Principal structural materials are wood, masonry (stone, brick, and concrete block), steel and reinforced concrete.

The principal elements of structures are walls, columns, and beams. Walls and columns carry the loads of the building down to the earth. Beams carry the loads generated on each floor of the building to the columns or walls.

Walls may be load-bearing, that is, carrying a load other than themselves, or be nonload-bearing, typically partitions and exterior veneer walls.

Columns carry vertical loads to the ground or foundation. Because columns take up space, suspension rods or cables in tension are sometimes used to "hang" certain loads in a building.

The system must, however, provide for the tensile load to be carried over into a column or wall and delivered to the earth in compression.

Floors and roofs are supported on beams and girders as well as on walls. A girder is a beam which supports other beams. Since beams must resist both tension (usually in the bottom of the beam) and compression forces (usually in the top), solid beams contain excess material. In many cases, the load can be carried on a lighter unit called a truss, which eliminates excess material. A trussconsists of a series of specially connected and designed load-carrying elements and open spaces, which makes it more vulnerable to fire and thus more likely to collapse than an equivalent solid beam.

Types of Building Construction

There are five basic construction types. Various building codes subdivide these types further (see table 1) The five types are:

Table 1 Types of Construction According to Model codes*

Construction Type	Basic Building Code, by Type (BOCA)	Standard Building Code, by Type (SBC)	Uniform Building Code, by type (UBC)	National Building Code, by Type (NBC)
Fire Resistive	1A	I	I	A
	1B	II	I	B
Noncombustiable Protected	2A		II (4 hr)	
	2B	IV (1 hr)	II (1 hr)	Protected Noncombustiable
None combustible Unprotected	2C	IV	II (N)	Unprotected Noncombustiable
Heavy Timber	3A	III	IV (HT)	Heavy Timber
Ordinary Protected	3B	V (1 hr)	III (1hr)	
Ordinary Unprotected	3C	V	III (N)	Ordinary
Wood Frame Protected	4A	VI (1hr)	V (1hr)	
Wood Frame Unprotected	4B	VI	V (N)	Wood Frame

* This Table indicates the type assigned by the respective codes to various construction types. It is not intended to indicate that different codes necessarily have identical requirements for any specific type.

Fire Resistive
Noncombustible
Heavy Timber
Ordinary Wood
Frame
Wood Frame

The investigator's report should use the terminology of the appropriate local code.

Note that the commonly used word "fireproof" does not appear in the list of types, though it may appear in some codes. When designers first considered fire as a problem they believed that all fire problems would be eliminated by constructing the building of noncombustible material. Such buildings were called "fireproof" and the misnomer has persisted. Early "fireproof" buildings were found deficient when put to the test of actual fires since all noncombustible materials will lose strength at sufficiently high temperatures. As technology improved, the term "fire resistive" emerged.

Fire Resistive buildings are ones in which specimens of the major structural components have been rated by standard fire endurance tests during which collapse and passage of fire, where appropriate, were resisted for prescribed periods of time. No direct relationship should be assumed between the "time" of the controlled test and an uncontrolled hostile fire. Whereas each of the elements of the building may meet fire resistance criteria, it is most unlikely that the building as a whole was ever analyzed for the total impact of a potential fire, and "the whole may be less than the sum of the parts". Fire resistance does not guarantee life safety. Fire resistance is not necessarily related to fire loss; in fact, while achieving its designed fire resistance, the structure may be damaged severely. Fire resistive assemblies are not necessarily noncombustible. Floors and walls of wood and gypsum board are assigned fire resistance ratings by UL (Underwriters Laboratories Inc.), even though the assemblies are combustible.

Depending upon how the fire resistance is achieved, different buildings of the same fire resistance rating may exhibit different characteristics in similar fires. For instance, a fire resistive floor of reinforced concrete absorbs considerable heat. A steel joist floor and ceiling assembly, of equal fire resistance, will not absorb as much heat. This can affect the propagation of a fire, as every Btu absorbed by the structure is one less available to keep the fire growing. As a second example, a rated reinforced concrete floor may act as a very effective smoke barrier. An equally rated floor and ceiling assembly with an integral air handling system could provide a path for travel of smoke and gases. This property is not considered in the test rating.

Noncombustible buildings are ones in which the walls, partitions and structural members are of noncombustible construction not qualifying as fire resistive construction.

Heavy Timber construction buildings have masonry exterior walls and heavy timber interiors. The concept is that the heavy timber is slow to ignite and burns at a slow enough rate that collapse may be delayed. The concept fails once the fire involves the building and the fire suppression forces cannot sustain an interior attack. The massive amount of timber then simply becomes a tremendous fire load.

Ordinary Construction buildings have masonry exterior walls and lightly constructed combustible interiors. The principal benefit of the masonry walls is to reduce the conflagration potential. The interior is expected to collapse in a fire and may be required by code to be so designed, the so-called fire cuts on wood joists are an example.

Wood Frame buildings are basically of wood construction. A noncombustible veneer, such as brick, does not change the nature or classification of the building.

Building Materials and Contents

Code regulations which limit the type and size of construction are predicated on the type of building, the type of occupancy anticipated, and the anticipated level of potential fire risk.

Estimates of the potential fire risk are based to a large extent on the fire load (or fuel load). For buildings of combustible construction the basic fire load is the building itself, thus such buildings are usually limited by code in area and height. In addition, for all buildings the weight of combustible contents per unit of floor area must be considered. Fire loads are usually expressed in the term pounds (of ordinary combustibles) per square foot. All weights are commonly converted to the equivalent of ordinary combustibles such as wood which has a heat value of about 8,000 Btu/lb. For instance, plastics which have a heat value of about 16,000 Btu/lb are converted at the rate of 1 lb of plastic to 2 lb ordinary combustibles.

Typical ranges of fire loads for the more common occupancy classes are shown in table 2. However, fire loads can vary considerably according to the occupancy the specific location in the building, and, other factors.

Table 2 Typical Fire Loads

Occupancy Classification	Typical Range of Fire Loads lb/sq ft
Residential	5 to 10
Educational	5 to 10
(Library)	(10 to 40)
Institutional	3 to 10
Assembly	5 to 10
Business (office)	5 to 10
(File, Storage)	(10 to 40)
Mercantile	10 to 20
Industrial	10 to 35
Storage	10 to 100
Hazardous	*

* No typical values available. Risk based on factors other than fire load

Structural fire protection requirements in building codes are based on fire resistance or fire endurance ratings expressed in hours. The ratings are basedon fire tests performed on the structural or compartmenting (separating) building components according to the NFPA 251 (ASTM E 119) standardized test procedure, The exposure is such that a temperature of 1000°F (538°C) is reached in 5 min, 1700°F (927°C) in 1 hr, 1850°F (1010°C) in 2 hrs, 2000°F (1093°C) in 4 hrs and 2300°F (1260°C) in 8 hrs. These temperatures-vs.-time points produce a curve which is referred to as the fire endurance standard time-temperature curve. The test is conducted in a special test furnace and continued until one of several criteria of failure, as appropriate, is reached: (a) structural failure (inability to sustain the applied load), (b) integrity failure (development of a crack or opening through which flames or hot gases may pass during the fire test, or a hose stream test) or, (c) insulation failure (heat transmission sufficient to raise the temperature on the unexposed surface by 250°F (139°C) average).

Although the standard fire test curve represents only one type of fire exposure, it serves as a useful means for the comparative rating of individual columns, beams, walls, partitions, and floor and ceiling assemblies. Again, it should be stressed that although the ratings are expressed in hours, the relationship between the rating hours and hours of an actual fire assault on a building may differ.

A relationship between fire load and equivalent fire endurance period was developed many years ago based on experimental burnouts of combustibles in special masonry test buildings and is shown in table 3. Table.3 indicates that the burning of a fire load of 10 lbs of ordinary combustibles per square foot (or 80,000 Btu/sq ft) is the approximate equivalent of 1 hour of the standard fire test ASTM E 119.

If these figures are used cautiously and broadly, rather than precisely, it is possible to estimate whether, in a given fire, the fire load was grossly excessive for the fire resistance of the building. Consider a building with floors rated two-hour fire-resistive. Such a building might reasonably be expected to successfully resist a fire involving a design fire load of 160,000 Btu/sq ft average. On the other hand, an investigator may estimate that in the affected area of an actual fire, the fire load was 300,000 Btu/sq ft average. It can be reasonably concluded that the fire area was overloaded from the fire endurance point of view, even though the total structural loading may have been within permissible limits.

Table 3. Fire Load versus Equivalent Fire Endurance Period in Standard Fire Test

Fire Load 1b sq ft	Equivalent Fire Endurance Period hr
5	½
7 ½	¾
10	1
15	1 ½
20	2
30	3
40	4 ½
50	6
60	7 ½

Structural members and floors are made fire resistive in a variety of ways.
Reinforced concrete has inherent fire resistance. This inherent fire resistance can be increased to the desired level by increasing the concrete cover over the "reinforcing" steel. If the depth of the concrete cover is not as specified, early failure may result.

Steel must be protected from the harmful effects of elevated temperatures (loss of strength, elongation and heat transmission). Protection can be accomplished in several ways, including encasement, sprayed fireproofing, membrane protection or by using water- filled columns. In a particular building more than one way may be used.

Encasement. Each structural steel member is encased in an insulating cover; hollow tile, poured concrete, concrete block, wire lath and plaster or gypsum board are typically used.

Sprayed "Fireproofing". In this case structural steel members are spraye or trowele with plaster containing inorganic fibers or cement. One common material formerly used, asbestos, is held responsible for health hazards due to inhalation in many buildings. In some cases this has caused its removal, sometimes without any provision for replacing the necessary fire resistance. Sprayed "fireproofing" may be poorly done and in many cases is found to have fallen off or been removed by other building trades

Membrane Protection. Large areas, such as entire floors, are protected by a membrane,"consisting typically of a wire lath and plaster ceiling or a suspended ceiling of individual panels. The problem is that, like all membranes, a single penetration may reduce the effectiveness of the entire membrane. Wire lath and plaster membranes are designed to be permanent and generally left in place but individual acoustical tile (panel) ceilings are readily removable.

The entire floor and ceiling assembly is fire rated as a unit. The presumption is that the unit is installed the same way as the unit tested. Even if this is accomplished, the ceiling tiles may be removed for many reasons. The fact that the ceiling tiles are part of the fire resistance of the building is unknown to many building owners and operators and fire inspectors. Untested penetrations as for sound system speakers are another weakness. Any tampering with the ceiling opens the entire floor area up to attack by fire. The void space between the ceiling and the floor above represents a potential for lateral fire spread between every floor of the building. There can be a substantial fire load in the void due to plastic insulation and piping, and lightweight merchandise is sometimes found stored in the void.

In one case, fire in one occupancy entered the void and extended downward to combustible shelves and contents in the next occupancy, This was detected early enough to clearly show what had happened. Had the extension not been detected, all appearances would have been of two separate fires. In fact, the fire was incendiary and successfully prosecuted. Failure to describe the development of the fire accurately might have led to a loss of the case.

Current lists of fire rated constructions and assemblies are maintained by Underwriters Laboratories -- the American Insurance Association -- and the Factory Mutual System.

Almost any structure has some degree of fire resistance, even though it is itself combustible. Table 4 is provided to enable the investigator to develop estimated fire resistance values for some common wall and floor assemblies. It consists of two parts. In the first part values are given for some common materials used as membranes (the surface finish). The second part gives values for framing members

For example, using table 4, unprotected open web steel joists are assigned a value of 7 minutes. With 1/2" gypsum wallboard properly attached and sealed, the combination could be assigned a time of 22 minutes (7 minutes for the steel joists, 15 minutes for the gypsum wallboard).

A wood stud wall with 1/2" gypsum board on both sides could be assigned a value of 50 minutes (20 minutes for the studs plus 15 minutes for each layer of the wallboard). It should be stated here again that the times referred to are estimates of how long the structure in question would continue to meet the standards of ASTM E 119 (NFPA 251) when tested in accordance with that standard. There is no necessary relationship to elapsed time in a hostile fire.

Table 4 Time Assigned to wallboard membranes

	Description of Finish	Time Assigned to Membrane in Minutes
(i)	½ in Fiberboard	5
(ii)	³/₈ in Douglas Fir Plywood Phenolic bonded	5
(iii)	½ in Douglas Fir Plywood Phenolic bonded	10
(iv)	⁵/₈ in Douglas Fir Plywood Phenolic bonded	15
(v)	³/₈ in Gypsum Wallboard	10
(vi)	½ in Gypsum Wallboard	15
(vii)	⁵/₈ in Gypsum Wallboard	30
(viii)	Double ³/₈ in gypsum Wallboard	25
(ix)	½ + ³/₈ in Gypsum Wallboard	35
(x)	Double ½ in Gypsum Wallboard	50(1)
(xi)	³/₁₆ in Asb. Cem. + in Gypsum Wallboard	40(2)
(xii)	³/₁₆ in asb. Cem. + ½ in Gypsum Wallboard	50(2)
(xiii)	Composit 1/8 in Asb. Cem. ⁷/₁₆ in Fibreboard	20

1) No. 16 s.w.g. 1 in sq wire mesh must be fastened between the two sheets of wallboard.
2) Values shown apply to walls only.

Time Assigned for Contribution of Wood or Light Steel Frame

Description of Frame	Time Assigned to from in Minutes
i. Wood Stud walls	20
ii. Steel Stud Wall	10
iii. Wood Joist Floors and Roofs	10
iv. Open Web Steel Joist Floors and roofs	10(07)

Building Code Requirements

In many cases a building is not required by code to be fire resistive but the designer chooses to use components which resemble rated fire resistive units (or which may in fact be rated). For instance, structures recently observed in the Washington, DC area are rated as Type 3C (unprotected ordinary) under the BOCA (Building Officials and Code Administrator's International, Inc.) Basic Building Code. The floors are of bar joist construction with concrete topping on corrugated metal. The suspended ceilings need only meet Fire Hazard (flame spread) requirements. When the job is finished its appearance will be similar to a rated floor and ceiling assembly and protected with the same surface finish. Wood joists would have been acceptable under the code and the floor as installed may not be as resistive to collapse as a wood joisted floor.

In a fire investigation it may be necessary to determine whether or not a fire-resistive structure or structural element reacted to the fire in a manner consistent with its rating. This can be extraordinarily difficult. Assuming that the building was required to meet fire resistance standards, there can be several reasons for determination of the reason for failure to perform adequately. Information developed may be of use in prosecution, civil actions, code changes or fire suppression planning.

Did the building meet code requirements? This requires a thorough knowledge of code requirements at the time the building was built and access to original drawings, change orders and officially authorized variances.

Possibly, in fact, the building met modern code requirements but when given the ultimate test, the fire, the code requirements were proven inadequate. Such information, properly developed and carefully documented, is vital to translating costly experience into recommended code revisions.

Valuable information also can be developed to aid fire suppression forces in preplanning and combating future fires in the same or similar buildings. For example, the investigation may develop information that the sealant of the floor slab to the panel exterior walls was made of foamed plastic which lacks "dimensional stability" (that is, it melts). If this was permitted in one building, it may exist in other buildings built about the same time.

Involvement of Ceilings

Fires generally burn upward. Thus, the ceilings and upper parts of walls are generally exposed to higher temperatures than the lower parts of walls and floors. Fire exposed ceilings can fail early in fires, sometimes considerably earlier than a fire test rating would indicate. The fact that a particular ceiling fell may be an important element in an investigation. It cannot be assumed that the ceiling stayed in place for as long as one might conclude from its quoted fire rating.

Recently there have been a number of cases of fires burning downward (10). Many plastics when ignited form a pool of fire on the floor. The plastic may be from building contents or it may have been installed as part of the wall or ceiling.

Material falling from the ceiling may extend the fire beyond the area of origin. Consider a noncombustible building with steel bar joists with combustible tile ceiling mounted on the bottom side of the joists. There is a gap atop the masonry partition wall equal to the height of the top chord of the joist. Heated gases passing through this gap into the adjacent space may ignite the combustible tiles on their upper side. They may fall, extending the fire beyond the masonry wall.

Building Elements

Historically the chief consideration in building fire problems has been given to the Structural Elements of the building, but in building fires three elements can be identified:

- Structural Elements
- Nonstructural Elements
- Contents

The structural elements are those which are necessary to the stability of the building. The nonstructural elements may be more important in the development and extension of a fire than the structural elements. Nonstructural elements which contribute to the fire are independent of the type of construction and may be found in any of the five structural types discussed. For instance, a high flame spread interior finish of plywood and fiber tile may be found in any type building. The life hazard due to rapid flame spread over the surface will be the same. In the case of a combustible building the interior finish may be the kindling which ignites the structure. In the case of a noncombustible or fire-resistive structure, the structure will not be ignited, but substantial damage may be done to structural elements.

Nonstructural elements can include the electrical system, interior finish on ceilings, walls, and floors, air handling systems, openings from floor to floor such as shafts, stairways, interior courts, and combustible exterior surfaces and insulation.

In the majority of fires the initial fuel is the contents. Only rarely is the building directly ignited.

Interior Finish
Up to World War II there was only one significant interior finish, plaster installed over either wood lath or metal lath. It is noncombustible and, when properly installed, provides a degree of fire resistance for combustible structural elements. If the plaster is penetrated and if wood lath is present, the wood lath may provide substantial fuel.

The interior finish of the building may be the most important single element in the development and spread of a fire. In a number of cases interior finish has been a major factor in the rapid spread of fire and resultant loss of life.

Interior finish may be applied to the ceiling, walls or floors. Building codes have applied specific limitations on the flame spread classification of wall and ceiling materials. Floor coverings are less likely to be regulated but flame spread over carpeting, for example, has been an important factor in a number of serious fires. Standards and techniques for measuring carpeting flame spread have been developed recently and these regulations have begun to appear in the codes.

There are a number of ways in which the restriction of high flame spread interior finishes can be circumvented which do not appear in the code regulations. Materials which would not be permitted by the code if attached to the building may appear in significant amounts as furniture, in exhibits, as free standing office dividers, and in merchandise displays.

Alterations are sometimes accomplished without a building permit and buildings properly built have been altered with the use of high flame spread ceiling or wall materials.

Even the building permit does not guarantee safety. Consider a building with a combustible acoustical tile ceiling. It is planned to "modernize" the room by installing a ceiling grid with tiles and light fixtures mounted below the existing ceiling. A local code may require the new tiles to meet flame spread requirements but there is no requirement to remove the old combustible ceiling hidden in the void. Such a hidden ceiling can generate heat and gases which can move upward through available openings.

The investigator must try to get an accurate description of the wall and ceiling surfaces before the fire. Often only very slight clues are available, for example, nails holding scraps of furring strip to joists may indicate that there was a combustible acoustical ceiling. Adhesive beading on a wall may indicate where paneling had been secured with adhesive. Small pieces may be found behind unburned baseboard.

Table 5 contains a listing of selected materials commonly used for interior finish in buildings and a rough classification according to flame spread rating by ASTM E 84. This tabulation is intended only as a general guide and the reader should not assume that all material of the same

Table 5 Approximate Spread Raing (E-84 Tunnel Test)

Ceilings

Gypsum Plaster	0
Sprayed Mineral-base plaster	0-20
Enameled metal	0-20
Mineral fiber tile	10-25
Glass or mineral fiber bord or title, coated	10-40
Wood-base acousical tile (flame proofed)	20-75
Wood-base acoustical tile (untreated)	75-300

Walls

Brick, concrete, asbestos-cement board, ceremic tile, gypsum plaster	0
Enameled st eel, aluminum	0-20
Gypsum board, various facings	10-50
Wood, fiberboard (flame-retardant treated)	20-75
Plastic Paneling (flame-retardant-treated)	20-75
Wood, at least 0.5 in thick, various species	70-200
Plywood paneling	70-300
Hardoard	100-250
Cork	200-500
Cloth, paper, wood veneer, fiberboard (untreated)	200-500
Shellac finish on wood	500+

Floors*

Concrete, terrazzo	0
Vinyl Asbestos Tile	10-50
Red oak	100
Linoleum	100-300
Carpeting**	50-600

---

* Use of E 84 Tunnel Test on Floor Covering Materials is no longer recommended. See other Methods, for example, NFPA 253 and ASTM E648

** Depends on type of face fiber, uunderlayment, method of attachment if glued down, loose, etc.

---

all materials of the same generic type will perform in a similar manner. Furthermore, although a flame spread classification rating or label denotes that a test has been performed on a sample of the material, there is no assurance that the material will not contribute in a major way to the spread of a fire in an actual building situation. A fire investigator should not hesitate to request that tests be performed on samples of unburned material removed from the building where the finish material appears to have contributed significantly to the fire.

In removing materials for testing the investigator should understand how the test is done so that proper samples will be obtained. If it is possible that criminal proceedings will develop, the samples must be treated as any other criminal evidence.

ASTM E 84, the Steiner Tunnel Test, is the usual basis for legal regulation of flame spread. The sample required is about 22 in width and 24 ft (565 mm x 7.32 m) in length. It may not be easy to get a sample of this size, but it may be necessary.

The fact that the method of attachment is important to the actual flame spread of combustible tiles was discovered when a full size sample of tiles glued to gypsum board showed a much greater flame spread than the same tiles, removed from the board for shipment

ASTM E 162 requires a sample only 6 x 18 in (15 x 46 cm). Samples this size is easier to get. For some materials, results from this test can be correlated in a general way with ASTM E 84 but no direct relationship should be assumed. The information developed can be useful in developing better code requirements. If the question of discrepancy in the installed material is going to be criminally significant, the prosecutor should be made aware of the difference in these tests because it might be critical to the case that the test be performed under the same conditions as the code requires, which would almost invariably be ASTME 84.

Carpeting should first be tested to the requirements of FF 1-70 (11), al so known as the "pill test". The "pill test" only measures the ignitability of the carpet from small flame sources, such as a dropped, burning match. If the carpet passed the "pill test", and it was thought to have contributed significantly to the fire, it may be useful to test the flame spread properties of the carpet, properties which are not involved in the "pill test". One flame spread test procedure is that given in NFPA 253, Standard Method of Test for Critical Radiant Flux of Floor Covering Systems Using a Radiant Heat Energy Source. For this test, samples 10 x 42 in (25 x 107 cm) are required. If a pad was used with the carpet, this pad should be included with the carpet in the test.

Nearly all carpets will spread fire if the exposure is sufficiently intense. However, some carpets spread fire under less heat exposure than others. If a pad is used under a carpet, the pad generally will cause an increase in the carpet's flame spread characteristics. The purpose of conducting the NFPA 253 test is to determine whether the carpet spreads fire easily or is more resistant to this spread than other carpets. The results of NFPA 253 will be a number called the critical radiant flux (CRF). To compare this number against other carpets, one should then refer to reference which lists the CRF's for many different types of carpets, with and without padding.

MATERIALS

Introduction

Knowledge of the effect of fire and high temperature on all types of materials -- construction, interior finish, furnishings and contents is essential to the job of the fire investigator. In searching through a burned building, the investigator should make note of the materials which were relatively unaffected as well as those which burned, charred and melted. The historical patterns of fires in buildings should be recognized and comparative differences or similarities noted.

Properties of Materials

There are many properties of materials which determine their response to fire and high temperature, as well as the contribution they may make to the growth of a fire. The principal fire properties of organic materials are heat of combustion and ignition temperature. Other thermal and mechanical properties include heat conductivity: ·specific heat (heat absorption capacity), melting and softening points, coefficient of expansion (elongation due to heating), shrinkage, cracking, etc. Some typical thermal properties are listed in table 6.

The high thermal conductivity of metals can be a means of spreading fire, for example, through sheets, ducts, joints, connectors and fasteners. Specific heat (or more accurately volumetric heat capacity) is a measure of the capacity to absorb and store heat. A material with a high heat capacity will heat up slower and may keep the maximum air temperatures lower but it will also retain the heat longer. Where high temperatures exists, thermal radiation is important and shiny surfaces (aluminum, steel, mirrors) may reflect the heat to other surfaces. While reflective surfaces would be expected to remain cooler, in most cases smoke deposition, oxidation and other changes often occur on shiny surfaces so that they eventually absorb as well as most other materials. Melting and softening points are obvious indicators of fire scene temperatures, provided allowance is made for fallen ceilings (which may protect materials at floor level), heat sinks (metals, for example, or water) and exposure to heat prior to the fire.

Classes of Materials

Masonry. In common usage, this term includes precast or cast-in-place concrete, concrete and cinder block, brick, stone, cement and clay tiles (terra cotta). Under fire exposure, many masonry walls will remain intact. However, due to thermal expansion caused by severe heating of the exposed surface (usually the interior surface), ordinary brick, block and stone walls may sometimes lean out at the top and collapse. The integrity of masonry walls depends to a large extent on the quality of the mortar bond at the joints. Collapse also may occur for other reasons, including failure of a non-masonry supporting element, thermal expansion of floors, beams or trusses, or impact loading due to collapse of a floor, a roof, another building, or an explosion. A brick veneer wall depends for its integrity on the wooden structural wall to which it is fastened. If the wooden wall is damaged, the brick wall may collapse.

Table 6 Typical Thermal Properties of Selected Materials

Materials	Density Lbs/Cu Ft	Thermal[1] Conductivity Btu-in Hr ft2 °F	Spefic[2] Heat Btu/lb °F	Percent Increase in Length for each 100° Temp Rise	Melting Point °F
Air	0.06	0.2	0.24		
Water	62	5	1.0	0.01	32
Aluminum	165	1400	0.22	0.14	1220
Brass	530	720	0.09	0.11	1650
Copper	560	2600	0.09	0.09	1980
Cast iron	440	320	0.13	0.06	2466-2550
Steel	490	310	0.12	0.06-0.15[3]	2370-2550
Glass	160	6	0.20	0.04-0.06	2600
Brick	120	5	0.22	0.05	--
Concrete, normal	140	9-12	0.16-0.25	0.06-0.08	--
Weight	120	4	0.2		
Asbestos-cement	45	1.1	0.30-0.55	0.03-0.05	--
board	32	0.8	0.33-0.45	0.02-0.03	--
Wood (oak, maple)	65	1.0	0.33	--	--
Wood (fir, pine)	35	0.8	0.29	--	--
Hardboard	15	0.35	0.30	--	--
Plywood	70	3-6	0.23	--	--
Fiberboard (wood	50-60	1.5	0.26	--	--
or cane)	0.6	0.5	0.2	--	--
Plaster	3	0.3	0.2	--	--
Gypsum Board	3	0.3	0.25	--	--
Glass fiber batt					
	-	1-2	0.2-0.3	0.3-1.0	--
Mineral wool	-	0.7-1.0	0.32-0.35	0.3-0.4	--
Plastics, rigid	2	0.26	0.32	0.3-04	--
Vinyls	2	0.18	0.38	0.4	--
Styrene					
Polystyrene foam					
Polyurethand foam					

Note: Values listed are estimated values at ordinary temperatures, or over typical temperature ranges in fires, if available.
    Actual values vary considerably with temperature, particularly where moisture is involved.
[1]The number of Btu transmitted in one hour, through one square foot, one inch thick, for each degree of temperature difference.
[2]Specific Heat is the number of Btu required to increase the temperature of one pound of the material one degree F.
[3]Steel elongation increases at higher temperatures.

Concrete. Concrete is typically composed of portland cement, sand and coarse aggregate, for example, gravel, stone, cinders, slag, shale, vermiculite. The proportions may vary, for example, from 1:1:3 for columns to 1:3:6 for foundations. Concrete has high compressive strength but low tensile or shear strength. When exposed to elevated temperature under load, the compressive strength decreases and is one-half of its normal value at a temperature of about 1100°F (593°C). When exposed to rapidly rising temperatures, concrete is susceptible to spalling which is the (sometimes violent) loss of surface material. Spalling is attributed to the rapid generation of steam and depends upon moisture content (generally above 5%) in the concrete, type of aggregate and compressive load. Spalling is more likely in concrete which has not had sufficient time to lose its initial water of hydration, a process which continues for years in heavy concrete sections.

Ordinary concrete contains no steel reinforcement (or only light reinforcement). Concrete blocks may be made from cement sand and gravel, or from cement and sand alone, or from cement, sand and cinders.

Reinforced concrete is a composite mixture in which steel rods or bars are used to provide tensile and flexural strength. Fire may cause the concrete to spall away from the reinforcing steel. The strength of the concrete structural element depends upon the close bond between the steel and the concrete. Damaged concrete may be structurally unsafe. The tendons used in prestressed concrete totally lose their prestress at 800°F (427°C).

Steel. Steel has high tensile and compressive strength and is used in buildings in many sizes, shapes and products. Steel loses strength at elevated temperatures. When used as a structural member its yield, tensile and compressive strengths decrease to one-half of its normal value at a temperature of about 1000 to 1100°F (538° to 593°C). The color of heated iron and steel is sometimes used as a measure of temperature (see table 7). Steel is used in rolled or built-up members, in bar and thin sheet "C" joists, as channels, tees and angles, and as a variety of connectors such as nails, screws, bolts, hangars, and gusset plates. The fire characteristics of the steel, including high heat conductivity, substantial thermal expansion and decrease in yield strength at high temperatures, may be critical factors in a fire. For instance, a 20 ft steel member will elongate almost 2 in when heated to 1000°F (538°C). If restrained, it will buckle to accommodate the expansion. The buckling may cause structural collapse and may be well removed from the point of origin of the fire.

Gypsum. Gypsum is used both for plaster and for manufactured wall boards. Gypsum is one of the few materials which absorb heat from a fire, rather than contributing to the fire. It performs well in fires. It is widely used in fire-resistive assemblies. If the question of fire resistance is an issue, careful examination of the rear of several full sections should be made to determine if the board has a label or marking indicating it was listed by UL (Underwriters Laboratories Inc.) or FM (Factory Mutual Research Corp.). If the board is listed, then the installation should be compared with the code requirements, particularly in type and spacing of nails, cement cover over the nails, taping of all joints and firestopping of the structure.

Wood. Lumber is sawn wood used for construction purposes, although the word timber is often applied to large cross sectional pieces of lumber. Under fire exposure, wood undergoes dehydration, followed normally by a burning and/or charring process. Charred wood has readily defined layers or zones. The charring rate is roughly 0.025 or 1/40 in/min, but varies significantly with species, density and moisture content. The relatively thin wood members of frame construction may lose structural strength rapidly on fire exposure. Thick structural members may retain their strength for long periods but the structure itself may fail because of failure of the connections.

Table 7 Approximate color of Glowing Hot, Solid Objects

Appearance	Temperature	
	°F	°C
No emission detectable	Less than 885	Less than 475
Dark red	885-1200	475-650
Dark red to cherry red	1200-1380	650-750
Cherry red to bright cherry red	1380-1500	750-815
Bright cherry red to orange	1500-1650	815-900
Orange to yellow	1650-200	900-1090
Yellow to light yellow	2000-2400	1090-1315
Light yellow to white	2400-2800	1315-1540
Brighter white	higher than 2800	Higher than 1540

Wood cannot be "fire proofed" or made "noncombustible". However, it can be treated to reduce its rate of burning by a variety of surface treatments and impregnations with mineral salts. Pressure impregnation is one of the most effective methods of reducing surface flame spread, rate of heat release and smoke generation. If there is an apparent poor performance of impregnated or surface-treated wood, samples should be removed and tested for adequacy of the treatment.

Plastics. This term refers to a group of organic substances (resins) of high molecular weight which can be shaped or molded into finished solid products. Cellulosic plastics, which include cellulose acetate, ethyl cellulose, methyl cellulose and cellulose nitrate, are produced by chemical modification of cellulose. Some plastic products are blends, combinations or composites with unique properties; some can be compounded to be thermoplastic or thermosetting. Thermosetting plastics are those which undergo chemical reaction and cure during molding and do not melt. Some thermoplastics melt at temperatures only slightly above 212°F (100°C) and may form liquid pools and burn intensely in a manner similar to flammable liquids. Examples of the two types of plastics and quoted values of service temperatures and ignition temperatures are given in table 8. These temperatures may not relate directly to actual performance of products in fires, since the test methods do not take into account specimen size, heat transfer properties, aging, etc.

The fire performance of plastics depends upon type, use and level) of exposure. Some plastics form a char structure which may inhibit further burning, but most plastics will burn rapidly and generate heat, smoke and potentially toxic gases at fire temperatures. The plastics may be almost completely consumed, and the investigator should investigate for the presence of plastics in fires which reached high intensity early.

Table 8 Pastics

	Typical Uses	Continuous Service Temp [1] °F	Ignition Temp [2] Flash °F	Ignition Temp [2] Self °F	Decomposition Temp Range °F
Thermoplastics					
ABS	Piping, refrigerators, telephones	175-212	--	--	--
Acrylic/Methyl Methacrylate	Glazing, light diffusers, furnishing	170-23	540-570	830-860	340-570
Cellulose Nitrate	Throwaway test tubes	120-160	285	285	--
Polyamide (Nylon)	Carpeting, clothing, appliances	180-250	790	795	590-715
Polycarbonate	Glazing, appliances, light diffusers	250	--	930	--
Polyethylene	Containers, vapor barriers	160-230	645	660	635-840
Polypropylene	Wire insulation, appliances, piping	190-280	650	730	625-770
Polystyrene	Appliances, furnishings, thermal insulation (foam)	140-175	650-680	910-925	570-750
Polytetrafluorethylene (Teflon)	Cooking utensils, wire insulation	500	--	985	950-1000
Polyurethane	Furniture cushioning, coating, thermal Insulation (foam)	250-300	590	780	--
Polyvinyl chloride	Floor and wall covering, wire insulation, piping, Upholstery, clothing, coating	150-175	735	850	390-570
Thermosetting					
Alkyd	Paints, lacquers				
Epoxy	Protective coating, reinforced plastics	350	--	--	
Melamine	Tableware, laminates	210	885-930	1150-1190	
Phenolic	Laminates, appliances	280		900	
Polyster	Partitions (Glass-reinforced), boats	250-350	635-750	810-910	
Silicone	Electrical Insulation, coatings, grease	350-525	--	--	
Urea Formaldehyde	Thermal insulation	120			

16

154

Flame retardants added in manufacture may be used to reduce the ease of ignition and flammability of some plastics.

Insulation. The principal types of thermal insulation used in buildings are (1) mineral wool batts, blankets and fibrous loose fill, (2) foamed plastics, (3) inorganic (vermiculite, perlite) loose fill, (4) organic (wood or cane fiber) boards and (e) organic (macerated paper) loose fill.

Batts and blankets may be supplied with an integral vapor barrier (asphalt-treated or aluminum-foil-faced Kraft paper) which is intended for application to the warm-in-winter surface of the wall or ceiling interior finish board. The paper facing"is flammable and should never be left exposed. The batts are held together with a combustible binder. Plastic foam, which is combustible, should never be left exposed and most building codes require that a layer of 1/2 in (1.3 cm) gypsum board or equivalent barrier protection be provided.

Loose fill cellulosic insulation is commonly made of ground-up paper with chemicals added to reduce flammability. The more common chemicals used are boric acid, borax, and various sulfates and phosphates and these are added in amounts ranging generally from 15 to 30% by weight. If the chemicals are not added properly, they may segregate and leave portions of untreated paper. Loose fill insulation may be poured or blown into attics or blown into walls. Unless care is taken to maintain clearances around light and heat fixtures, and around flues and other heated surfaces and heat-producing appliances, smoldering of the cellulosic insulation may occur.

UTILITY SYSTEMS

Introduction

Brief descriptions of the types of utility systems found in buildings are provided. Those features and materials of the various systems which have resulted in fires and fire spread are discussed. The principal utility systems are:

1. Plumbing systems;
2. heating, ventilation, and air conditioning systems;
3. electrical systems.

Plumbing Systems

Plumbing systems include water supply and waste removal (sewage). Water supply systems, as the wording indicates, supply water to the building's fixtures and equipment. Sewage systems remove the waste products, usually accompanied by water for ease in movement, from the building.

Piping for both water supply and waste removal systems may be either metallic (copper, steel, or cast iron) or nonmetallic (plastics such as chlorinated polyvinyl chloride, polyvinyl chloride and acrylonitrile-butadiene-styrene, or CPVC, PVC, and ABS, respectively).

In some code jurisdictions, gas piping is included under the local plumbing code provisions and, as such, is a plumbing system. Piping for gas supply systems includes wrought iron (black pipe) and zinc-coated pipe (galvanized).

The major concerns with plumbing systems from a fire standpoint are with:

1. Piping, if metallic, providing an accidental ground for stray electrical currents;
2. piping, if nonmetallic, providing a fuel for nearby fires with the resultant spread of the fire;
3. penetration of fire-resistive walls and floors without proper protection (firestopping) leading to the spread of the fire;
4. leaks or ruptures in fuel gas piping and the possibility of ignition of the leaking gas.

Gas leaks have contributed too many accidental fires. The leak does not have to be within the building to pose a fire problem. Gas from leaks in the underground piping outside of a building has been known to follow the piping through the wall of the building and contact an ignition source within the structure. Also, gas leaking outside of the building has been known to have entered the sewage system and flowed back into the building through untrapped floor drains, reach an ignition source within the building and explode. Natural gas and liquefied petroleum gas have no natural odor. They are odorized artificially. The odorant may be removed as gas leaks through the earth or it may be absorbed in the scale in the inside of the pipeline. As a consequence, the absence of any reported gas odor does not necessarily mean that gas was not present. Gas leaks in the underground gas utility systems which result in accidents should be reported to the National Transportation Safety Board. While the Board must investigate any accident in which a fatality occurs, the Board also will assist in the investigation of any serious gas utility accident.

The major concerns from fire in plumbing systems are with:
(1) leakage from joints, especially in gas piping or sewer systems, where sewer wastes may produce methane; and (2) improperly constructed penetrations of fire-rated assemblies by the piping or appurtenances. Under fire exposure certain installations of plastic piping, either water or waste, may contribute to spread of fire or emit toxic gases.

Heating, Ventilation and Air Conditioning

Heating. The basic types of heating systems are hot water, steam, hot air and electricity. Hot water and steam systems utilize water usually heated by coal, gas, or oil-fired boilers. The hot water or steam is conveyed to radiators and/or convectors by piping. In hot-air systems, the air is heated by coal, oil, or gas-fired burners, or electric-resistance heaters, and conveyed throughout the building through ducts. Electrical heating systems generally utilize either radiant panels (resistance heating cables) built into the floor or ceiling or baseboard heating coils (convective panels) with electrical service supplied directly to the heating units.

Ventilation. Mechanical ventilation is provided either in conjunction with the air conditioning systems, or is in the form of ventilating fans installed in exterior walls or roofs and exhausting directly to the outdoors or into exhaust shafts which lead to the outdoors. Supply or makeup air is usually obtained through grills in doors or exterior walls, or by air leakage through openings.

Air Conditioning. There are two primary types of air conditioning: (1) central systems with distribution ducts or piping, utilizing compression or absorption-type refrigeration equipment or (2) packaged room or zonal air conditioners with free air discharge.

Central air conditioning systems utilize electricity, natural gas, or fuel oil to operate the compressors and a refrigerant as coolant in the coils and condensers. Either cooled air is circulated through ducts or chilled water is circulated through piping to individual room or zone convectors.

Individual packaged room or zonal units are generally electrically operated with closed refrigerant circuits self-contained within the units and may, depending on the conditions of usage, take fresh air from the outside or recirculate the inside air.

Heating, ventilation and air conditioning systems may be the cause of the original fire or the systems may contribute to the growth and spread of the fire. Fire initiation may include:

1. Explosive ignition due to the accumulation of gas or oil vapors within the equipment from failure of equipment controls;
2. ignition of fuel gases or oils from leaks in the piping or in the equipment;
3. ignition of combustibles near flue pipes, combustion chambers, and radiant heating units.

In air duct systems, most codes require fire dampers at points where ducts pierce fire-resistive walls and floors (where not in a shaft). In fire investigations, it is sometimes important to determine whether these dampers operated properly. As noted below, air conditioning and ventilation systems are sometimes designed to perform specific functions, such as smoke removal from the area of the fire. It is sometimes necessary for the fire investigator to determine whether such a system was installed and whether the system operated as intended.

Smoke Movement

The explanation of heated smoke and gases rising and mushrooming under the roof, if not vented, is adequate for simple structures. In tall buildings a number of factors may cause the movement of smoke to locations far beyond the area of origin, without necessarily affecting the areas in between.

Smoke movement may be caused by:
1. Thermal energy of the fire;
2. wind;
3. stack effect;
4. air handling system;
5. special built in smoke removal equipment;
6. openings in the building;
7. atmospheric conditions.

Wind. The wind exerts a pressure on one side and suction on the opposite side of the building. It may be powerful enough to overcome any of the other forces discussed here. It may change direction a number of times during the fire. It may blow in different directions at different levels of a high-rise building, particularly in congested areas where "canyon effects" may occur. The effect of the wind is increased when openings occur in the building. It is important to note that the wind at the fire may not have conformed to the information recorded at the nearest official weather station.

Stack Effect. This is due to differences between the inside and outside temperatures. The greater the difference, the greater the stack effect. Under cold weather conditions, normal air flow in the lower part of the building is from floors into shafts. The flow will decrease on successively higher floors until there is a "neutral zone", one or more floors where the flow is minimal. In the absence of wind, this generally will be from 1/3 to 1/2 the height of the building. Above the neutral zone the flow reverses, from the shafts onto-the floors, with the pressure (and thus the flow) increasing with height. The greatest flow therefore is from the lowest floors into the shafts and out from the shafts onto the highest floors. Thus top floor occupants sometimes may be the first to report a lower floor fire. In air conditioned buildings on a hot summer day, the flow may be reversed, that is downward. It should be kept in mind that the stack effect exists due to temperature difference and height. The fire does not cause it, the fire gases simply are transported by it. As an example of stack effect on fire gases, a rubbish fire on the ninth floor of a high-rise building under construction ignited PVC (polyvinyl chloride) air conditioning connectors. The fumes greatly distressed workmen on the 35th floor. They started to walk down the stairs but the stairwell was so full of noxious fumes that they got out at the 25th floor. They smashed the glass windows to get relief. This movement of gases from a lower to an upper floor was due to stack effect.

Air Conditioning. The investigator should determine the effect of the system on the fire. If the system was supposed to react to the fire in some way, the suggestions in the next paragraph are pertinent.

Special Smoke Removal Equipment In some buildings special equipment is provied to vent the fire area. It may be triggered automatically or manually. In other buildings the air conditioning system may have been designed to assist in controlling the spread of smoke.

There are two questions the investigator can ask:

"Did the special smoke removal equipment operate as designed? If it did operate as designed, were the results adequate?"

Openings in the building. Openings in the building, particularly large ones, can disrupt stack effect, multiply the wind effect, and disrupt the operation of mechanical equipment. When and why openings occurred might be important information as the fire investigation develops.

Atmospheric Conditions. When the temperature of the atmosphere is constantly decreasing as height increases, the condition is called "lapse". Under "lapse" conditions smoke will move up and away from the fire. If there is a layer of air warmer than the air below, this layer is called the "inversion layer". It acts as a roof to rising smoke. A high rise building may penetrate an inversion layer. This causes substantial differences in the smoke situation above and below the layer.

Wood-Burning Stoves and Furnaces

In recent years, there has been a growth in the use of wood-burning stoves and furnaces to provide either primary or supplemental heating. Such equipment, if not installed with adequate clearances to nearby combustible materials is potential sources of accidental fires. The burning of wood leads to the production of creosote which tends to deposit in the flue pipes and chimneys. This is particularly true of the newer so-called air-tight stoves. Operation of these stoves at low-firing rates enhances the production of creosote. The buildup of creosote in the flue pipes and chimneys can lead to a severe fire in the flue and chimney as the creosote is combustible. Flues and chimneys, be they masonry or the newer all-fuel triple-wall metal variety, should be able to withstand a total burnout. However, they may not due to deficiencies which may have been built in or have occurred with the passage of time.

ELECTRICAL

Electrical service consists of the following:

1. Service drop wires, either overhead or underground (from the public utilities' lines to the building);

2. service-entrance wires (from outside of building to equipment on the inside);

3. meter;

4. service entrance switch (to disconnect entire installation from public utilities' lines);

5. panel boards providing fuse or circuit breaker protection as well as disconnect means for each of the individual branch circuits;

6. grounding system;

7. distribution system - individual circuits, for lighting, appliance, and equipment operation.

There are six different types of wiring systems in common use. They are: (1) rigid conduit; (2) thin wall conduit; (3) flexible conduit; (4) nonmetallic-sheathed cable; (5) armored cable; and (6) knob-and-tube (which is seldom used today). Electrical codes are very specific with regard to where each of these systems may be used.

Junction boxes and outlet boxes are required at every location where wiring is spliced or insulation is removed, and at fixture locations.

In older buildings, electrical installations may have been made without outlet boxes at all splices and where insulation had been removed. In these locations, and where the wiring has been run in joist or stud spaces, dust, cobwebs and other easily ignitable materials may be present. If the splices and joints have not been properly made, there is a possibility of either short circuits or overheating of wire junctions thus leading to fire.

Another common cause of electrical fires, particularly in single-family dwellings, is the replacement of fuses of one rating with those of higher rating, that is, replacement of 15 ampere fuses with 20 or 30 ampere fuses. This practice may result in the overloading of the electrical wiring causing overheating and breakdown of insulation, and, if in close proximity to combustibles, eventually to smoldering and possible flaming ignition.

BUILDING ASPECTS OF A HOUSING INSPECTION

CONTENTS

		Page
I.	Background Factors	1
II.	Housing Construction Terminology	1
III.	Structure	4
IV.	Discussion of Inspection Techniques	15
V.	Noise as an Environmental Stress	17

BUILDING ASPECTS OF A HOUSING INSPECTION

The principle function of a house is to furnish protection from the elements. In its current stage, however, our civilization requires that a home provide not only shelter but also privacy, safety, and reasonable protection of our physical and mental health. A living facility that fails to offer these essentials through adequately designed and properly maintained interiors and exteriors cannot be termed "healthful housing."

I. Background Factors

In this chapter, a building will be considered in terms of its major components: heating, plumbing, and electrical systems. Each of these items will be examined in detail in future chapters. Attention will be given in this chapter to the portions of a building not visible upon completion of the ceiling, roof, and interior and exterior walls in order to give the reader an understanding of generally accepted construction practices. Emphasis, however, will be placed upon the visible interior and exterior parts of a completed dwelling that have a bearing on the soundness, state of repair, and safety of the dwelling both during intended use and in the event of a fire. These are some of the elements that the housing inspector must examine when making a thorough housing inspection.

II. Housing Construction Terminology

(Key to Component Parts Numbered in Figure 1)

A Fireplace

1 **Chimney** - A vertical masonry shaft of reinforced concrete or other approved noncombustible, heat resisting material enclosing one or more flues. It removes the products of combustion from solid, liquid, or gaseous fuel.

2 **Flue Liner** - The flue is the hole in the chimney. The liner, usually of terra cotta, protects the brick from harmful smoke gases.

3 **Chimney Cap** - This top is generally of concrete. It protects the brick from weather.

4 **Chimney Flashing** - Sheet-metal flashing provides a tight joint between chimney and roof.

5 **Firebrick** - An ordinary brick cannot withstand the heat of direct fire, and so special firebrick is used to line the fireplace.

6 **Ash Dump** - A trap door to let the ashes drop to a pit below, from where they may be easily removed.

7 **Cleanout Door** - The door to the ash pit or the bottom of a chimney through which the chimney can be cleaned.

8 **Chimney Breast** - The inside face or front of a fireplace chimney.

9 **Hearth** - The floor of a fireplace that extends into the room for safety purposes.

B Roof

10 **Ridge** - The top intersection of two opposite adjoining roof surfaces.

11 **Ridge Board** - The board that follows along under the ridge.

12 **Roof Rafters** - The structural members that support the roof.

13 **Collar Beam** - Really not a beam at all. A tie that keeps the roof from spreading. Connects similar rafters on opposite side of roof.

14 **Roof Insulation** - An insulating material (usually rock wool or fiberglas) in a blanket form placed between the roof rafters for the purpose of keeping a house warm in the winter, cool in the summer.

15 **Roof Sheathing** - The boards that provide the base for the finished roof.

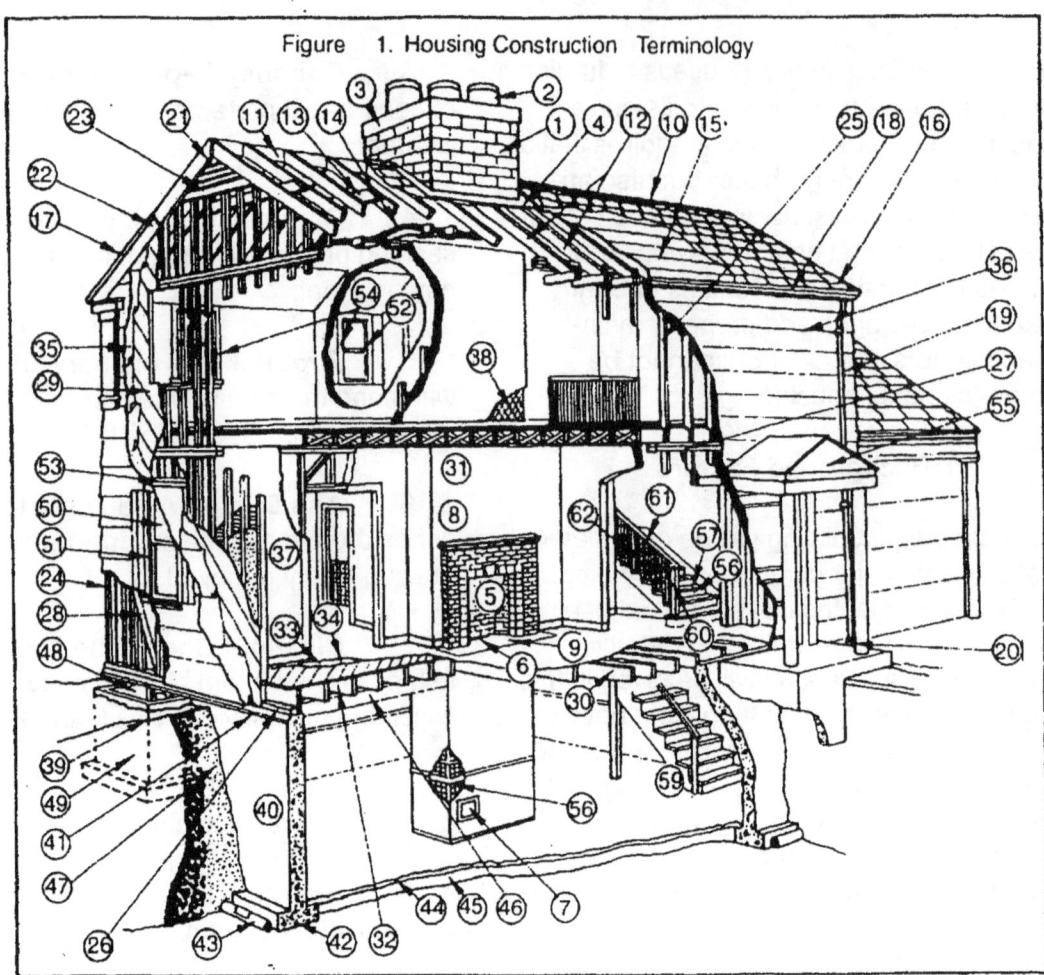

Figure 1. Housing Construction Terminology

16 **Roofing** - The wood, asphalt, or asbestos shingles - or tile, slate or metal - that form the outer protection against the weather.

17 **Cornice** - A decorative element made up of molded members usually placed at or near the top of an exterior or interior wall.

18 **Gutter** - The trough that gathers rainwater from a roof.

19 **Downspouts** - The pipe that leads the water down from the gutter.

20 **Storm Sewer Tile** - The underground pipe that receives the water from the downspouts and carries it to the sewer.

21 **Gable** - The triangular end of a building with a sloping roof.

22 **Barage Board** - The fascia or board at the gable just under the edge of the roof.

23 **Louvers** - A series of slanted slots arranged to keep out rain, yet allow ventilation.

C   Walls and Floors

24 **Corner Post** - The vertical member at the corner of the frame, made up to receive inner and outer covering materials.

25 **Studs** - The vertical wood members of the house, usually 2 X 4's generally spaced every 16 inches.

26 **Sill** - The board that is laid first on the foundation, and on which the frame rests.

27 **Plate** - The board laid across the top ends of the studs to hold them even and rigid.

164

28   **Corner Bracing** - Diagonal strips to keep the frame square and plumb.

29   **Sheathing** - The first layer of outer wall covering nailed to the studs.

30   **Joist** - The structural members or beams that hold up the floor or ceiling, usually 2 X 10's or 2 X 12's spaced 16 inches apart.

31   **Bridging** - Cross bridging or solid. Members at the middle or third points of joist spans to brace one to the next and to prevent their twisting.

32   **Subflooring** - The rough boards that are laid over the joist. Usually laid diagonally.

33   **Flooring Paper** - A felt paper laid on the rough floor to stop air infiltration and, to some extent, noise.

34   **Finish Flooring** - Usually hardwood, of tongued and grooved strips.

35   **Building Paper** - Paper placed outside the sheathing, not as a vapor barrier, but to prevent water and air from leaking in. Building paper is also used as a tarred felt under shingles or siding to keep out moisture or wind.

36   **Beveled Siding** - Sometimes called clapboards, with a thick butt and a thin upper edge lapped to shed water.

37   **Wall Insulation** - A blanket of wool or reflective foil placed inside the walls.

38   **Metal Lath** - A mesh made from sheet metal onto which plaster is applied.

D   **Foundation and Basement**

39   **Finished Grade Line** - The top of the ground at the foundation.

40   **Foundation Wall** - The wall of poured concrete (shown) or concrete blocks that rests on the footing and supports the remainder of the house.

41   **Termite Shield** - A metal baffle to prevent termites from entering the frame.

42   **Footing** - The concrete pad that carries the entire weight of the house upon the earth.

43   **Footing Drain Tile** - A pipe with cracks at the joints to allow underground water to drain in and away before it gets into the basement.

44   **Basement Floor Slab** - The 4- or 5-inch layer of concrete that forms the basement floor.

45   **Gravel Fill** - Placed under the slab to allow drainage and to guard against a damp floor.

46   **Girder** - A main beam upon which floor joists rest. Usually of steel, but also of wood.

47   **Backfill** - Earth, once dug out, that has been replaced and tamped down around the foundation.

48   **Areaway** - An open space to allow light and air to a window. Also called a light well.

49   **Area Wall** - The wall, of metal or concrete, that forms the open area.

E   **Windows and Doors**

50   **Window** - An opening in a building for admitting light and air. It usually has a pane or panes of glass and is set in a frame or sash that is generally movable for opening and shutting.

51   **Window Frame** - The lining of the window opening.

52   **Window Sash** - The inner frame, usually movable, that holds the glass.

53   **Lintel** - The structural beam over a window or door opening.

54   **Window Casing** - The decorative strips surrounding a window opening on the inside.

F   Stairs and Entry

55   **Entrance Canopy** - A roof extending over the entrance door.

56   **Furring** - Falsework or framework necessary to bring the outer surface to where we want it.

57   **Stair Tread** - The horizontal strip where we put our foot when we climb up or down the stairs.

58   **Stair Riser** - The vertical board connecting one tread to the next.

59   **Stair Stringer** - The sloping board that supports the ends of the steps.

60   **Newel** - The post that terminates the railing.

61   **Stair Rail** - The bar used for a handhold when we use the stairs.

62   **Balusters** - Vertical rods or spindles supporting a rail.

III. Structure

A   Foundation

The word **foundation** is used to mean:
1   Construction below grade such as footings, cellar or basement walls.
2   The composition of the earth on which the building rests.
3   Special construction such as pilings and piers used to support the building.

The foundation bed may be composed of solid rock, sand, gravel, or unconsolidated sand or clay. Rock, sand, or gravel are the most reliable foundation materials. Unconsolidated sand and clay, though found in many sections of the country, are not as desirable, because they are subject to sliding and settling.

The footing (see Figure 2) distributes the weight of the building over a sufficient area of ground so as to ensure that the foundation walls will stand properly. Footings are usually constructed of a masonry-type material such as concrete; however, in the past wood and stone have been used. Some older houses have been constructed without footings.

Although it is usually difficult to determine the condition of a footing without excavating the foundation, a footing in a state of disrepair or lack of a footing will usually be indicated either by large

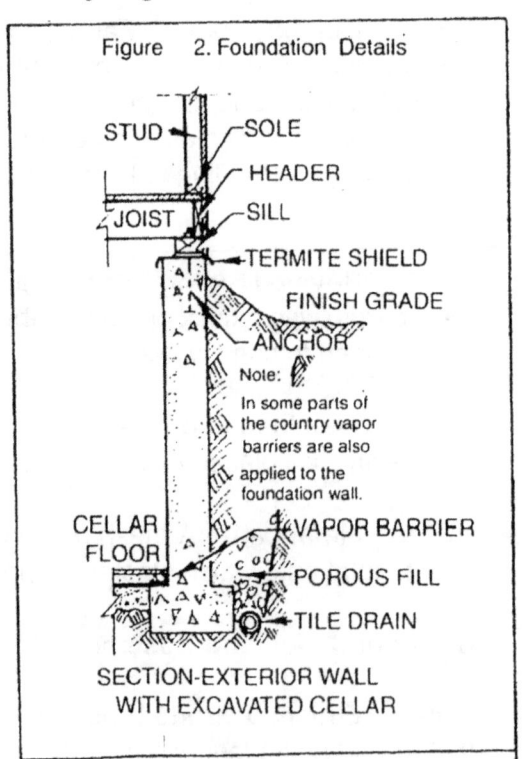

Figure 2. Foundation Details
SECTION-EXTERIOR WALL WITH EXCAVATED CELLAR

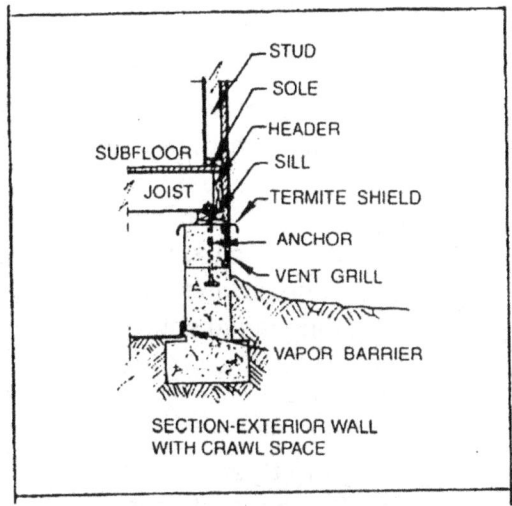

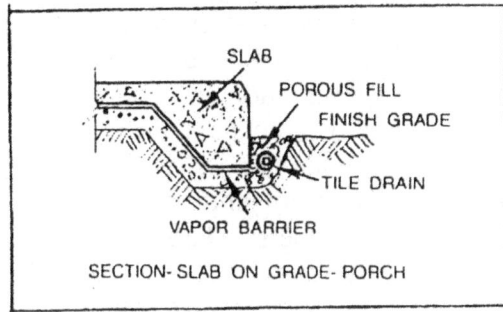

cracks or by settlement in the foundation walls (see Figure 3).

Foundation wall cracks are usually diagonal, starting from the top, the bottom, or the end of the wall. Cracks that do not extend to at least one edge of the wall may not be caused by foundation problems. Such wall cracks may be due to other structural problems and should also be reported.

The foundation walls support the weight of the structure and transfer this weight to the footings. The foundation walls may be made of stone, brick, concrete, or concrete blocks and should be moisture proofed with either a membrane of water-proof material or a coating of portland cement mortar. The membrane may consist of plastic sheeting or a sandwich of standard roofing felt joined and covered with tar or asphalt. The purpose of waterproofing the foundation walls is to prevent water from penetrating the wall material and leaving the basement or cellar walls damp.

Holes in the foundation walls are a common finding in many old houses. These holes may be caused by missing bricks or blocks. Holes and cracks in a foundation wall are undesirable because they make a convenient entry for rats and other rodents and also indicate the possibility of further structural deterioration. These holes should not be confused with adequately installed vents in the foundation wall that permit ventilation and prevent moisture entrapment.

The basement or cellar floor should be made of concrete placed on at least 6 inches of gravel. The purpose of a concrete floor is to protect the basement or cellar from invasion by rodents or from flooding. The gravel distributes ground water movements under the concrete floor, reducing the possibility of the water's penetrating the floor. A waterproof membrane, such as plastic sheeting, should be laid before the concrete is placed for additional protection against flooding.

The basement or cellar floor should be gradually but uniformly sloped towards a drain or a series of drains from all directions. These drains permit the basement or cellar floor to be drained if it becomes flooded.

Evidence of ineffective waterproofing or moisture proofing will be indicated by water or moisture marks on the floor and walls.

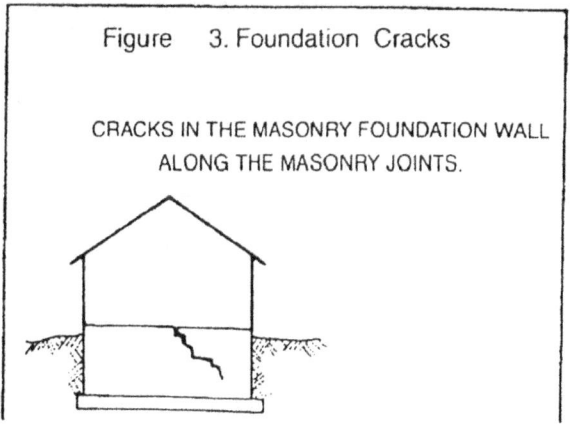

Figure 3. Foundation Cracks

CRACKS IN THE MASONRY FOUNDATION WALL ALONG THE MASONRY JOINTS.

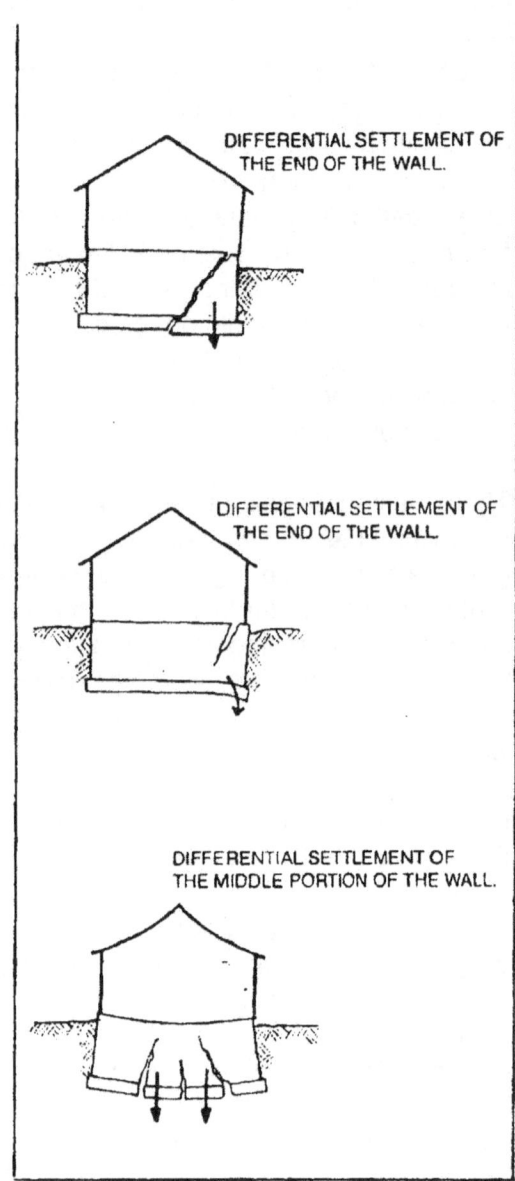

Cellar doors, hatchways, and basement windows should be weathertight and rodent proof. A hatchway can be inspected by standing at the lower portion with the doors closed; if daylight can be seen, the door probably needs repair.

B Framing
Many different types of house-framing systems are found in various sections of the country; however, the majority of the members in each framing system are the same. They include:

1 **Foundation Sills:** (see Figure 4 and 5). The purpose of the sill is to provide support or a bearing surface for the outside walls of the building. The sill is the first part of the frame to be placed and rests directly on the foundation wall. It is bolted to the foundation wall by sill anchors. It is good practice to protect the sill against termites by extending the foundation wall to at least 18 inches above the ground and using a non-corroding metal shield continuously around the outside top of the foundation wall.

2 **Flooring Systems:** (see Figure 5). The flooring system is composed of a combination of girders, joists, sub-flooring, and finished flooring that may be made up of concrete, steel, or wood. Joists are laid perpendicular to the girders, at about 16 inches on centers, and are the members to which the sub-flooring is attached. When the subfloor is wood, it may be nailed at either right angles or diagonally to the joists.

As shown in Figure 5, a girder is a member that in certain framing systems supports the joists and is usually a larger section than the joists it supports. Girders are found in framing systems where there are no interior bearing walls or where the span between bearing walls is greater than the joists are capable of spanning. The most common application of a girder is to support the first floor in residences. Often a board known as a ledger is applied to the side of a wood girder or beam to form a ledge for the joists to rest upon. The girder, in turn, is supported by wood posts or steel "lally columns" which extend from the cellar or basement floor to the girder.

3 **Studs:** (see Figure 4 and 5). Wall studs are almost always 2 by 4

inches; studs 2 by 6 inches are occasionally used to provide a wall thick enough to permit the passage of waste pipes. There are two types of walls or partitions: bearing and nonbearing. A bearing wall is constructed at right angles to and supports the joists. A nonbearing wall or partition acts as a screen or enclosure; hence, the headers in it are often parallel to the joists of the floor above.

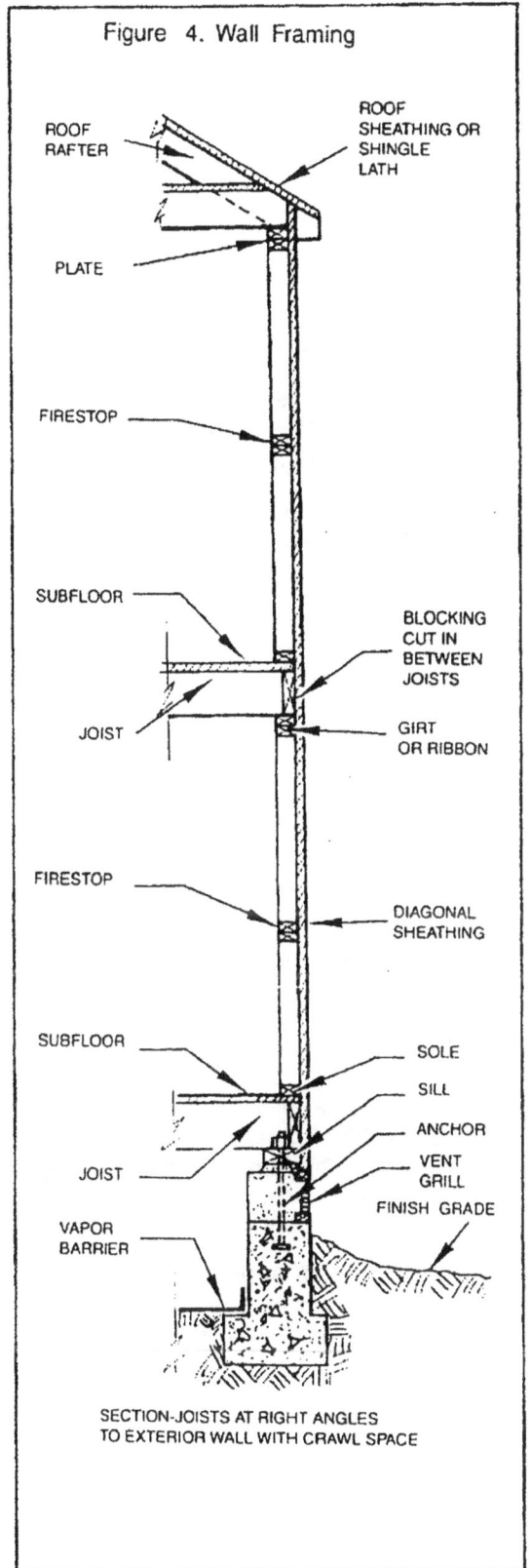

Figure 4. Wall Framing

In general, studs like joists are spaced 16 inches on center. In light construction such as garages and summer cottages where plaster is omitted, or some other material is used for a wall finish, wider spacing on studs is common.

Openings for windows or doors must be framed in studs. This framing consists of horizontal members called "headers," and vertical members called "trimmers" (see Figure 1).

Since the vertical spaces between studs can act as flues to transmit flames in the event of a fire, "fire stops" are important in preventing or retarding fire from spreading through a building by way of air passages in walls, floors, and partitions. Fire stops are wood obstructions placed between studs or floor joists to prevent fire from spreading in these natural fluespaces.

4 **Interior Wall Finish:** Many types of materials are used for covering interior walls and ceilings, but the principal types are plaster and dry-wall construction. Plaster is a mixture, usually lime, sand, and water, applied in two or three coats to lath to form a hard-wall surface. Dry-wall finish is a material that requires little, if any, water for application. More specifically, dry-wall finish may be gypsum board, plywood, fiberboard, or wood in various sizes and forms.

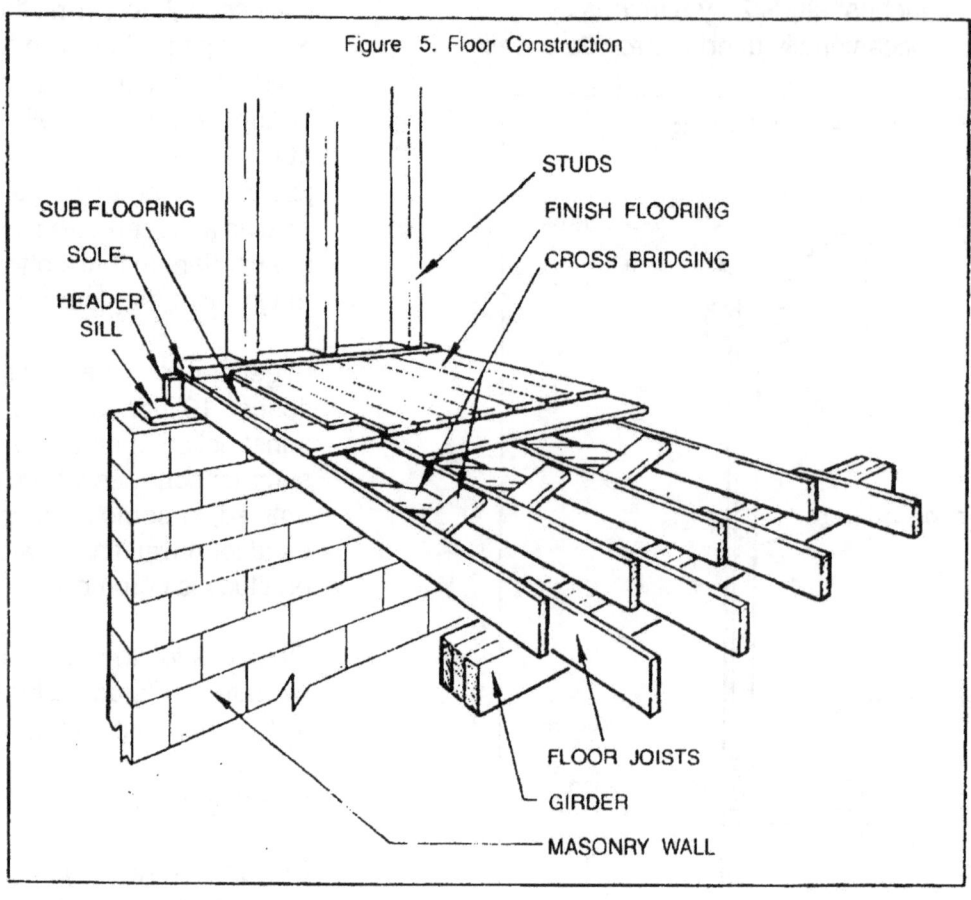

Figure 5. Floor Construction

Gypsum board is a sheet material composed of a gypsum filler faced with paper. Sheets are usually 4 feet wide and can be obtained in lengths up to 12 feet. In dry-wall construction, gypsum boards are fastened to the studs either vertically or horizontally and then painted. The edges along the length of the sheet are recessed to receive joint cement and tape.

A plaster finish requires a base upon which plaster can be spread. Wood lath at one time was the plaster base most commonly used, but today gypsum-board lath is more popular. It has paper faces with a gypsum filler. Such lath is 16 by 48 inches and 1/2 or 3/8 inches thick.

It is applied horizontally across the studs. Gypsum lath may be perforated to improve the bond and thus lengthen the time the plaster can remain intact when exposed to fire. The building codes in some cities require that gypsum lath be perforated. Expanded-metal lath may also be used as a plaster base. Expanded-metal lath consists of sheet metal slit and expanded to form openings to hold the plaster. Metal lath is usually 27 by 96 inches and is fastened to the studs.

Plaster is applied over the base to a minimum thickness of 1/2 inch. Because some drying may take place in wood-framing members after the house is completed, some shrinkage can be expected, which, in turn, may cause plaster cracks to develop around openings and in corners. Strips of lath imbedded in the plaster at these locations prevent cracks.

On the inside face of studs that form an exterior wall, vapor barriers are used to prevent condensation on the wall. The vapor barrier is an asphalted paper or metal foil through which moisture-laden air cannot travel.

5 **Stairways:** (see Figure 6). The general purpose of the standards for stairway dimensions is to ensure that there is adequate headroom, width, and uniformity in riser and tread size of every step to accommodate the expected traffic on each stairway safely.

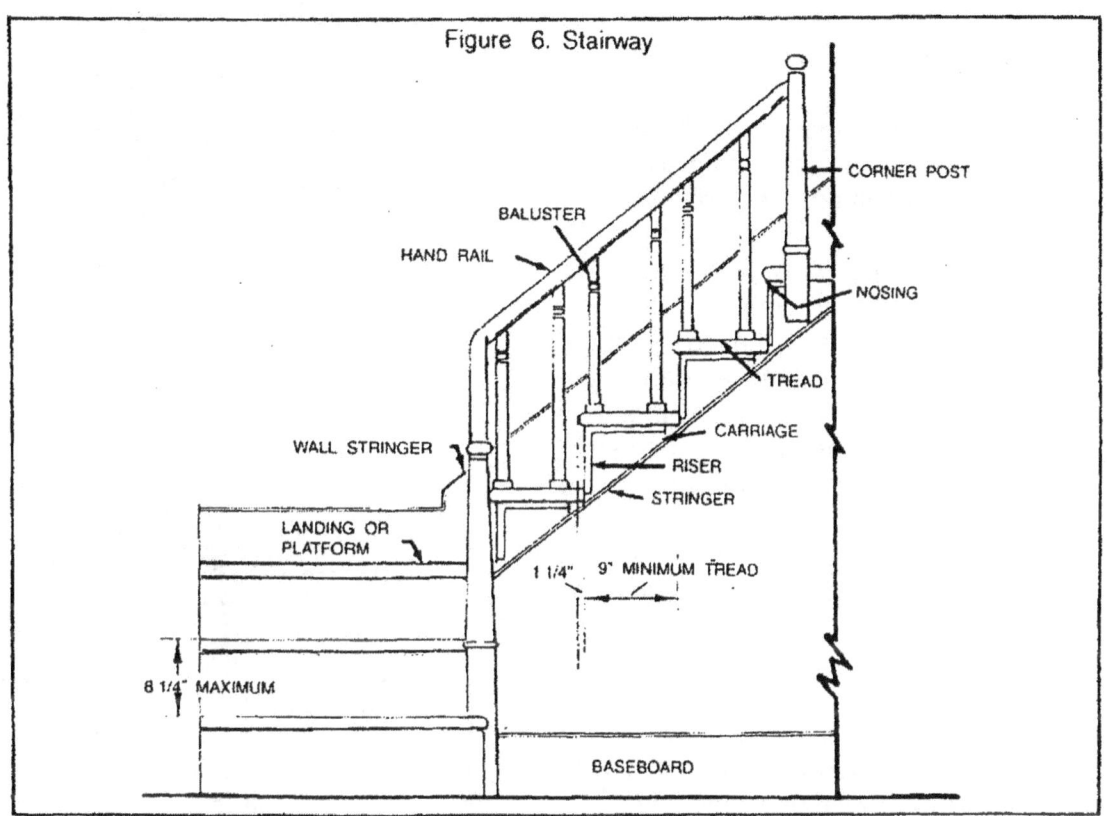

Figure 6. Stairway

Interior stairways should be not less than 44 inches in width. The width of a stairway may be reduced to 36 inches in one- and two-family dwellings. Stairs with closed risers should have maximum risers of 8 1/4 inches and a minimum tread of 9 inches plus 1 1/4-inch nosing. Basement stairs are often constructed with open risers. These stairs should have maximum risers of 8 1/4 inches and minimum treads of 9 inches plus 1/2-inch nosing. The headroom in all parts of the stair enclosure should be no less than 80 inches.

Exterior stairway dimensions should be the same as those called for in interior stairways, except that the headroom requirement does not apply.

6 **Windows:** The four general classifications of windows for residences are:

a Double-hung sash window that moves up or down, balanced by weights hung on chains or ropes, or springs on each side.

b Casement window sash is hinged at the side and can be hung so that it will swing outward or inward.

c Awning window - usually has two or more glass panes that are hinged at the top and swing about a horizontal axis.

d Sliding window - usually has two or more glass panes that slide past one another on a horizontal track.

The principal parts of a double-hung window (see Figure 4-7) are the lights, the top rail-framing members, bars or muntins that separate the lights, stiles - side-framing members, bottom rail, sash weights, and sash cords or chains. (All rails are horizontal, all stiles vertical.) The casement window's principal parts include: top and bottom rails, muntins, butt hinges, and jamb. All types of windows should open freely and close securely.

The exterior sill is the bottom projection of a window. The drip cap is a separate piece of wood projecting over the top of the window and is a component of the window casing.

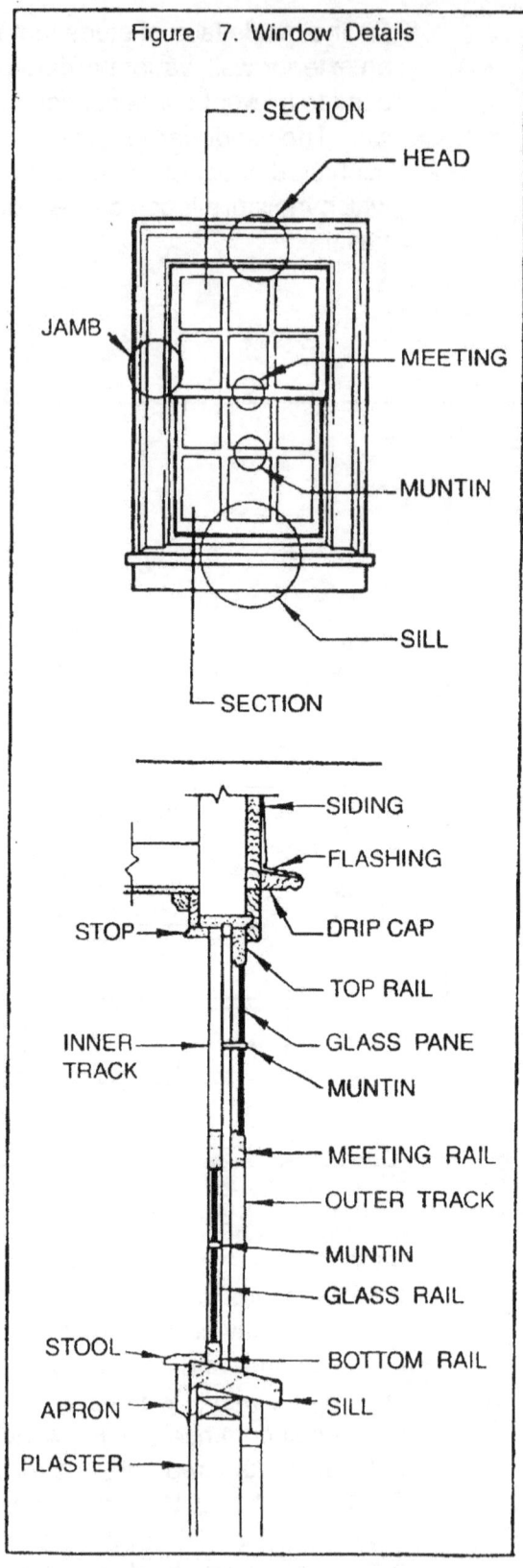

Figure 7. Window Details

7 **Doors**: There are many styles of doors both for exterior and interior use. Interior doors should offer a rea-

sonable degree of privacy. Exterior doors must, in addition to offering privacy, protect the interior of the structure from the elements. The various parts of a door have the same definitions as the corresponding parts of a window.

The most common types of doors are:

a **Batten door**: This consists of boards nailed together in various ways. The simplest is two layers nailed to each other at right angles, usually with each layer at 45 degrees to the vertical.

Another type of batten door consists of vertical boards nailed at right angles to several (two to four) cross strips called ledgers, with diagonal bracing members nailed between ledgers. If vertical members corresponding to ledgers are added at the sides, the verticals are called frames.

Batten doors are often found in cellars and other places where appearance is not a factor and economy is desired.

b **Flush doors**: Solid flush doors are perfectly flat, usually on both sides, although occasionally they are made flush on one side and paneled on the other. Flush doors sometimes are solid planking, but they are commonly veneered and possess a core of small pieces of white pine or other wood. These pieces are glued together with staggered end joints. Along the sides, top, and bottom are glued 3/4-inch edge strips of the same wood, used to create a smooth surface that can be cut or planed. The front and back faces are then covered with a 1/8-to 1/4-inch layer of veneer.

Solid flush doors may be used on both the interior and exterior.

c **Hollow-core doors**: These, like solid flush doors, are perfectly flat, but unlike solid doors, the core consists mainly of a grid of crossed wooden slats or some other type of grid construction. Faces are 3-ply plywood instead of one or two plies of veneer, and the surface veneer may be any species of wood, usually hardwood. The edges of the core are solid wood and are made wide enough at the appropriate places to accommodate locks and butts. Doors of this kind are considerably lighter than solid flush doors.

Hollow-core doors are usually used as interior doors.

d **Paneled doors**: Most doors are paneled, with most panels consisting of solid wood or plywood, either "raised" or "flat," although exterior doors frequently have one or more panels of glass, in which case they are called "lights." One or more panels may be employed although the number seldom exceeds eight. Paneled doors may be used both on the interior or exterior.

In addition to the various types of wood doors, metal is often used as a veneer or for the frame.

In general, the horizontal members are called rails and the vertical members are called stiles. Every door has a top and bottom rail, and some may have intermediate rails. There are always at least two stiles, one on each side of the door. The frame of a doorway is the portion to which the door is hinged. It consists of two side jambs and a head jamb, with an integral or attached stop against which the door closes.

Exterior door frames are ordinarily of softwood plank, with side rabbitted to receive the door in the same way as casement windows. At the foot is a sill, made of hardwood to withstand the wear of traffic, and sloped down and out to shed water.

Interior door frames are similar to exterior, except that they are often set directly on the hardwood flooring without a sill.

Building codes throughout the country call for doors in various locations within the structure to be fire resistant. These doors are often covered with metal or some other fire-resistant materials, and some are completely constructed of metal. Fire-resistant doors are usually located between a garage and a house, stairwells and hallways, all boiler rooms. The fire resistance rating required for various doors differs with local fire codes

C **Roof Framing** (see Figures 1, 4, 8, and 9)

Rafters serve the same purpose for the roof as joists do for floors, i.e., providing support for sheathing and roofing material. Rafters are usually spaced 20 inches on center.

1. **Collar Beam:** Collar beams are ties between rafters on opposite sides of the roof. If the attic is to be used for rooms, the collar beam may double as the ceiling joist.

2. **Purlin:** A purlin is the horizontal member that forms the support for the rafters at the intersection of the two slopes of a gambrel roof.

3. **Ridge Board:** A ridge board is a horizontal member against which the rafters rest at their upper ends; it forms a lateral tie to make them secure.

4. **Hip:** Like a ridge except that it slopes. The intersection of two adjacent, rather than two opposite, roof planes.

5. **Roof Boards:** The manner in which roof boards are applied depends upon the type of roofing material. Roof boards may vary from tongue-and-groove lumber to plywood panels.

6. **Dormer:** The term dormer window is applied to all windows in the roof of a building, whatever their size and shape.

D **Exterior Walls and Trim** (see Figure 4 and 9)

Exterior walls are enclosure walls whose purpose is to make the building weathertight. In most one- to three-story buildings they also serve as bearing walls. These walls may be made of many different materials.

Frequently used framed exterior walls appear to be of brick construction. In this situation, the brick is only one course thick and is called a brick veneer. It supports nothing but itself and is kept from toppling by ties connected to the frame wall.

In frame construction the base material of the exterior walls is called "sheathing." The sheathing material may be square-edge, shiplap, or tongue-and-groove boards.

In recent construction there has been a strong trend toward the use of plywood or composition panels.

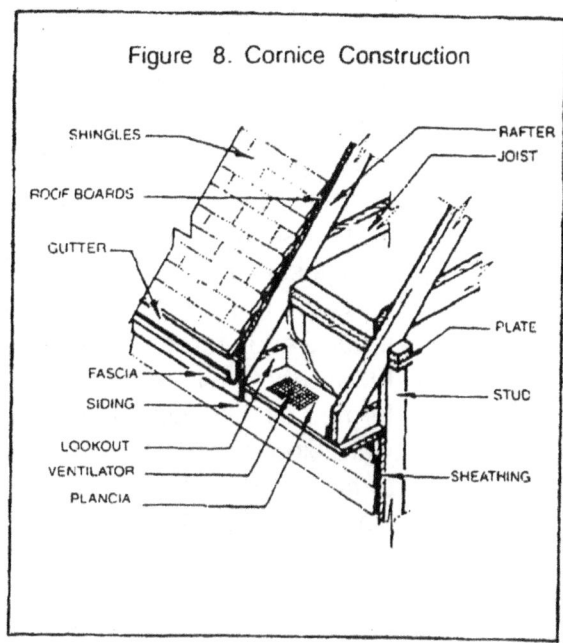

Figure 8. Cornice Construction

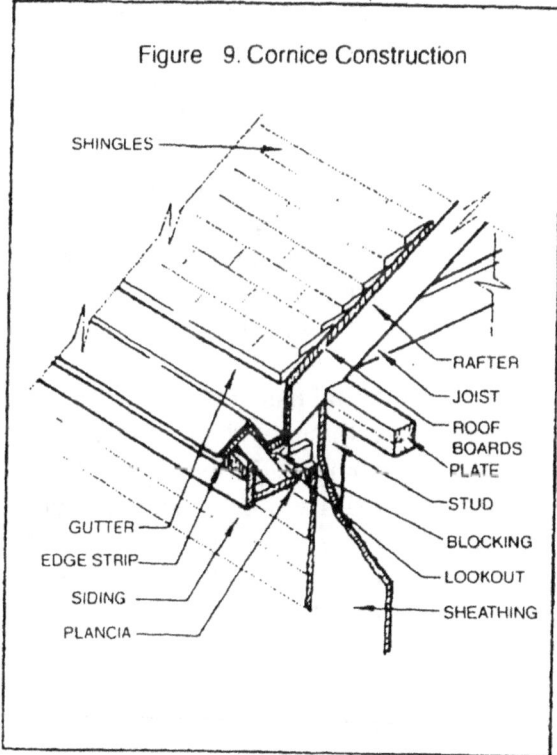

Figure 9. Cornice Construction

Sheathing, in addition to serving as a base course for the finished siding material, stiffens the frame to resist sway caused by wind. It is for this reason that sheathing has been applied diagonally on frame buildings.

The finished siding may be clapboard, shingles, aluminum, brick asphalt, wood, and so forth, or a combination thereof. Good aluminum siding has a backer board that serves as added insulation and affords rigidity to the siding. Projecting cornices are a decorative trim found at the top of the building's roofline. A parapet wall is that part of the masonry wall that extends up and beyond the roofline and is capped with a noncombustible material. It helps prevent spread of fire, provides a rest for fire department ladders, and helps prevent people on the roof from falling off.

Many types of siding, shingles, and other exterior coverings are applied over the sheathing. Wood siding, cedar, and other wood shingles or shakes, clapboard, common siding (called bevel siding), composition siding, asbestos, cement shingles, asbestos-cement siding, and the aforementioned aluminum siding are commonly used for exterior coverings. Clapboards and common siding differ only in the length of the pieces. Clapboards are 4 feet long while panel siding comes in lengths from 6 to 16 feet. Composition siding is made of felt and asphalt, which are often shaped to look like brick. Asbestos and cement shingles are rigid and produce a covering that is fire resistant. Cedar wood shingles are also manufactured with a backer board that gives insulation and fire-resistant qualities. Asbestos cement siding made of asbestos fiber and portland cement has good fire-resistant qualities and is a rigid covering.

E Roof Coverings (Flexible Material Class)

1 **Asphalt Shingle:** The principal damage to asphalt shingle roofs is caused by the action of strong winds on shingles nailed too high. Usually the shingles affected by winds are those in the four or five courses nearest the ridge and in the area

extending about 5 feet down from the edge or rake of the roof.

2. **Asphalt Built-up Roofs:** These may be un-surfaced, the coating of bitumen being exposed directly to the weather, or they may be surfaced having slag or gravel imbedded in the bituminous coating. The use of surfacing material is desirable as a protection against wind damage and the elements. This type of roof should have enough pitch to drain water readily.

3. **Coal Tar Pitch Built-up Roofs:** This type roof must be surfaced with slag or gravel. Coal tar pitch built-up roof should always be used on deck pitched less than 1/2 inch per foot; that is, where waler may collect and stand. This type roof should be inspected on completion, 6 months later, and then at least once a year, preferably in the fall. When the top coating of bitumen shows damage or has become badly weathered, it should be renewed (rigid material class).

4. **Slate Roofs:** The most common problem with slate roofs is the replacement of broken slates. Roofs of this type normally render long service with little or no repair.

5. **Tile Roofs:** Replacement of broken shingle tiles is the main maintenance problem. This is one of the most expensive roofing materials. It requires very little maintenance and gives long service.

6. **Copper Roofs:** Usually are of 16-ounce copper sheeting and applied to permanent structures. When properly installed, they require practically no maintenance or repair. Proper installation allows for expansion and contraction with changes in temperature.

7. **Galvanized Iron Roofs:** Maintenance is done principally by removing rust and keeping roof well painted. Leaks can be corrected by re-nailing, caulking, or replacing all or part of the sheet or sheets in disrepair.

8. **Wood Shingle Roofs:** The most important factors of this type roof are its pitch and exposure, the character of wood, kind of nails used, and preservative treatment given shingles. Creosote and coal tar preservative are satisfactory for both treated and untreated shingles.

9. **Flashing:** Valleys in roofs that are formed by the junction of two downward slopes may be finished, open, or closed. In a closed valley the slates, tiles, or shingles of one side meet those of the other, and the flashing below them may be comparatively narrow. In an open valley, the flashing, which may be made of zinc, copper, or aluminum, is laid in a continuous strip, extending 12 to 18 inches on each side of the valley, while the tiles or slates do not come within 4 to 6 inches of it.

The ridges built up on a sloping roof where it runs down against a vertical projection, like a chimney or a skylight, should be weather-proofed with flashing.

Metal flashings are generally used with slate, tile, metal, and wood shingles. Failure of roof flashing is usually due to exposed nails that have come loose. The loose nails allow the flashing to lift with leakage resulting.

10. **Gutters and Leaders:** Gutters and leaders should be of noncombustible materials. They should be securely fastened to the structure and spill into a storm sewer if the neighborhood is so provided. When there is no storm sewer, a concrete or stone block placed on the ground beneath the leader prevents water from eroding the lawn. This store

block is called a splash block. Gutters will not become plugged if protected against clogging of leaves and twigs. Gutters should be checked every spring and fall and then cleaned out when necessary.

IV. Discussion of Inspection Techniques

A serious building defect may often be observed during a housing inspector's routine examination. In many cases it is beyond the scope of the housing inspector's background to analyze the underlying causes and to recommend a course of action that will facilitate repair in an efficient and economical manner. In situations such as this, it is important that the inspector realize his limitations and refer the matter to the proper expert.

A prime example of a technically complex situation that a housing inspector might observe is a leaning, buckling, or bulging foundation or bearing wall. This problem may be the result of a number of hidden or interacting problems. For example, it may be the result of differential building settlement or failure of a structural beam or girder. It is beyond the scope of the housing inspector's responsibilities to discover the cause of the defect, but it is his responsibility to note the problem and refer it to the proper authority. In this case the proper authority would be a building inspector.

In the aforementioned situation where a bulging foundation wall was discovered, this would obviously constitute a violation of the housing ordinance and should be written up as such by the housing inspector. Since the housing inspector is generally not qualified to determine whether the house should be evacuated because it is in danger of imminent collapse, he should seek the advice of a building inspector.

A question that frequently arises is *which violations should be referred to an expert?* Needless to say, circumstances that obviously fall within the jurisdiction of another department should be referred to the department. The housing inspector should discuss with his supervisor any situation in which he feels inadequate to make a decision. In all cases the inspector should inform his supervisor before referring a problem to another agency or expert.

Another reason for referral to other departments is that when a remedial action is completed the other department will be in a better position to determine whether the job is satisfactory.

This principle of referral should be applied to every portion of the inspection, whether it deals with health, heating, plumbing, gas, or electrical as well as structural defects.

Certain structural items should be recognized as unsafe by the housing inspector. For example, a beam that has sagged or slanted may cause a portion of or an entire floor to sag or slope. Where a sagging or sloping floor is found, examine the ceiling of the room below or the basement for a broken or dropped girder or joist.

Doors and windows that are out of level will not close completely. It may be possible to see outside light through openings around window rails and door jambs. If an inspector detects such a situation, the condition of the supporting girders, girts, posts, and studs should be questioned, since this condition is evidence that some of these members may be termite infested or rotted and may be causing the outside wall to sag. Glass panes in doors and windows should be replaced if found to be broken or missing. Windows should also be checked for proper operation, and items such as broken sash cords or chains noted.

If the roof of the structure appears to be sagging, the inspector should make a special effort to examine the rafters, purlin, collar beams, and ridge boards if these members are exposed as in unfinished attics. The condition of the roof boards may be examined while he is in the attic. If light can be seen between these boards the roof is unsound. Evidence of a leaking roof will be indicated by loose plaster or peeling or stained paint and wall paper. Areas of the roof where flashing occurs, such as around the chimney, are frequent origins of roof leaks. It is essential that the leak be found and repaired, not only to prevent the entrance of moisture into the building, but also to prevent the loosening of the plaster, rotting of timbers, and extension of damage to the remainder of the house.

Gutters and rain leaders should be placed around the entire building to insure proper drainage of water. This will lessen the possibility of seepage of water through siding and window frames, and entrance of water into the cellar or basement. Lack of or leaking gutters may result in rotting of the siding or erosion of the exposed portion of the cellar or basement walls. This situation commonly exists where the mortar between bricks or concrete blocks in foundation walls is found to be heavily eroded. Gutters should be free from dirt and leaves.

The exterior siding should be in sound, weathertight condition. Peeled or worn paint on wood siding will expose the bare wood to the elements and result in splitting and warping of siding. This condition will eventually lead to the entrance of rain water with resultant rotting of the sheathing and studs as well as inside dampness and falling plaster. Sound and painted siding will prevent major repairs and expenses in the future. This condition will often be particularly prevalent on the north face of the structure.

Roof and chimneys should be inspected for tilting, missing bricks, deterioration of flashing, and pointing of chimney bricks. In addition, roof covering should be checked for broken spots and missing shingles or tiles. Roof doors should be metal clad, self-closing, tight fitting, and unlockable. The roof should also be examined for weather-tightness and broken TV antennas.

Porches should be carefully examined for weakened treads, missing or cracked boards, holes, and holes covered with tin plates, railing rigidity, missing posts, handrail rigidity, condition of the columns that support the porch roof, and the condition of the porch roof itself. The open section beneath the porch should be inspected for broken lattice-work. Check under the porch for accumulation of dirt and debris that can offer a harborage for vermin and rodents.

Loose plaster and missing or peeling wallpaper or paint should be noted. Bugs and cockroaches eat the paste from the wallpaper while leaving behind loose paper.

The basic parts of a stairway that a housing inspector should be able to identify correctly are the following:

A   Riser

B   Tread

C   Nosing

D   Handrail

E   Balustrade and Balusters, the Vertical Members that Support the Handrail, and

F   The Soffit, Underpart of the Stairway.

In the examination of a stairway (be careful to turn the light on) initially check the underside, if visible, to see if it is intact. Then proceed slowly up the stairs placing full weight on each tread and checking for loose, wobbling, or uneven treads and risers. Regardless of the size of the treads or risers they should all be of uniform size. For all stairs that rise 3 or more feet, a handrail should be present and in a sound and rigid condition.

Any fireplace should conform to the requirements of the local code. An unused fireplace that has its opening covered with wallpaper or other material should have a solid seal behind the paper. Operable fireplaces should have a workable damper and a fire screen, and should be clean.

Garages and accessory structures should be inspected in the same manner as the main building.

Sidewalks and driveways, whether constructed of flagstone, concrete, or asphalt, should be checked for creaking, buckling, and other conditions dangerous to pedestrian travel.

Stone, brick, or concrete steps should be inspected for cracks, deterioration, and pointing.

Fences should be in a sound condition and painted. Fire escapes should be checked for paint condition, loose or broken treads and rails, proper operating condition, and proper connection to the house.

V. Noise as an Environmental Stress

People feel comfortable in an environment with a low-level, soothing, steady, unobstrusive level of sound, typical of the natural undisturbed environment. All of us have experienced the anguish that noise can cause, whether it be noise from a neighbor's television, the grinding of truck gears while asleep, the persistent whine of a fan motor, or the sound of children racing down the halls. These annoyances experienced in the home are producing public demands for noise control legislation.

Not only is noise disturbing, but studies also indicate that extreme noise can cause deafness and perhaps interfere with other bodily functions.

While few existing housing ordinances contain enforceable noise provisions, noise problems must be considered by the building inspector because they intimately affect and are affected by his decisions. As a housing inspector, you can help residents by suggesting corrective noise measures that can be taken; you can refer them to agencies, if needed, for corrective action; you can help them to understand that their noisy environment can place limitations on their behavior, capabilities, and satisfaction with their home.

Noise is unwanted sound. Noise can travel through air or through the building structure. The first stage of noise control is the control of sound at its source. If attempts to quiet the source are not completely successful, then other, more expensive corrective measures will be required.

Although a visual examination of a dwelling may detect some sources of noise leaks (see Figure 10) such as wide gaps or cracks at ceiling, floor, or adjoining wall edges, it is usually inadequate since it fails to detect sources of noise leaks hidden from the eye. A far more effective test is to be alert for the operation of some noisy device like a vacuum cleaner in a closed room and listen near the other side of the wall for any noise leakage. The ear is a reasonably good sensing device. If a noise leak is noticed, the partition may be surveyed at critical points with a bright flashlight while an observer looks for light leakage in a darkened room on the other side. Detection of any light leakage in the darkened room will signify a noise leak.

Noise carried as vibration by a building structure is called structure-borne noise. Detecting structure-borne noise caused by the operation of mechanical equipment is somewhat more difficult (see Figure 11). With noisy equipment in operation, the inspector can sometimes locate noise leaks or structure-borne noise paths by conducting similar hearing tests along with pressing the ear against various room surfaces or using fingertips to sense the vibration of these surfaces.

A Airborne Noise

The sources of airborne noise that cause the most frequent disturbances in the home are audio instruments such as televisions, radios, phonographs, or pianos; adults and children speaking loudly, singing, crying and shouting; household appliances such as garbage disposals, dishwashers, vacuum cleaners, clothes washers, and dryers; plumbing noises such as pipes knocking, toilets flushing, and water running.

The disturbing influences of airborne noise are generally limited to the areas near the noise source. For example, a phonograph may cause annoyance in rooms of a neighbor's apartment adjacent to the phonograph but rarely in rooms farther removed unless doors or passageways are left open. Sound absorption materials such as carpeting, acoustical tile, drapery, and upholstered furniture in the intervening rooms may often provide a significant reduction in the disturbing noise before it reaches rooms where quiet is desired.

Under no conditions should sound-absorptive materials be used on the surfaces of walls and ceilings for the sole purpose of preventing the transmission of sound as structure-borne noise. To do so would be a complete waste of effort. To illustrate, imagine the noise conducted by a wall constructed solely of drapery or acoustical tile attached to studs. The noise level in the room would be reduced, but sound produced in the room would pass through the wall to adjoining rooms with little, if any, reduction in noise level. Sound absorptive materials should be used in and near areas of high noise levels to limit airborne noise at the source of the noise and reduce the effects of noise along corridors.

The transmission of noise from one completely enclosed room to an adjoining room separated by a partition wall may be either direct transmission through the wall, indirect transmission through other walls, ceilings, and floors common to both rooms, or through corridors adjacent to such rooms.

In some older wood frame houses, the open troughs between studs and joists are efficient sound transmission paths. This noise transmission by indirect paths is known as "flanking transmission" (see Figure 10 and 11). In addition to the flanking paths, there may be noise leaks particularly along the ceiling, floor, and sidewall edges of the wall. In order to obtain the highest sound insulation performance, a partition wall must be of airtight construction. Care must be exercised to seal all openings, gaps, holes, joints, and penetrations of piping and conduits with a nonsetting caulking compound. Even hairline cracks, particularly at adjoining wall, floor, and ceiling edges, transmit a substantially greater amount of noise than would normally be expected on the basis of the size of the crack.

Figure 10. Flanking Transmission of Airborne Noise

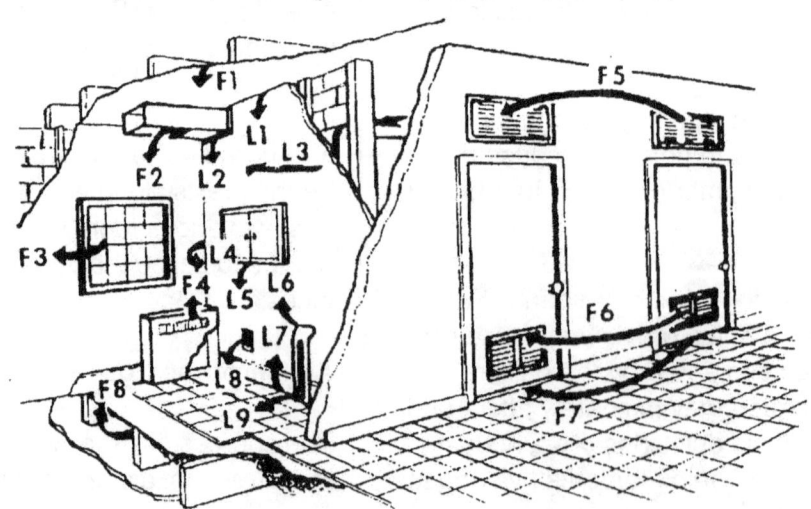

FLANKING NOISE PATHS	NOISE LEAKS
F1 Open plenums over walls, false ceilings	L1 Poor seal at ceiling edges
F2 Unbaffled duct runs	L2 Poor seal around duct penetrations
F3 Outdoor path, window to window	L3 Poor mortar joints, porous masonry block
F4 Continuous unbaffled inductor Units	L4 Poor seal at sidewall, filler panel, etc.
F5 Hall path, open vents	L5 Back-to-back cabinets, poor workmanship
F6 Hall path, louvered doors	L6 Holes, gaps at wall penetrations
F7 Hall path, openings under doors	L7 Poor seal at floor edges
F8 Open troughs in floor-ceiling structure	L8 Back-to-back electrical outlets
	L9 Holes, gaps at floor penetrations

Other points to consider are these: leaks are (a) batten strip A/O post connections of prefabricated walls, (b) under-floor pipe or service chases, (c) recessed, spanning light fixtures, (d) ceiling and floor cover plates of movable walls, (e) unsupported A/O unbacked wall-board joints (f) edges and backing of built-in cabinets and appliances, (g) prefabricated, hollow metal, exterior curtain walls.

It is often helpful to use one sound to drown out another disturbing noise; for example, music on the radio can be used to drown out the noise of traffic. The use of sound to drown out noise is particularly useful in masking noises that occur infrequently, such as accelerating or braking vehicles, periodic mechanical equipment noise, barking dogs, laughter, or shouting.

B **Structure-Borne Noise**

Structure-borne noise occurs when wall, floor, or other building elements are set into vibration by direct contact with vibrating sources such as mechanical equipment or domestic appliances. A small, vibrating pipe firmly attached to a plywood or gypsum wall panel will amplify the vibration noise. An illustration of this amplification of structure-borne noise is provided by the sound board of a piano. The major sources of structure-borne noise are the impact of walking on wood floors or of slamming doors, plumbing system noises, heating and air-conditioning system noises, noise from mechanical equipment or appliances, and vibration from sources outside the building. If the vibration is severe enough, it may have adverse effects not only on the occupants of a building but also on the building structure. Household appliances such as refrigerators, washing machines, sewing machines, clothes dryers, televisions, and pianos should be vibration isolated from the floor by means of rubber mounts placed under them if disturbing structure-borne noise is to be avoided. Residents should also be cautioned against locating these noise sources along party walls and in particular against mounting these appliances and kitchen cabinets directly on party walls so that the walls act as sounding boards in adjoining apartments. Window air-conditioners should be completely vibration isolated from the surrounding window frame by rubber gaskets and padding. The importance of isolating a vibrating source from the structure in the control of equipment noise cannot be overemphasized.

Another source of disturbing structure-borne noise is squeaking of wood floors. Some squeaks can be eliminated by lubricating the tongues of wood floor boards with mineral oil applied sparingly to the openings between adjacent boards. Loose finish flooring may be securely fastened to subflooring by surface nailing into the

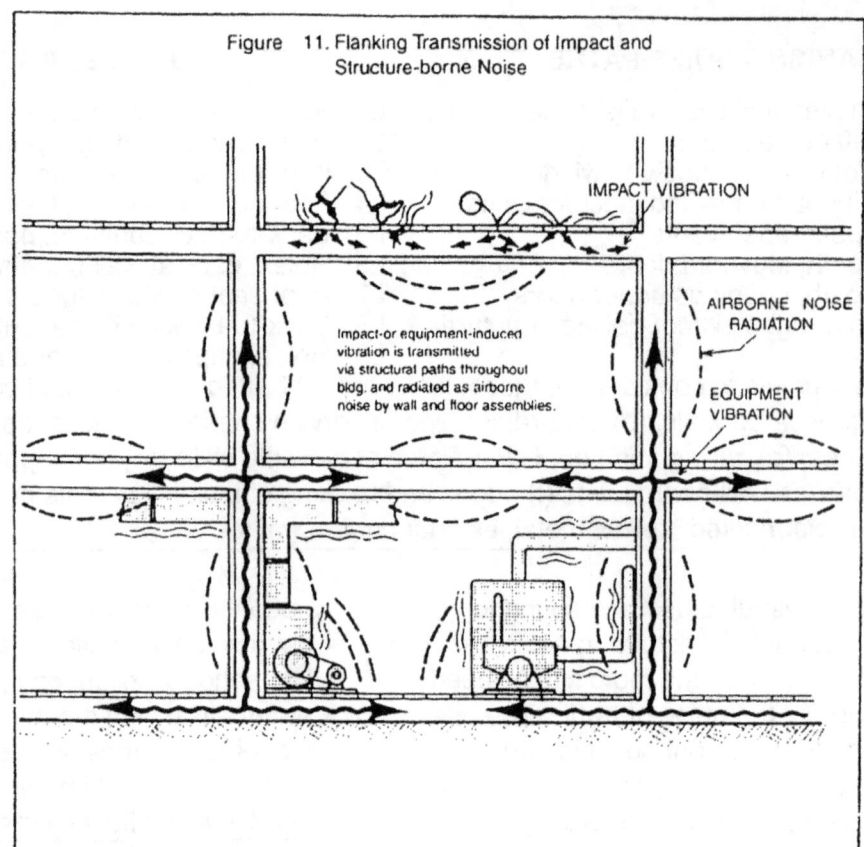

Figure 11. Flanking Transmission of Impact and Structure-borne Noise

subfloor and preferably the joists. Ring-type nails or sawtooth staples properly spaced should be used in nailing finish flooring to subflooring. In an exposed joist structure, where finish flooring is warped, driving screws up through the subfloor and into the finish floor will be effective in drawing the layers of flooring tightly together to reduce noise.

Of course, noise caused by the impact of walking or scraping can be substantially reduced by the use of carpets. In the case of door slams, the impact noise may be eliminated by the use of door closers or rubber bumpers.

The noisy hammering of a plumbing system is usually caused by the sudden interruption of water-flow, for example, by a quick closing or opening of a tap.

Air chambers can be built into the plumbing system to reduce water hammer. The air pockets, rubber inserts, or spring elements in air chambers act to reduce noise. Air chambers are explained in Chapter 6.

Defective, loose, or worn valve stems create intense chattering of the plumbing system. The defective device can frequently be found without difficulty, since immediate use of the device causes the vibration, which generally occurs at some low-flow-velocity setting and diminishes or disappears at a higher flow setting. For example, if a chattering noise occurs when a particular faucet or tap is opened partially and diminishes when fully opened, the faucet more than likely has some loose or defective parts and should be repaired.

Noise can be a very complex problem. The housing inspector is not expected to be an acoustics expert. Nor is he expected to be able to analyze and solve the noise problems that an acoustics consultant would normally handle. He can, however, help teach the public that the annoyances and stress caused by noise can be partially alleviated by a simple awareness of common noise problems found in many residences.

Although the housing inspector is not an expert in the fields of zoning, plumbing, building, and electrical systems, he should be familiar with the applicable code in each of the respective fields. Familiarization with these codes will better enable him to recognize violations.

BASIC FUNDAMENTALS OF DRAWINGS AND SPECIFICATIONS

A building project may be broadly divided into two major phases: (1) the DESIGN phase, and (2) the CONSTRUCTION phase. In accordance with a number of considerations, of which the function and desired appearance of the building are perhaps the most important, the architect first conceives the building in his mind's eye, as it were, and then sets his concept down on paper in the form of PRESENTATION drawings. Presentation drawings are usually done in PERSPECTIVE, by employing the PICTORIAL drawing techniques.

Next the architect and the engineer, working together, decide upon the materials to be used in the structure and the construction methods which are to be followed. The engineer determines the loads which supporting members will carry and the strength qualities the members must have to bear the loads. He also designs the mechanical systems of the structure, such as the lighting, heating, and plumbing systems. The end-result of all this is the preparation of architectural and engineering DESIGN SKETCHES. The purpose of these sketches is to guide draftsmen in the preparation of CONSTRUCTION DRAWINGS.

The construction drawings, plus the SPECIFICATIONS to be described later, are the chief sources of information for the supervisors and craftsman responsible for the actual work of construction. Construction drawings consist mostly of ORTHOGRAPHIC views, prepared by draftsmen who employ the standard technical drawing techniques, and who use the symbols and other designations

You should make a thorough study of symbols before proceeding further with this chapter. Figure 1 illustrates the conventional symbols for the more common types of material used on structures. Figure 2 shows the more common symbols used for doors and windows.

Before you can interpret construction drawings correctly, you must also have some knowledge of the structure and of the terminology for common structural members.

I. STRUCTURES

The main parts of a structure are the LOAD-BEARING STRUCTURAL MEMBERS, which support and transfer the loads on the structure while remaining in equilibrium with each other. The places where members are connected to other members are called JOINTS. The sum total of the load supported by the structural members at a particular instant is equal to the total DEAD LOAD plus the total LIVE LOAD.

The total dead load is the total weight of the structure, which gradually increases, of course, as the structure rises, and remains constant once it is completed. The total live load is the total weight of movable objects (such as people, furniture, bridge traffic or the like) which the structure happens to be supporting at a particular instant.

The live loads in a structure are transmitted through the various load-bearing structural members to the ultimate support of the earth as follows. Immediate or direct support for the live loads is provided by HORIZTONAL members; these are in turn supported by VERTICAL members; which in turn are supported by FOUNDATIONS and/or FOOTINGS; and these are, finally, supported by the earth.

The ability of the earth to support a load is called the SOIL BEARING CAPACITY; it is determined by test and measured in pounds per square foot. Soil bearing capacity varies considerably with different types of soil, and a soil of given bearing capacity will bear a heavier load on a wide foundation or footing than it will on a narrow one.

VERTICAL STRUCTURAL MEMBERS

Vertical structural members are high-strength columns; they are sometimes called PILLARS in buildings. Outside wall columns and inside bottom-floor columns, usually rest directly on footings. Outside-wall columns usually extend from the footing or foundation to the roof line. Inside bottom-floor columns extend upward from footings or foundations to horizontal members which in turn support the

185

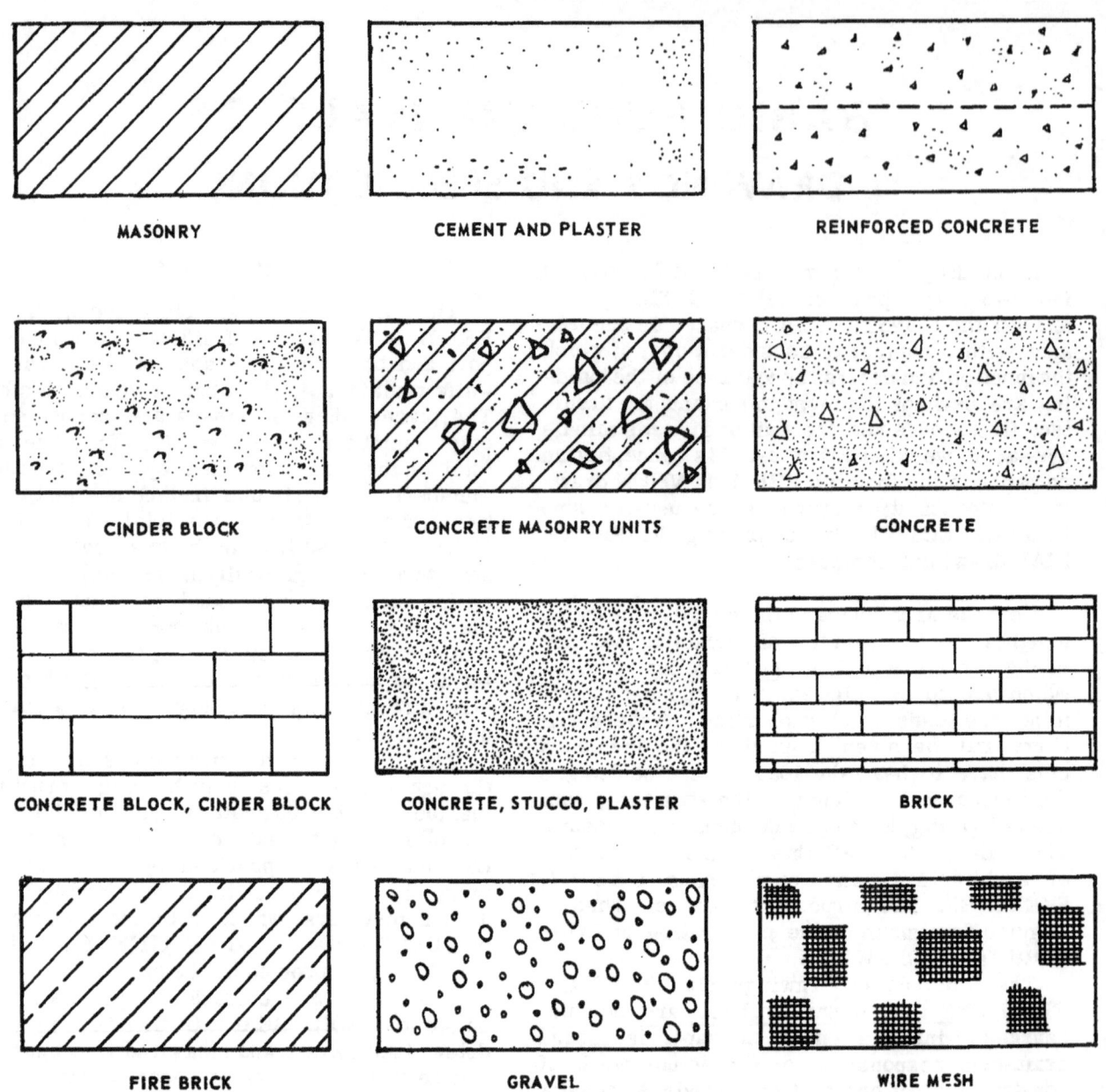

Figure 1.—Material symbols.

first floor. Upper floor columns usually are located directly over lower floor columns.

A PIER in building construction might be called a short column. It may rest directly on a footing, or it may be simply set or driven in the ground. Building piers usually support the lowermost horizontal structural members.

In bridge construction a pier is a vertical member which provides intermediate support for the bridge superstructure.

The chief vertical structural members in light frame construction are called STUDS. They are supported on horizontal members called SILLS or SOLE PLATES, and are topped by horizontal members called TOP PLATES or RAFTER PLATES. CORNER POSTS are enlarged studs, as it were, located at the building corners. In early FULL-FRAME construction a corner post was usually a solid piece of larger timber. In most modern construction BUILT-UP

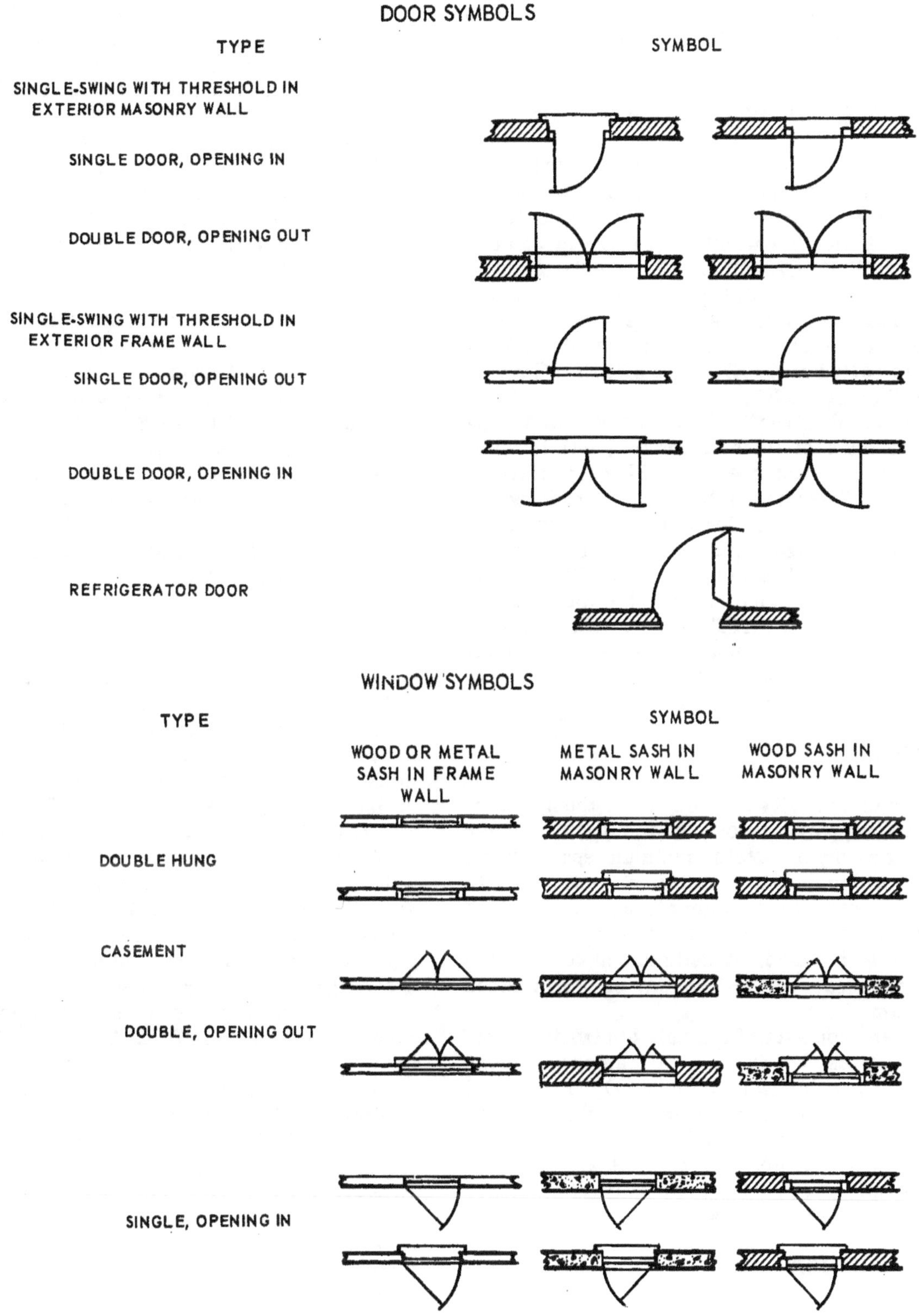

DOOR SYMBOLS

TYPE	SYMBOL
SINGLE-SWING WITH THRESHOLD IN EXTERIOR MASONRY WALL	
SINGLE DOOR, OPENING IN	
DOUBLE DOOR, OPENING OUT	
SINGLE-SWING WITH THRESHOLD IN EXTERIOR FRAME WALL	
SINGLE DOOR, OPENING OUT	
DOUBLE DOOR, OPENING IN	
REFRIGERATOR DOOR	

WINDOW SYMBOLS

TYPE	SYMBOL		
	WOOD OR METAL SASH IN FRAME WALL	METAL SASH IN MASONRY WALL	WOOD SASH IN MASONRY WALL
DOUBLE HUNG			
CASEMENT			
DOUBLE, OPENING OUT			
SINGLE, OPENING IN			

Figure 2 —Architectural symbols (door and windows).

corner posts are used, consisting of various numbers of ordinary studs, nailed together in various ways.

HORIZONTAL STRUCTURAL MEMBERS

In technical terminology, a horizontal load-bearing structural member which spans a space, and which is supported at both ends, is called a BEAM. A member which is FIXED at one end only is called a CANTILEVER. Steel members which consist of solid pieces of the regular structural steel shapes are called beams, but a type of steel member which is actually a light truss is called an OPEN-WEB STEEL JOIST or a BAR STEEL JOIST.

Horizontal structural members which support the ends of floor beams or joists in wood frame construction are called SILLS, GIRTS, or GIRDERS, depending on the type of framing being done and the location of the member in the structure. Horizontal members which support studs are called SILL or SOLE PLATES. Horizontal members which support the wall-ends of rafters are called RAFTER PLATES. Horizontal members which assume the weight of concrete or masonry walls above door and window openings are called LINTELS.

TRUSSES

A beam of given strength, without intermediate supports below, can support a given load over only a certain maximum span. If the span is wider than this maximum, intermediate supports, such as a column must be provided for the beam. Sometimes it is not feasible or possible to install intermediate supports. When such is the case, a TRUSS may be used instead of a beam.

A beam consists of a single horizontal member. A truss, however, is a framework, consisting of two horizontal (or nearly horizontal) members, joined together by a number of vertical and/or inclined members. The horizontal members are called the UPPER and LOWER CHORDS; the vertical and/or inclined members are called the WEB MEMBERS.

ROOF MEMBERS

The horizontal or inclined members which provide support to a roof are called RAFTERS. The lengthwise (right angle to the rafters) member which support the peak ends of the rafters in a roof is called the RIDGE. (The ridge may be called the Ridge board, the Ridge PIECE, or the Ridge pole.) Lengthwise members other than ridges are called PURLINS. In wood frame construction the wall ends of rafters are supported on horizontal members called RAFTER PLATES, which are in turn supported by the outside wall studs. In concrete or masonry wall construction, the wall ends of rafters may be anchored directly on the walls, or on plates bolted to the walls.

II. CONSTRUCTION DRAWINGS

Construction drawings are drawings in which as much construction information as possible is presented GRAPHICALLY, or by means of pictures. Most construction drawings consist of ORTHOGRAPHIC views. GENERAL drawings consist of PLANS AND ELEVATIONS, drawn on a relatively small scale. DETAIL drawings consist of SECTIONS and DETAILS, drawn on a relatively large scale.

PLANS

A PLAN view is, as you know, a view of an object or area as it would appear if projected onto a horizontal plane passed through or held above the object or area. The most common construction plans are PLOT PLANS (also called SITE PLANS), FOUNDATION PLANS, FLOOR PLANS, and FRAMING PLANS.

A PLOT PLAN shows the contours, boundaries, roads, utilities, trees, structures, and any other significant physical features pertaining to or located on the site. The locations of proposed structures are indicated by appropriate outlines or floor plans. By locating the corners of a proposed structure at given distances from a REFERENCE or BASE line (which is shown on the plan and which can be located on the site), the plot plan provides essential data for those who will lay out the building lines. By indicating the elevations of existing and proposed earth surfaces (by means of CONTOUR lines), the plot plan provides essential data for the graders and excavators.

A FOUNDATION PLAN (fig. 3) is a plan view of a structure projected on a horizontal plane passed through (in imagination, of course) at the level of the tops of the foundations. The plan shown in figure 3 tells you that the main foundation of this structure will consist of a rectangular 12-in. concrete block wall, 22 ft

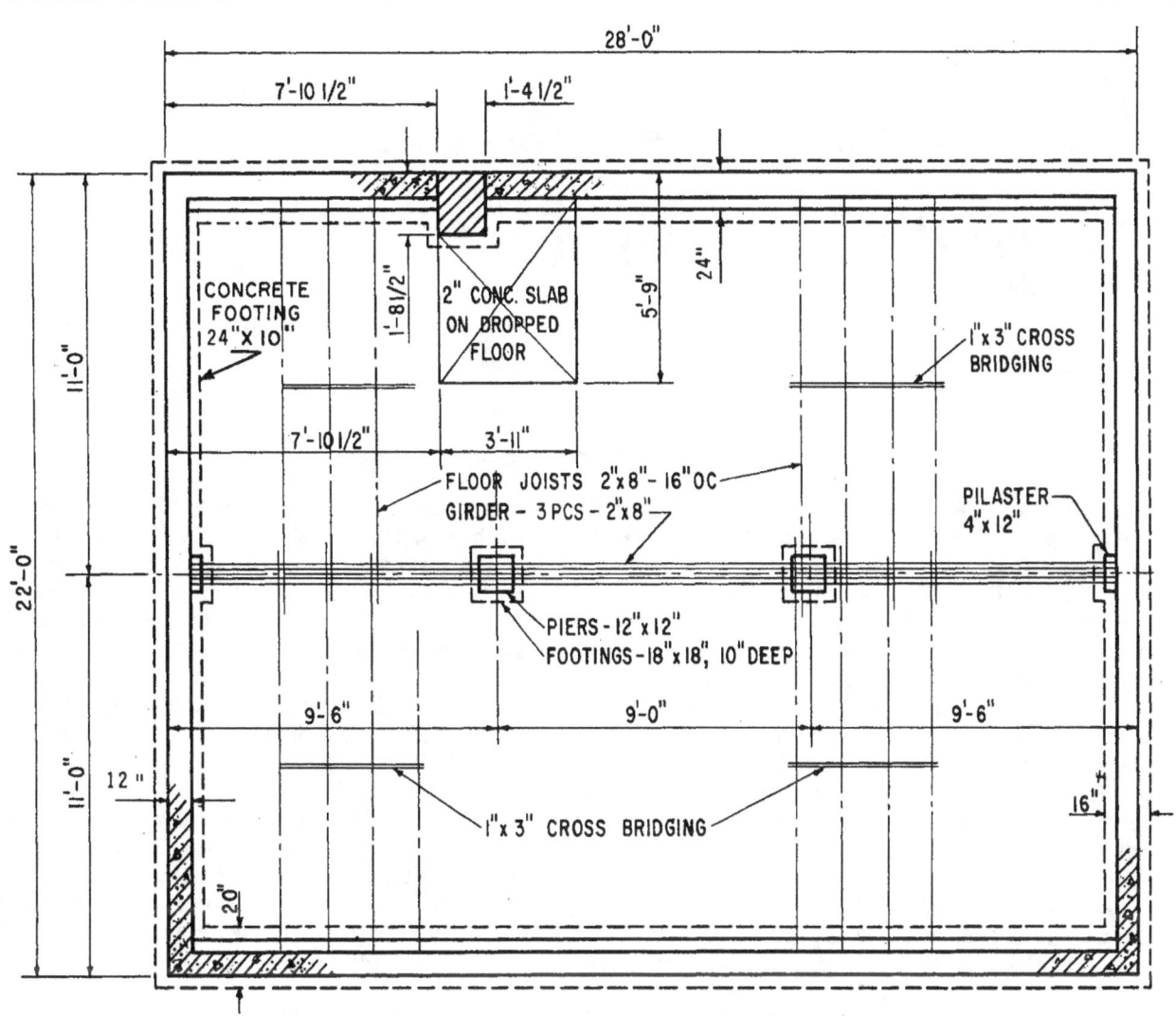

Figure 3.—Foundation plan.

wide by 28 ft long, centered on a concrete footing 24 in. wide. Besides the outside wall and footing, there will be two 12-in. square piers, centered on 18-in. square footings, and located on center 9 ft 6 in. from the end wall building lines. These piers will support a ground floor center-line girder.

A FLOOR PLAN (also called a BUILDING PLAN) is developed as shown in figure 4. Information on a floor plan includes the lengths, thicknesses, and character of the building walls at that particular floor, the widths and locations of door and window openings, the lengths and character of partitions, the number and arrangement of rooms, and the types and locations of utility installations. A typical floor plan is shown in figure 5.

FRAMING PLANS show the dimensions, numbers, and arrangement of structural members in wood frame construction. A simple FLOOR FRAMING PLAN is superimposed on the foundation plan shown in figure 3. From this foundation plan you learn that the ground-floor joists in this structure will consist of 2 x 8's, lapped at the girder, and spaced 16 in. O. C. The plan also shows that each row of joists is to be braced by a row of 1 x 3 cross bridging. For a more complicated floor framing problem, a framing plan like the one shown in figure 2-6 would be required. This plan

  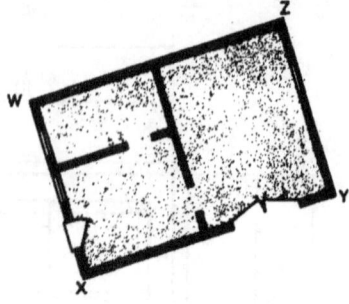

PERSPECTIVE VIEW OF A BUILDING SHOWING CUTTING PLANE WXY

PREVIOUS PERSPECTIVE VIEW AT CUTTING PLANE WXYZ, TOP REMOVED

DEVELOPED FLOOR PLAN WXYZ

Figure 4.—Floor plan development.

shows, among other things, the arrangement of joists and other members around stair wells and other floor openings.

A WALL FRAMING PLAN gives similar information with regard to the studs, corner posts, bracing, sills, plates, and other structural members in the walls. Since it is a view on a vertical plane, a wall framing plan is not a plan in the strict technical sense. However, the practice of calling it a plan has become a general custom. A ROOF FRAMING PLAN gives similar information with regard to the rafters, ridge, purlins, and other structural members in the roof.

A UTILITY PLAN is a floor plan which shows the layout of a heating, electrical, plumbing, or other utility system. Utility plans are used primarily by the ratings responsible for the utilities, but they are important to the Builder as well. Most utility installations require the leaving of openings in walls, floors, and roofs for the admission or installation of utility features. The Builder who is placing a concrete foundation wall must study the utility plans to determine the number, sizes, and locations of the openings he must leave for utilities.

Figure 7 shows a heating plan. Figure 8 shows an electrical plan.

ELEVATIONS

ELEVATIONS show the front, rear, and sides of a structure projected on vertical planes parallel to the planes of the sides. Front, rear, right side, and left side elevations of a small building are shown in figure 9.

As you can see, the elevations give you a number of important vertical dimensions, such as the perpendicular distance from the finish floor to the top of the rafter plate and from the finish floor to the tops of door and window finished openings. They also show the locations and characters of doors and windows. Dimensions of window sash and dimensions and character of lintels, however, are usually set forth in a WINDOW SCHEDULE.

A SECTION view is a view of a cross-section, developed as indicated in figure 10. By general custom, the term is confined to views of cross-sections cut by vertical planes. A floor plan or foundation plan, cut by a horizontal plane, is, technically speaking, a section view as well as a plan view, but it is seldom called a section.

The most important sections are the WALL sections. Figure 11 shows three wall sections for three alternate types of construction for the building shown in figures 3, 5, 7 and 8. The angled arrows marked "A" in figure 5 indicate the location of the cutting plane for the sections.

The wall sections are of primary importance to the supervisors of construction and to the craftsmen who will do the actual building. Take the first wall section, marked "masonry construction," for example. Starting at the bottom, you learn that the footing will be concrete, 2 ft wide and 10 in. high. The vertical distance of the bottom of the footing below FINISHED GRADE (level of the finished earth surface around the house) "varies"—meaning that it will depend on the soil-bearing capacity at the particular site. The foundation wall will consist of

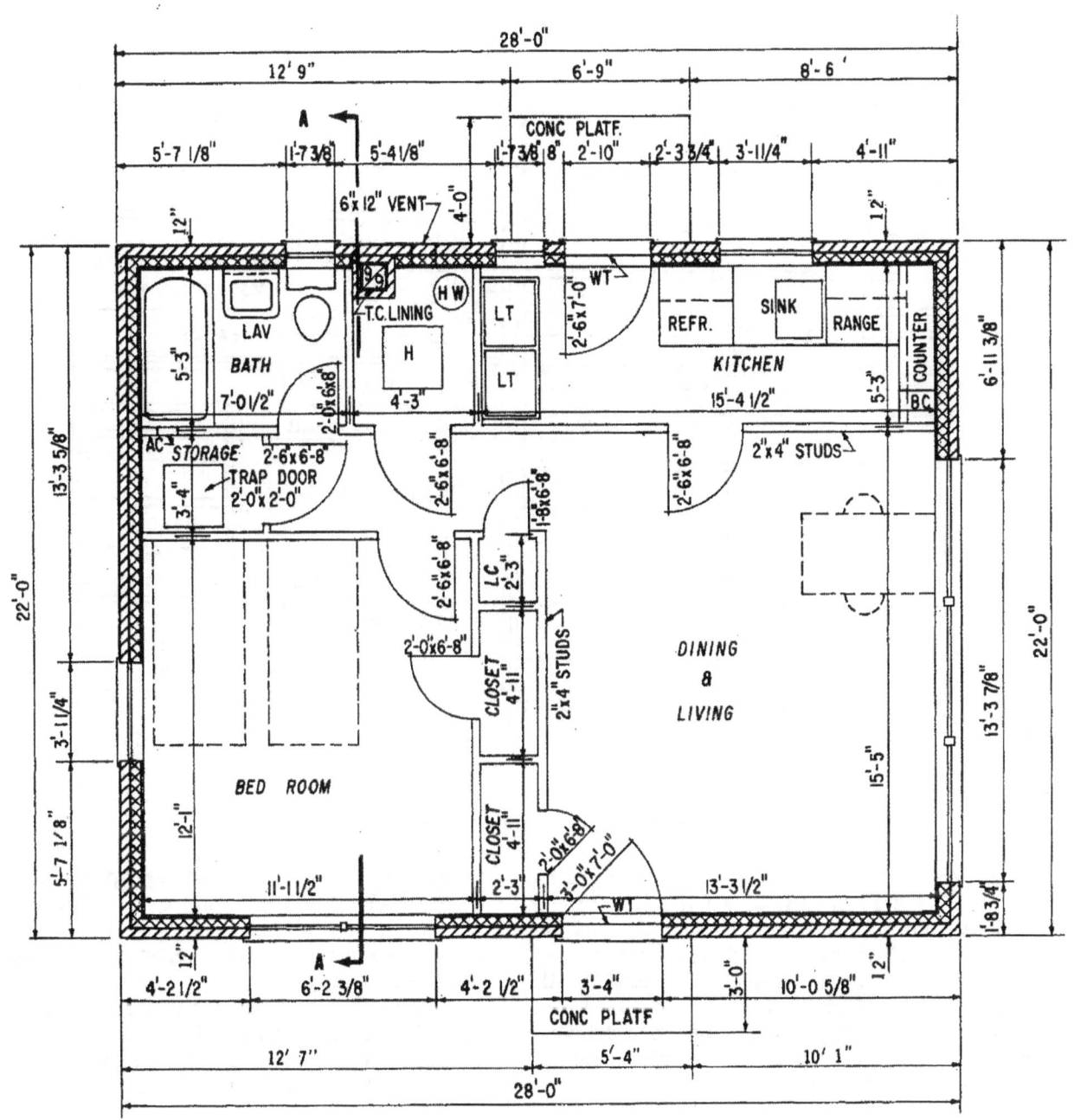

Figure 5.—Floor plan.

12-in. CMU, centered on the footing. Twelve-inch blocks will extend up to an unspecified distance below grade, where a 4-in. brick FACING (dimension indicated in the middle wall section) begins. Above the line of the bottom of the facing, it is obvious that 8-in. instead of 12-in. blocks will be used in the foundation wall.

The building wall above grade will consist of a 4-in. brick FACING TIER, backed by a BACKING TIER of 4-in. cinder blocks. The floor joists, consisting of 2 x 8's placed 16 in. O.C., will be anchored on 2 x 4 sills bolted to the top of the foundation wall. Every third joist will be additionally secured by a 2 x 1/4 STRAP ANCHOR embedded in the cinder block backing tier of the building wall.

The window (window B in the plan front elevation, fig. 9) will have a finished opening

DRAWINGS AND SPECIFICATIONS

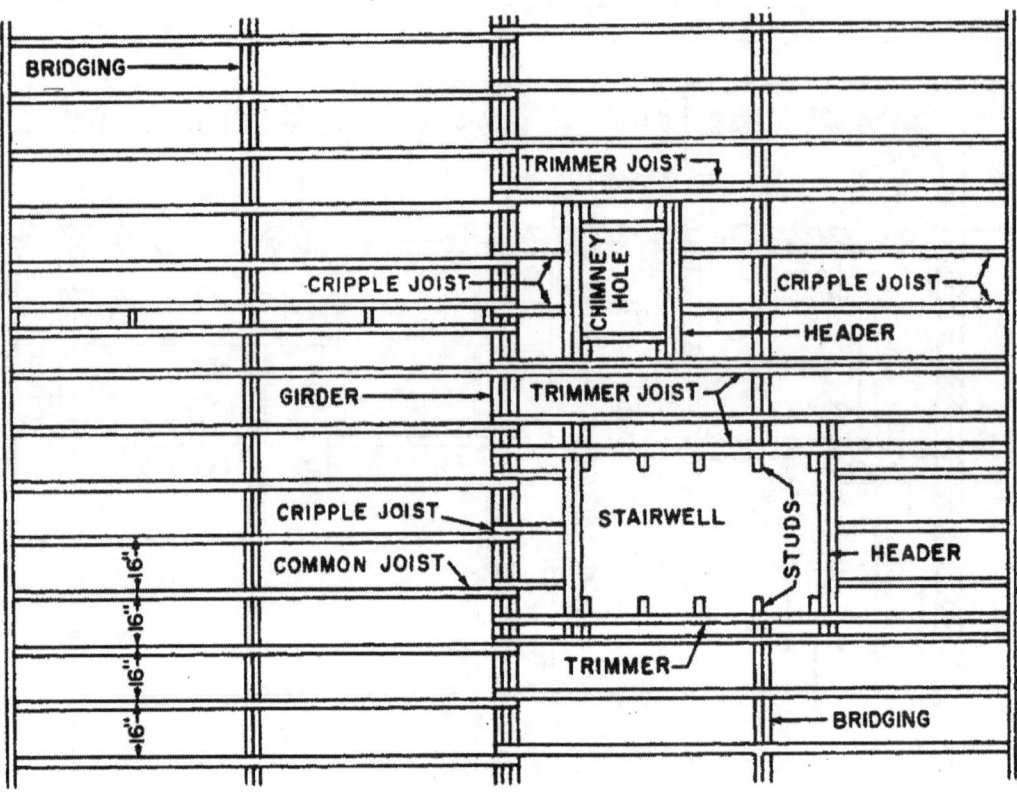

Figure 6.—Floor framing plan.

4 ft 2-5/8 in. high. The bottom of the opening will come 2 ft 11-3/4 in. above the line of the finished floor. As indicated in the wall section, (fig. 11) 13 masonry COURSES (layers of masonry units) above the finished floor line will amount to a vertical distance of 2 ft 11-3/4 in. As also indicated, another 19 courses will amount to the prescribed vertical dimension of the finished window opening.

Window framing details, including the placement and cross-sectional character of the lintel, are shown. The building wall will be carried 10-1/4 in., less the thickness of a 2 x 8 RAFTER PLATE, above the top of the window finished opening. The total vertical distance from the top of the finished floor to the top of the rafter plate will be 8 ft 2-1/4 in. Ceiling joists and rafters will consist of 2 x 6's, and the roof covering will consist of composition shingles laid on wood sheathing.

Flooring will consist of a wood finisher floor laid on a wood subfloor. Inside walls will be finished with plaster on lath (except on masonry wall which would be with or without lath as directed). A minimum of 2 vertical feet of crawl space will extend below the bottoms of the floor joists.

The middle wall section in figure 2-11 gives you similar information for a similar building constructed with wood frame walls and a DOUBLE-HUNG window. The third wall section shown in the figure gives you similar information for a similar building constructed with a steel frame, a casement window, and a concrete floor finished with asphalt tile.

DETAILS

DETAIL drawings are drawings which are done on a larger scale than that of the general drawings, and which show features not appearing at all, or appearing on too small a scale, on the general drawings. The wall sections just described are details as well as sections, since

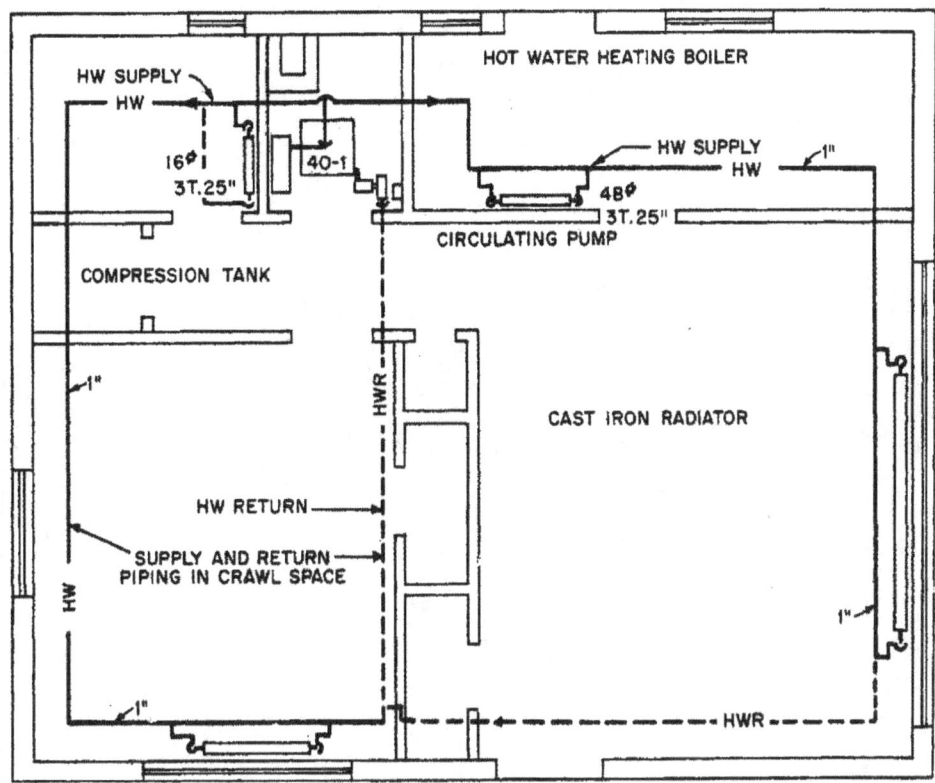

Figure 7.—Heating plan.

they are drawn on a considerable larger scale than the plans and elevations. Framing details at doors, windows, and cornices, which are the most common types of details, are practically always sections.

Details are included whenever the information given in the plans, elevations, and wall sections is not sufficiently "detailed" to guide the craftsmen on the job. Figure 12 shows some typical door and window wood framing details, and an eave detail for a very simple type of CORNICE. You should study these details closely to learn the terminology of framing members.

III. SPECIFICATIONS

The construction drawings contain much of the information about a structure which can be presented GRAPHICALLY (that is, in drawings). A very considerable amount of information can be presented this way, but there is more information which the construction supervisors and artisans must have and which is not adaptable to the graphic form of presentation. Information of this kind includes quality criteria for materials (maximum amounts of aggregate per sack of cement, for example), specified standards of workmanship, prescribed construction methods, and the like.

Information of this kind is presented in a list of written SPECIFICATIONS, familiarly known as the "SPECS." A list of specifications usually begins with a section on GENERAL CONDITIONS. This section starts with a GENERAL DESCRIPTION of the building, including the type of foundation, type or types of windows, character of framing, utilities to be installed, and the like. Next comes a list of DEFINITIONS of terms used in the specs, and next certain routine declarations of responsibility and certain conditions to be maintained on the job.

SPECIFIC CONDITIONS are grouped in sections under headings which describe each of the major construction phases of the job. Separate specifications are written for each phase, and the phases are then combined to more or less follow the usual order of construction sequences on the job. A typical list of sections under "Specific Conditions" follows:

DRAWINGS AND SPECIFICATIONS

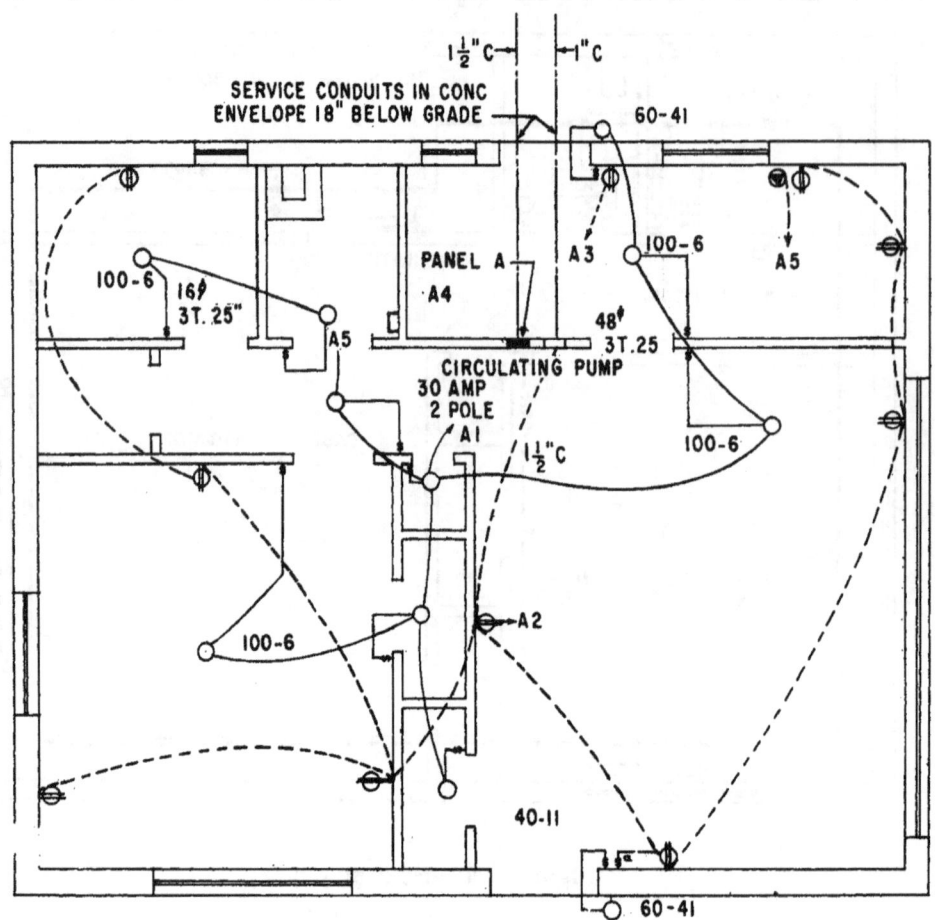

Figure 8.—Electrical plan.

2.—EARTHWORK 3.—CONCRETE 4.—MASONRY 5.—MISCELLANEOUS STEEL AND IRON 6.—CARPENTRY AND JOINERY 7.—LATHING AND PLASTERING 8.—TILE WORK 9.—FINISH FLOORING 10.—GLAZING 11.—FINISHING HARDWARE 12.—PLUMBING 13.—HEATING 14.—ELECTRICAL WORK 15.—FIELD PAINTING.

A section under "Specific Conditions" usually begins with a subsection of GENERAL REQUIREMENTS which apply to the phase of construction being considered. Under Section 6, CARPENTRY AND JOINERY, for example, the first section might go as follows:

6-01. GENERAL REQUIREMENTS. All framing, rough carpentry, and finishing woodwork required for the proper completion of the building shall be provided. All woodwork shall be protected from the weather, and the building shall be thoroughly dry before the finish is placed. All finish shall be dressed, smoothed, and sandpapered at the mill, and in addition shall be hand smoothed and sandpapered at the building where necessary to produce proper finish. Nailing shall be done, as far as practicable, in concealed places, and all nails in finishing work shall be set. All lumber shall be S4S (meaning, "surfaced on 4 sides"); all materials for millwork and finish shall be kiln-dried; all rough and framing lumber shall be air- or kiln-dried. Any cutting, fitting, framing, and blocking necessary for the accommodation of other work shall be provided. All nails, spikes, screws, bolts, plates, clips, and other fastenings and rough hardware necessary for the proper completion of the building shall be provided.

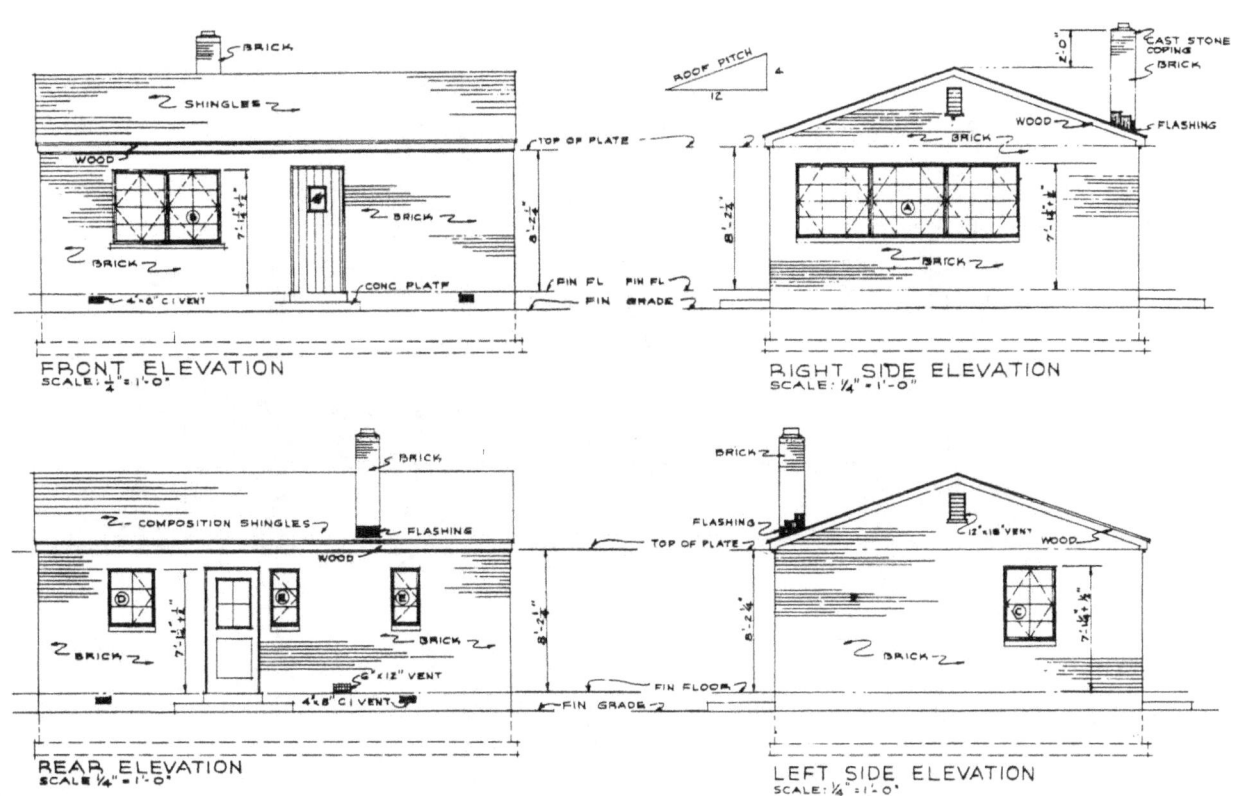

Figure 2-9.—Elevations.

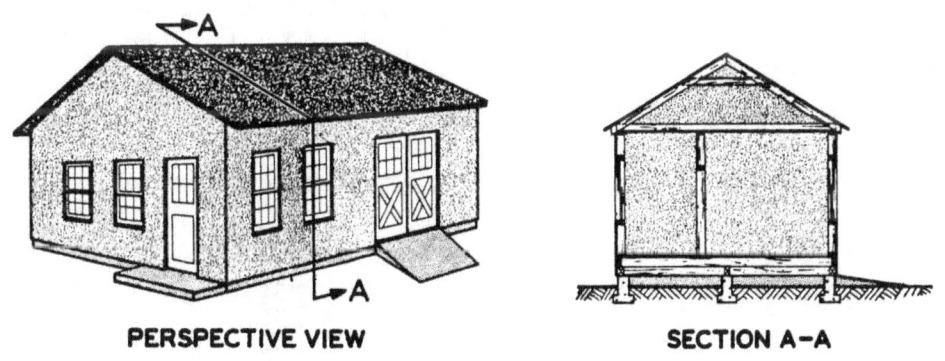

Figure 10.—Development of a section view.

All finishing hardware shall be installed in accordance with the manufacturers' directions. Calking and flashing shall be provided where indicated, or where necessary to provide weathertight construction.

Next after the General Requirements for Carpentry and Joinery, there is generally a subsection on "Grading," in which the kinds and grades of the various woods to be used in the structure are specified. Subsequent subsections

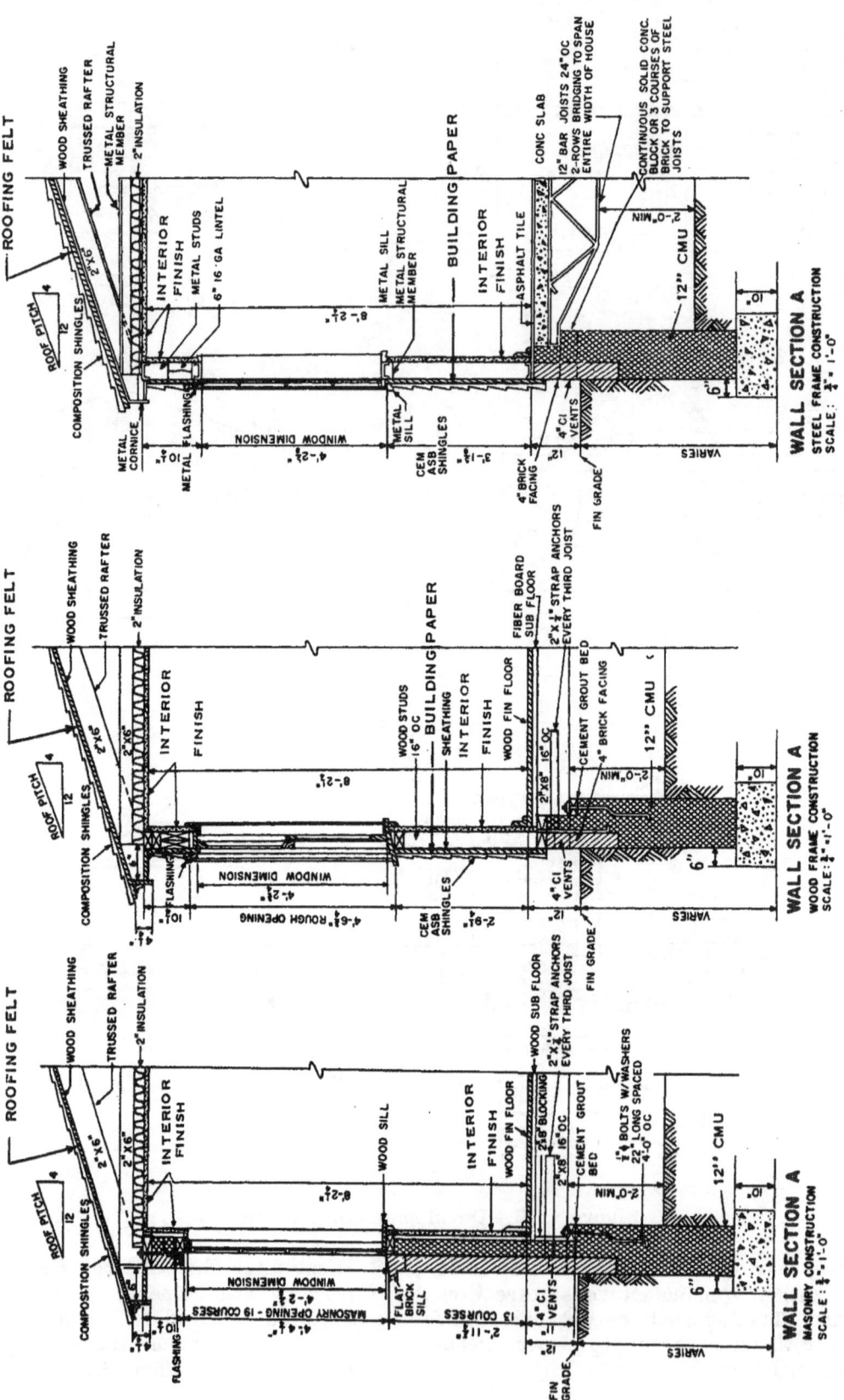

Figure 11.—Wall sections

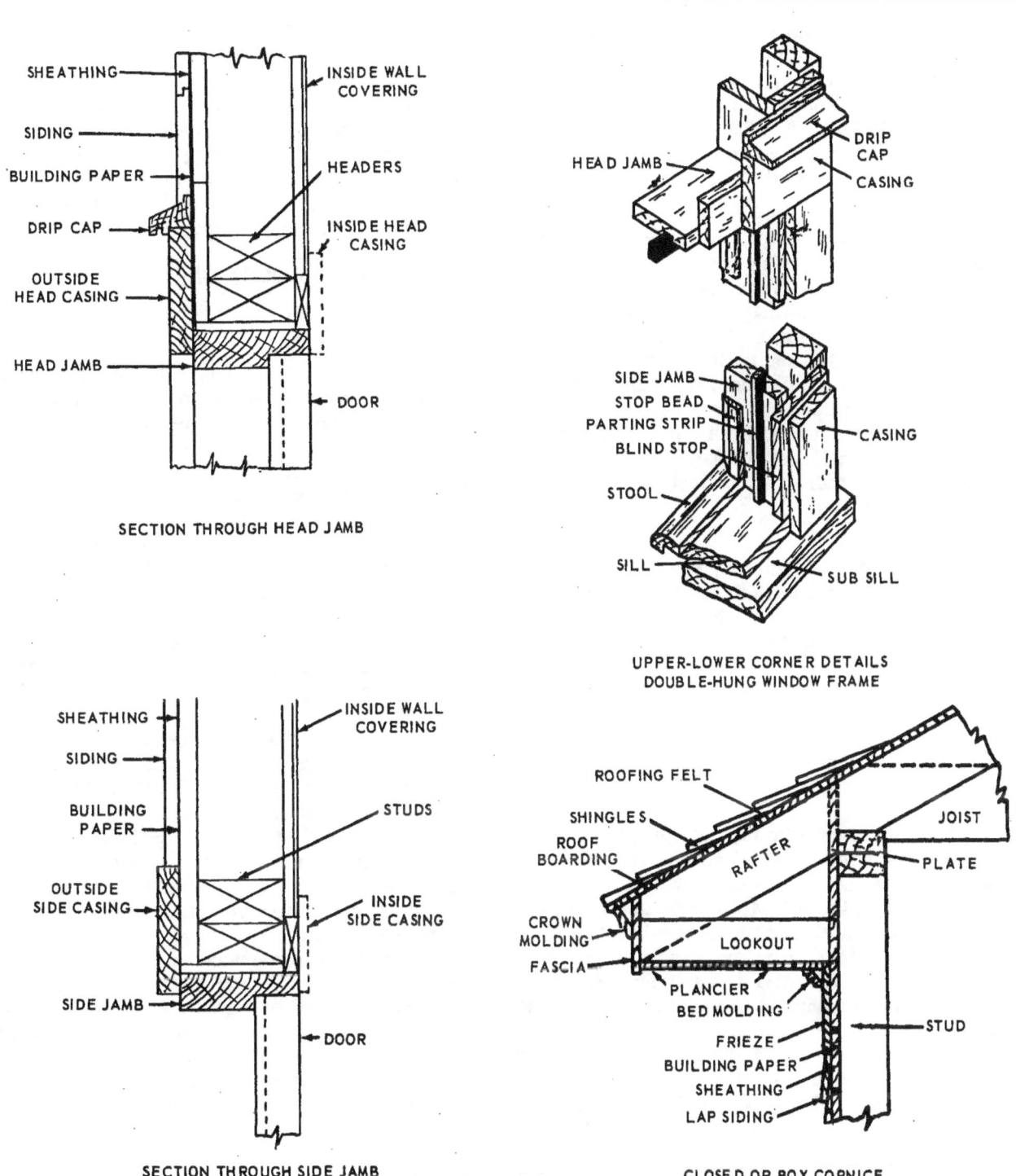

Figure 12.—Door, window and eave details.

specify various quality criteria and standards of workmanship for the various aspects of the rough and finish carpentry work, under such headings as FRAMING; SILLS, PLATES, AND GIRDERS; FLOOR JOISTS AND ROOF RAFTERS; STUDDING; and so on. An example of one of these subsections follows:

STUDDING for walls and partitions shall have doubled plates and doubled stud caps. Studs shall be set plumb and not to exceed 16-in. centers and in true alignment; they shall be bridged with one row of 2 x 4 pieces, set flatwise, fitted tightly, and nailed securely to each stud. Studding shall be doubled around openings and the heads of openings shall rest on the inner studs. Openings in partitions having widths of 4 ft and over shall be trussed. In wood frame construction, studs shall be trebled at corners to form posts.

From the above samples, you can see that a knowledge of the relevant specifications is as essential to the construction supervisor and the construction artisan as a knowledge of the construction drawings.

It is very important that the proper spec be used to cover the material requested. In cases in which the material is not covered by a Government spec, the ASTM (American Society for Testing Materials) spec or some other approved commercial spec may be used. It is EXTREMELY IMPORTANT in using specifications to cite all amendments, including the latest changes.

As a rule, the specs are provided for each project by the A/E (ARCHITECT-ENGINEERS). These are the OFFICIAL guidelines approved by the chief engineer or his representative for use during construction. These requirements should NOT be deviated from without prior approval from proper authority. This approval is usually obtained by means of a change order. When there is disagreement between the specifications and drawings, the specifications should normally be followed; however, check with higher authority in each case.

IV. BUILDER'S MATHEMATICS

The Builder has many occasions for the employment of the processes of ordinary arithmetic, and he must be thoroughly familiar with the methods of determining the areas and volumes of the various plane and solid geometrical figures. Only a few practical applications and a few practical suggestions, will be given here.

RATIO AND PROPORTION

There are a great many practical applications of ratio and proportion in the construction field. A few examples are as follows:

Some dimensions on construction drawings (such as, for example, distances from base lines and elevations of surfaces) are given in ENGINEER'S instead of CARPENTER's measure. Engineer's measure is measure in feet and decimal parts of a foot, or in inches and decimal parts of an inch, such as 100.15 ft or 11.14 in. Carpenter's measure is measure in yards, feet, inches, and even-denominator fractions of an inch, such as 1/2 in., 1/4 in., 1/16 in., 1/32 in., and 1/64 in.

You must know how to convert an engineer's measure given on a construction drawing to a carpenter's measure. Besides this, it will often happen that calculations you make yourself may produce a result in feet and decimal parts of a foot, which result you will have to convert to carpenter's measure. To convert engineer's to carpenter's measure you can use ratio and proportion as follows:

Let's say that you want to convert 100.14 ft to feet and inches to the nearest 1/16 in. The 100 you don't need to convert, since it is already in feet. What you need to do, first, is to find out how many twelfths of a foot (that is, how many inches) there are in 14/100 ft. Set this up as a proportional equation as follows: x:12::14:100.

You know that in a proportional equation the product of the means equals the product of the extremes. Consequently, 100x = (12 x 14), or 168. Then x = 168/100, or 1.68 in. Next question is, how many 16ths of an in. are there in 68/100 in.? Set this up, too, as a proportional equation, thus: x:16::68:100. Then 100x = 1088, and x = 10 88/100 sixteenths. Since 88/100 of a sixteenth is more than one-half of a sixteenth, you ROUND OFF by calling it 11/16. In 100.14 ft, then, there are 100 ft 1 11/16 in. For example:

A. $\underbrace{x:12::14:100}_{\text{Extremes}}$ means

Product of extremes = product of means:

$$100\ x = 168$$
$$x = 1.68 \text{ IN.}$$

B. x:16::68:100

$$100\ x = 1088$$
$$x = 10.88$$
$$x = 10\frac{88}{100} \text{ sixteenths}$$

Rounded off to 11/16

Another way to convert engineer's measurements to carpenter's measurements is to multiply the decimal portion of a foot by 12 to get inches; multiply the decimal by 16 to get the fraction of an inch.

There are many other practical applications of ratio and proportion in the construction field. Suppose, for example, that a table tells you that, for the size and type of brick wall you happen to be laying, 12,321 bricks and 195 cu ft of mortar are required per every 1000 sq ft of wall. How many bricks and how much mortar will be needed for 750 sq ft of the same wall? You simply set up equations as follows; for example:

Brick: x:750::12,321:1000
Mortar: x:750::195:1000

Brick: $\frac{X}{750} = \frac{12,321}{1000}$ Cross multiply

$$1000\ X = 9,240,750 \quad \text{Divide}$$
$$X = 9,240.75 = 9241 \text{ Brick.}$$

Mortar: $\frac{X}{750} = \frac{195}{1000}$ Cross multiply

$$1000\ X = 146,250 \quad \text{Divide}$$
$$X = 146.25 = 146\ 1/4 \text{ cu ft}$$

Suppose, for another example, that the ingredient proportions by volume for the type of concrete you are making are 1 cu ft cement to 1.7 cu ft sand to 2.8 cu ft coarse aggregate. Suppose you know as well, by reference to a table, that ingredients combined in the amounts indicated will produce 4.07 cu ft of concrete. How much of each ingredient will be required to make a cu yd of concrete?

Remember here, first, that there are not 9, but 27 (3 ft x 3 ft x 3 ft) cu ft in a cu yd. Your proportional equations will be as follows:

Cement: x:27::1:4.07

Sand: x:27::1.7:4.07

Coarse aggregate: x:27::2.8:4.07

Cement: x:27::1:4.07

$$\frac{x}{27} = \frac{1}{4.07}$$
$$4.07\ x = 27$$
$$x = 6.63 \text{ cu ft Cement}$$

Sand: x:27::1.7:4.07

$$\frac{x}{27} = \frac{1.7}{4.07}$$
$$4.07\ x = 45.9$$
$$x = 11.28 \text{ cu ft Sand}$$

Coarse aggregate: x:27::2.8:407

$$\frac{x}{27} = \frac{2.8}{4.07}$$
$$4.07\ x = 75.6$$
$$x = 18.57 \text{ cu ft Coarse aggregate}$$

ARITHMETICAL OPERATIONS

The formulas for finding the area and volume of geometric figures are expressed in algebraic equations which are called formulas. A few of the more important formulas and their mathematical solutions will be discussed in this section.

DRAWINGS AND SPECIFICATIONS

To get an area, you multiply 2 linear measures together, and to get a volume you multiply 3 linear measures together. The linear measures you multiply together must all be expressed in the SAME UNITS; you cannot, for example, multiply a length in feet by a width in inches to get a result in square feet or in square inches.

Dimensions of a feature on a construction drawing are not always given in the same units. For a concrete wall, for example, the length and height are usually given in feet and the thickness in inches. Furthermore, you may want to get a result in units which are different from any shown on the drawing. Concrete volume, for example, is usually expressed in cubic yards, while the dimensions of concrete work are given on the drawings in feet and inches.

You can save yourself a good many steps in calculating by using fractions to convert the original dimension units into the desired end-result units. Take 1 in., for example. To express 1 in. in feet, you simply put it over 12, thus: 1/12 ft. To express 1 in. in yards, you simply put it over 36, thus: 1/36 yd. In the same manner, to express 1 ft in yards you simply put it over 3, thus 1/3 yd.

Suppose now that you want to calculate the number of cu yd of concrete in a wall 32 ft long by 14 ft high by 8 in. thick. You can express all these in yards and set up your problem thus:

$$\frac{32}{3} \times \frac{14}{3} \times \frac{8}{36}$$

Next you can cancel out, thus:

$$\frac{\overset{16}{\cancel{32}}}{3} \times \frac{\cancel{14}}{3} \times \frac{8}{\underset{9}{\cancel{\underset{18}{\cancel{36}}}}} = \frac{896}{81}$$

Dividing 896 by 81, you get 11.06 cu yds of concrete in the wall.

The right triangle is a triangle which contains one right (90°) angle. The following letters will denote the parts of the triangle indicated in figure 2-13—a = altitude, b = base, c = hypotenuse.

In solving a right triangle, the length of any side may be found if the lengths of the other two sides are given. The combinations of 3-4-5 (lengths of sides) or any multiple of these combinations will come out to a whole number. The following examples show the formula for finding

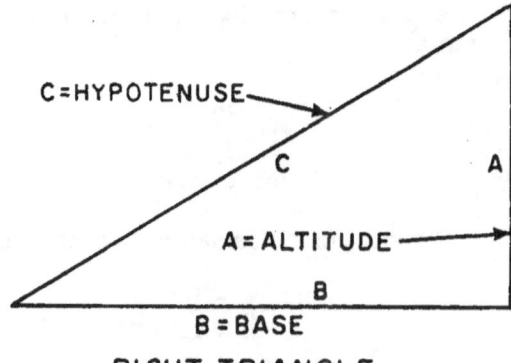

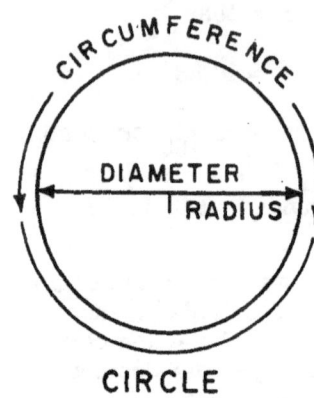

Figure 13.—Right triangle and circle.

each side. Each of these formulas is derived from the master formula $c^2 = a^2 + b^2$.

(1) Find c when a = 3, and b = 4.

$c = \sqrt{a^2 + b^2} = \sqrt{3^2 + 4^2} = \sqrt{9 + 16} = \sqrt{25} = 5$

(2) Find a when b = 8, and c = 10.

$a = \sqrt{c^2 - b^2} = \sqrt{10^2 - 8^2} = \sqrt{100 - 64} = \sqrt{36} = 6$

(3) Find b when a = 9, and c = 15.

$b = \sqrt{c^2 - a^2} = \sqrt{15^2 - 9^2} = \sqrt{225 - 81} = \sqrt{144} = 12.$

There are tables from which the square roots of numbers may be found; otherwise, they may be found arithmetically as explained later in this chapter.

Areas And Volumes Of
Geometric Figures

This section on areas and volumes of geometric figures will be limited to the most commonly used geometric figures. Reference books, such as Mathematics, Vol. 1, are available for additional information if needed. Areas are expressed in square units and volumes in cubic units.

1. A circle is a plane figure bounded by a curved line every point of which is the same distance from the center.
   a. The curved line is called the circumference.
   b. A straight line drawn from the center to any point on the circumference is called a radius. (r = 1/2 the diameter.)
   c. A straight line drawn from one point of the circumference through the center and terminating on the opposite point of the circumference is called a diameter. (d = 2 times the radius.) See figure 2-13.
   d. The area of a circle is found by the following formulas: $A = \pi r^2$ or $A = .7854 d^2$. (π is pronounced pie = 3.1416 or 3 1/7, .7854 is 1/4 of π.) Example: Find the area of a circle whose radius is 7". $A = \pi r^2 = 3\ 1/7 \times 7^2 = 22/7 \times 49 = 154$ sq in. If you use the second formula you obtain the same results.
   e. The circumference of a circle is found by multiplying π times the diameter or 2 times π times the radius. Example: Find the circumference of a circle whose diameter is 56 inches. $C = \pi d = 3.1415 \times 56 = 175.9296$ inches.

2. The area of a right triangle is equal to one-half the product of the base by the altitude. (Area = 1/2 base x altitude.) Example: Find the area of a triangle whose base is 16" and altitude 6". Solution:

$$A = 1/2\ bh = 1/2 \times 16 \times 6 = 48 \text{ sq in.}$$

3. The volume of a cylinder is found by multiplying the area of the base times the height. ($V = 3.1416 \times r^2 \times h$). Example: Find the volume of a cylinder which has a radius of 8 in. and a height of 4 ft. Solution:

$$8 \text{ in} = \frac{2}{3} \text{ ft and } \left(\frac{2}{3}\right)2 = \frac{4}{9} \text{ sq ft.}$$

$$V = 3.1416 \times \frac{4}{9} \times 4 = \frac{50.2656}{9} = 5.59 \text{ cu ft.}$$

4. The volume of a rectangular solid equals the length x width x height. (V = lwh.) Example: Find the volume of a rectangular solid which has a length of 6 ft, a width of 3 ft, and a height of 2 ft. Solution:

$$V = lwh = 6 \times 3 \times 2 = 36 \text{ cu ft.}$$

5. The volume of a cone may be found by multiplying one-third times the area of the base times the height.

$$\left(V = \frac{1}{3} \pi r^2 h\right)$$

Example: Find the volume of a cone when the radius of its base is 2 ft and its height is 9 ft. Solution:

$$\pi = 3.1416,\ r = 2,\ 2^2 = 4$$

$$V = \frac{1}{3} r^2 h = \frac{1}{3} \times 3.1416 \times 4 \times 9 = 37.70 \text{ cu ft.}$$

Powers And Roots

1. Powers—When we multiply several numbers together, as 2 x 3 x 4 = 24, the numbers 2, 3, and 4 are factors and 24 the product. The operation of raising a number to a power is a special case of multiplication in which the factors are all equal. The power of a number is the number of times the number itself is to be taken as a factor. Example: 2^4 is 16. The second power is called the square of the number, as 3^2. The third power of a number is called the cube of the number, as 5^3. The exponent of a number is a number placed to the right and above a base to show how many times the base is used as a factor. Example:

$$4^3 \leftarrow \text{exponent} \atop \leftarrow \text{base}$$

$$4 \times 4 \times 4 = 64.$$

2. Roots—To indicate a root, use the sign $\sqrt{\ }$, which is called the radical sign. A small figure, called the index of the root, is placed in the opening of the sign to show which root is to be taken. The square root of a number is one of the two equal factors into which a number is

divided. Example: $\sqrt{81} = \sqrt{9 \times 9} = 9$. The cube root is one of the three equal factors into which a number is divided. Example: $\sqrt[3]{125} = \sqrt[3]{5 \times 5 \times 5} = 5$.

Square Root

1. The square root of any number is that number which, when multiplied by itself, will produce the first number. For example; the square root of 121 is 11 because 11 times 11 equals 121.

2. How to extract the square root arithmetically:

```
                    95.
     √9025    √90'25.
              : -81

      180 :    925
       +5 :   -925

      185 :    000
```

a. Begin at the decimal point and divide the given number into groups of 2 digits each (as far as possible), going from right to left and/or left to right.
b. Find the greatest number (9) whose square is contained in the first or left hand group (90). Square this number (9) and place it under the first pair of digits (90), then subtract.
c. Bring down the next pair of digits (25) and add it to the remainder (9).
d. Multiply the first digit in the root by 20 and use it as a trial divisor (180). This trial divisor (180) will go into the new dividend (925) five times. This number, 5 (second digit in the root), is added back to the trial divisor, obtaining the true divisor (185).
e. The true divisor (185) is multiplied by the second digit (5) and placed under the remainder (925). Subtract and the problem is solved.
f. If there is still a remainder and you want to carry the problem further, add zeros (in pairs) and continue the above process.

Coverage Calculations

You will frequently have occasion to estimate the number of linear feet of boards of a given size, or the number of tiles, asbestos shingles, and the like, required to cover a given area. Let's take the matter of linear feet of boards first.

What you do here is calculate, first, the number of linear feet of board required to cover 1 sq ft. For boards laid edge-to-edge, you base your calculations on the total width of a board. For boards which will lap each other, you base your calculations on the width laid TO THE WEATHER, meaning the total width minus the width of the lap.

Since there are 144 sq in. in a sq ft, linear footage to cover a given area can be calculated as follows. Suppose your boards are to be laid 8 in. to the weather. If you divide 8 in. into 144 sq in., the result (which is 18 in., or 1.5 ft) will be the linear footage required to cover a sq ft. If you have, say, 100 sq ft to cover, the linear footage required will be 100 x 1.5, or 150 ft.

To estimate the number of tiles, asbestos shingles, and the like required to cover a given area, you first calculate the number of units required to cover a sq ft. Suppose, for example, you are dealing with 9 in. x 9 in. asphalt tiles. The area of one of these is 9 in. x 9 in. or 81 sq in. In a sq ft there are 144 sq in. If it takes 1 to cover 81 sq in., how many will it take to cover 144 sq in.? Just set up a proportional equation, as follows.

$$1:81::x:144$$

When you work this out, you will find that it takes 1.77 tiles to cover a sq ft. To find the number of tiles required to cover 100 sq ft, simply multiply by 100. How do you multiply anything by 100? Just move the decimal point 2 places to the right. Consequently, it takes 177 9 x 9 asphalt tiles to cover 100 sq ft of area.

Board Measure

BOARD MEASURE is a method of measuring lumber in which the basic unit is an abstract volume 1 ft long by 1 ft wide by 1 in. thick. This abstract volume or unit is called a BOARD FOOT.

There are several formulas for calculating the number of board feet in a piece of given dimensions. Since lumber dimensions are most frequently indicated by width and thickness in inches and length in feet, the following formula is probably the most practical.

$$\frac{\text{Thickness in in.} \times \text{width in in.} \times \text{length in ft}}{12}$$

= board feet

Suppose you are calculating the number of board feet in a 14-ft length of 2 x 4. Applying the formula, you get:

$$\frac{\overset{1}{\cancel{2}} \times \overset{2}{\cancel{4}} \times 14}{\underset{\underset{3}{\cancel{6}}}{\cancel{12}}} = \frac{28}{3} = 9\ 1/3 \text{ bd ft}$$

The chief practical use of board measure is in cost calculations, since lumber is bought and sold by the board foot. Any lumber less than 1 in. thick is presumed to be 1 in. thick for board measure purposes. Board measure is calculated on the basis of the NOMINAL, not the ACTUAL, dimensions of lumber.

The actual size of a piece of dimension lumber (such as a 2 x 4, for example) is usually less than the nominal size.

www.ingramcontent.com/pod-product-compliance
Lightning Source LLC
Chambersburg PA
CBHW081809300426
44116CB00014B/2297